WITHDRAWN

Transgressive Language in Medieval English Drama

Transgressive Language in Medieval English Drama

Signs of Challenge and Change

Lynn Forest-Hill

Ashgate

Aldershot • Burlington USA • Singapore • Sydney

This edition copyright © Lynn Forest-Hill, 2000

All rights reserved. No part of this publication may be reproduced, stored in a retrieval system, or transmitted in any form or by any means, electronic, mechanical, photocopying, recording or otherwise without the prior permission of the publisher.

Lynn Forest-Hill has asserted her moral right under the Copyright, Designs and Patents Act, 1988, to be identified as the author of this work.

Published by
Ashgate Publishing Limited
Gower House
Croft Road
Aldershot
Hants GU11 3HR
England

Ashgate Publishing Company
131 Main Road
Burlington
Vermont, 05401–5600
USA

Ashgate website: http://www.ashgate.com

British Library Cataloguing in Publication Data

Forest-Hill, Lynn.
    Transgressive Language in Medieval English Drama:
    Signs of Challenge and Change.
    1. English drama—To 1500—History and criticism. 2. Style,
    Literary. I. Title.
    822.1'09

US Library of Congress Cataloging in Publication Data

Forest-Hill, Lynn.
    Transgressive Language in Medieval English Drama:
    Signs of Challenge and Change / Lynn Forest-Hill.
       p.   cm.
    Includes bibliographical references and index.
    1. English drama—To 1500—History and Criticism. 2. English
    language—Middle English, 1100–1500—Discourse analysis.
    3. Literature and society—England—History—To 1500. 4. Language
    and culture—England—History—To 1500. 5. Discourse analysis,
    Literary. 6. Invective in literature. I. Title.
    PR641.F67 2000
    822'.209–dc21   99–042634

ISBN 0 7546 0086 6

This book is printed on acid free paper.

Printed and bound in Great Britain by Athenaeum Press Ltd, Gateshead, Tyne & Wear.

Contents

Preface		vii
Introduction		1
1	Language law and drama	6
2	Transgressive language and characterization	25
3	Social comment, religious dissent, and audience response in the biblical plays	50
4	Transgressive language in three fifteenth–century morality plays	85
5	*Magnyfycence*: signs of change in the sixteenth century	108
6	*The Play of the Weather*: entertainment and religious anxiety	136
7	*King Johan*: the language of virtue and reformation	165
Bibliography		197
Index		210

Preface

For present-day readers of late medieval religious and didactic drama the use of copious amounts of abusive, insulting and mocking language in some plays can come as a surprise, or even a shock, and poses problems of interpretation. While a number of excellent short critical studies have been published which shed light on the forms and possible functions of such 'bad language' in the drama, no full-length study of the topic has been done. This book is intended to redress that situation and to illuminate the skill and sophistication with which dramatists in the fifteenth and sixteenth centuries used a wide vocabulary of abuse, insults, oaths, curses and mocking language to create characterizations, define spiritual states, and drive home didactic points while providing entertaining drama.

My enthusiasm for medieval drama I owe to my former supervisors Dr John J. McGavin, of the English Department at the University of Southampton, and Dr Peter Happé, and I am deeply indebted to them for their help and encouragement, as I am to Dr Bella Millett, also of the English Department at Southampton, who was my adviser and constant intellectual inspiration throughout my research period. I also take this opportunity to thank Professor Greg Walker, of the English Department at the University of Leicester, for his generous help and advice during the preparation of this book.

I should like to record my gratitude to the School for Research and Graduate Studies and the Faculty of Arts, at the University of Southampton, who provided funding for my first year of research, to the University of Southampton for funding the remaining two years, to the Wessex Medieval Centre for additional funding, and to the Hartley Institute for providing funding and facilities during the preparation of this book.

However, without doubt the greatest debt of gratitude I owe is to my family for their constant support and encouragement, and so this book is dedicated to Neville, Diane, and David.

Introduction

In medieval society some forms of language broke the rules which governed its use. These were not rules of grammar, but concerned vocabulary and modes of expression, and language such as insults, abuse, oaths, and curses transgressed against these rules. The authors of biblical and morality plays in late medieval England used this familiar form of social transgression as a means of commenting on their society. New Historicism has encouraged us to examine texts for evidence of resistance to social authority, and the play texts reveal, through the use of transgressive language, many kinds of cultural behaviour which appear to resist that authority. However, the language, and sometimes the sentiments, which this study will focus on, function in complex ways which are not adequately illuminated by doctrinaire interpretations.

The significance of language is always determined by the contexts in which it is used. Although transgressive language remains indebted to its social significance, in the biblical, moral, and political drama of the fifteenth and sixteenth centuries it is subject to the artistic endeavour of the dramatists. Wherever transgressive language is used it contributes to the interactive relationship between words, action, and audience which is unique to drama, and prompts complex audience responses. Although the latter cannot be derived from non-dramatic sources, they can be inferred from the drama, and from knowledge of the auspices under which the plays were produced.

Transgressive language in didactic drama derives an important part of its significance from its social context, and an examination of the medieval sermons and laws which laid down the rules governing its use will show that language could be sinful, or conducive to sin, or illegal in secular terms, and was punished by penance, humiliation, and fines. These sermons and laws show that language had moral significance in medieval society, and this was used with subtlety by dramatists in both biblical and morality genres to create characterizations and draw spectators into relationships with characters. These would prompt emotional and intellectual responses from spectators, and change with the action of a play.

Dramatists created their characterizations using the moral significance of transgressive language in conjunction with prosodic style, costume, and action. By examining the diversity, complexity, and development of this language in the cycles of biblical plays commonly referred to as the mystery cycles; in the three fifteenth-century moralities known as the Macro plays; and then in three sixteenth-century political moralities: John Skelton's *Magnyfycence*, John Heywood's *The Play of the Wether*, and John Bale's *King Johan*, we will see how these characterizations create changing relationships between audiences and characters, and serve the didactic purposes of the plays.

Dramatists exploited the flexibility of transgressive language to create varied and subtle characterizations which mirrored for late medieval society its own imperfections. Such language used by any character defines the extent of that character's sinfulness and rejection of the social and religious ideals of medieval society, while changes in a character's use of transgressive language signal changes in his or her sinful condition. However, virtuous characters may use the same language to punish sinfulness. The ways in which characters use this language would provoke emotional and intellectual responses from spectators, which reflect, and contribute to, the didactic purposes of the plays.

When the condemnation of transgressive language in the sermons and laws is compared with its exploitation as a means of creating social, spiritual, or moral characterizations, a difference is revealed between the society represented in drama and the society producing the drama. In that gap between reality and representation social criticism and religious instruction flourish. The most extensive use of transgressive language for social and religious comment is in the cycles of biblical plays.

The manuscripts of the four extant cycles vary considerably in date, form, and auspices. The York 'Register', assembled between 1463 and 1477,[1] is known to have been used as an authoritative text against which performances were checked. The earliest manuscript of the Chester cycle dates from 1591, and post-dates its last performance in 1575.[2] The N-Town[3] and Towneley[4] manuscripts represent compilations of plays arranged in cycle form. While the differences in date and auspices may have contributed to diversity in the forms and functions of transgressive language in each cycle, it is the didactic intention of playwrights and redactors which appears to generate the greatest

---

[1] Richard Beadle, 'The York Cycle', in Richard Beadle, ed., *The Cambridge Companion to Medieval English Theatre* (Cambridge: Cambridge University Press, 1994), p. 90.

[2] David Mills, 'The Chester Cycle', in Beadle, ed., cited above, p. 110.

[3] Alan J. Fletcher suggests a date of compilation 'sometime after 1468'; Alan J. Fletcher, 'The N-Town Plays', in Beadle, ed., cited above, p. 164. Stephen Spector, ed., *The N-Town Play*, 2 vols, EETS SS 11, 12 (Oxford: Oxford University Press, 1991), suggests as a date 'the second half of the fifteenth century, and perhaps the early part of the sixteenth' (p. xxxviii). I am grateful to the Council of the Early English Text Society for permission to quote from the EETS editions of the plays cited in this work.

[4] Martin Stevens and A.C. Cawley, eds, *The Towneley Plays*, 2 vols, EETS SS 13, 14 (Oxford: Oxford University Press, 1994), suggest a date of 'about 1500' (p. xv), while Peter Meredith, 'The Towneley cycle', in Beadle, ed., cited above, places the manuscript 'either very late in the fifteenth century or ... into the sixteenth' (p. 136).

diversity. The plays nevertheless exhibit conformity to the genre's norms in their use of such language.

Only some of the biblical plays contain transgressive language, but it frequently occurs in different plays on the same biblical topic, as, for example, in the Cain plays. However, individual dramatists choose particular forms of that language to characterize Cain's wickedness in different ways, but always in terms made relevant to a contemporary medieval audience by the forms of language chosen.

The transgressiveness of language used by characters in the biblical plays is intended to provoke responses from the plays' eclectic audiences which challenge, for example, the wickedness of evil rulers, perversion of the law, social subversion, and the piety and Christian knowledge of the spectators themselves. These are all constant concerns.

In notable instances, the authors of the biblical plays created unique and important variations on conventional themes as they used transgressive language to represent the dissent of biblical characters. While this may be resolved within the action of an individual play, or by the redemptive theme of the cycle, the dramatists may have intended to expose unresolved areas of discontent in medieval society, or, regardless of their intention, their plays may have exposed such discontent. The gap between reality and the society represented in the drama, and the eclectic nature of the audiences attending the biblical plays, permits differing interpretations of transgressive language according to the life experiences and erudition of individual spectators. Thus the response created by a character's linguistic transgressions may not have been contained by the ludic context in which it is formed.

Understanding likely audience response is less problematic for the morality genre, which permits dramatists greater freedom than the biblical plays to address selected audiences on contentious social topics. Transgressive language is used in all three fifteenth-century moralities known as the Macro plays: *The Castle of Perseverance*, *Wisdom*, and *Mankind*. These represent a small body of dramatic material in comparison to the biblical plays in which similar language is used. Nevertheless, they significantly extend the diversity of transgressive language. The manuscripts show how this language is matched to the didactic purpose of a play, its allegorical framework, and possibly its particular audience.

Major differences exist between the use of transgressive language in the biblical plays and its use in the Macro plays. These differences reveal generic conventions in the use of this language, which distinguish the moralities from the biblical plays. The most important is the use of the moral significance of transgressive language to characterize tempters, and abstract representatives of humanity, and this defines their relationship to medieval society. These conventions are adapted and altered in the sixteenth-century moralities as dramatists offer instruction and persuasion in response to cultural and religious change.

Significant differences also exist between the moralities themselves, and these determine the forms and functions of transgressive language in each play. Unconstrained by biblical sources, morality dramatists used transgressive language to create widely differing allegorical frameworks, and characterizations, and to offer different forms of moral instruction and social comment which may be pitched to particular audiences. *Wisdom* uses subtle forms to involve spectators intellectually, as it shows how the rejection of the proper relationship between the Soul and Christ is manifested in medieval society in forms of legal perversion. In *Mankind*, highly entertaining scatological language serves the play's moral purpose as it tempts spectators to become involved in the sin of using such language. However, both *Wisdom* and *Mankind* use transgressive language to show that moral danger is not an abstract concept, but is present in everyday life.

The forms and functions of transgressive language used in the Macro plays, together with the diversity in characterization, allegory, and social didactic purposes, were developed with great sophistication in the sixteenth-century moralities. These plays reveal that developments in the use of transgressive language were driven not only by a dramatist's desire to create new forms of entertaining morality drama, but by a play's historical context. Three sixteenth-century morality plays: *Magnyfycence*, by John Skelton, *The Play of the Wether*, by John Heywood, and *King Johan*, by John Bale, illustrate how dramatic conventions of transgressive language were manipulated, adapted, and eventually inverted as the playwrights addressed cultural and religious changes.

In *Magnyfycence* John Skelton adapted the conventions by which the moral significance of language indicates the moral or spiritual status of a character, to create unstable characterizations, and discuss humanist challenges to the status of language. Through his manipulation of transgressive language, Skelton, like the *Mankind* dramatist, involves the audience, but in *Magnyfycence* they are confronted with the intellectual problem of judging the moral identity of characters. The confusion Skelton creates serves his instructional purpose as he shows that language itself can be judged according to its usefulness to society.

John Heywood, in his *Play of the Wether*, used transgressive language more conventionally as a means of signalling the moral status of the new characters he introduced to morality drama. He also extended the use of bawdy language and made entertaining use of scatological language, as the means by which he addressed the dangerous topic of religious change.

Heywood introduced characters, including two women, who are not obviously personifications, as the characters in earlier moralities were, but represent the estates of society. However, if a character's moral status, indicated conventionally by their use of transgressive language, is considered in the context of the contemporary religious controversy, it frequently suggests an underlying allegorical personification. This is particularly important in the case of Mery Report, Heywood's development of the vice characters of the morality tradition. When this character's highly entertaining bawdy, scatological, and insulting remarks are considered in the context of Henry VIII's divorce, and the religious debate which it provoked, they reveal the cautiously fragmented allegory which veils Heywood's serious comments. Mery Report's three forms of transgressive language create intellectual contexts which direct spectators towards controversial interpretations of the characters and their actions, but disguise these interpretations behind the entertainment.

Heywood's necessary caution controlled the changes and innovations he introduced in the use of transgressive language. John Bale's violently anti-Catholic language in *King Johan* might appear, by contrast, to lack control, but his Protestant polemic is only the most obvious manifestation of his views on Catholicism. He used subtle allusions to criticize those aspects of Catholic doctrine to which Henry VIII remained devoted, and he introduced radical changes in the use of transgressive language to create characterizations and didactic comments. However, he also modulated his vituperation to create more entertaining drama.

Bale's innovations in language are accompanied by his innovative choice of characters as he used historical figures as a means of representing the Protestant and Catholic factions. Bale's innovations constitute the most radical break with the traditions which governed the use of transgressive language in medieval drama, but that does not inhibit its use to create relationships between characters and audiences.

Transgressive language loses its traditional moral significance in *King Johan*. Characters are no longer identifiable as good or evil simply by their use of such language, but by the orientation of their language in favour of Protestantism or Catholicism. The most violent forms of traditional transgressive language are used in *King Johan* by characters whose virtue lies in their defence of Protestantism. Thus Bale redefines language in the play as good or evil according to the context in which it is used.

The freedom to develop and change the use of transgressive language, which Bale exploited, seems particular to the morality genre. Although the authors of the biblical plays used such language to comment on their society, chronological development in the use of this language in these plays is obscured by the manuscripts. In York, the persistent use of the Register reveals that the plays continued without major changes throughout the period when the morality dramatists were radically altering the significance of transgressive language. The two genres thus represent co-existing dramatic traditions which, through their use of transgressive language, provided entertainment and instruction for widely differing audiences, by remarkably different methods.

Chapter 1

Language law and drama

Transgressive language in both medieval drama and medieval society may be defined as language which was subject to constraint but nevertheless in some cases exceeded the limits of that constraint. This chapter sets out the social constraints on language, as these are revealed by a number of crucial medieval sermons and laws, in order to define the social significance of language. By comparing the condemnation of transgressive language in the sermons and laws with the punishments meted out for its misuse, and with the use of language in drama, the chapter will reveal that language used in drama differs from similar language used in society in the responses it produces.

In medieval society ecclesiastical and secular laws governed the use of language. These non-dramatic constraints would influence a spectator's response to transgressive language in drama. Medieval sermons provide definitions of sinful language which establish its moral significance. This was used to create characterizations in both biblical and morality plays where such language signifies a character's sinfulness. The moral significance of language remained unchanged in didactic drama until it was inverted and weakened by John Bale in the sixteenth-century morality *King Johan*.

While the laws themselves provide important contexts for the use of transgressive language in some biblical plays, legal cases which are contemporaneous with the drama show how the ideals set out in sermons were reflected in social practice, and provide insights into the social significance of transgressive language. The cases illustrate various forms of transgressive vocabulary, and draw attention to the functions of witnesses. Historical records reveal that the punishments for improper speech involved local communities. All these social contexts contribute to the significance of transgressive language in drama.

The functions transgressive language performs in drama are ultimately based on the moral significance accorded to language in medieval society. The drama not only reflects that significance, but exploits it and expands it as the foundation of important dramatic devices and conventions which dramatists in turn adapted in the service of entertainment, socio-political comment, and religious instruction.

A chronological progression towards increasingly complex uses of transgressive language can be traced through the fifteenth-century morality plays and the three sixteenth-century moralities, *Magnyfycence*, *The Play of the*

Wether, and *King Johan*. This progression was driven by cultural, political, and religious change in the sixteenth century, and reflects the sensitivity of the topics that this language was used to address. As part of this process of change, the major functions of transgressive language to characterize, to involve audiences, and to comment on social and theological topics increase in complexity.

This chapter begins the process of defining transgressive language by establishing its moral significance and non-dramatic context. Language is transgressive when it ignores religious teaching, or the ecclesiastical and secular laws governing speech in society. It may be transgressive according to the ways in which it is used, or in the forms it takes. This chapter reveals that theological and legal definitions of transgressive language provide an important social context for interpreting such language when it is used in drama, and shows that responses to its use in drama differ markedly from responses to its use in society.

Sermons and transgressive language

In the thirteenth century St Thomas Aquinas provided early and influential definitions of the sins of defamation, backbiting, and ridicule. He asserts that:

> *dehonoratio quae fit in verbis dicitur convicium vel improperium* ('disgrace which takes place in words is called insult or abuse').[1]

He continues:

> *convicium et improperium consistunt in verbis, sicut et contumelia ... per omnia haec repræsentatur aliquis defectus alicujus in detrimentum honoris ipsius* ('insult and abuse consist of words as does defamation ... through all of them someone's defect is exhibited to the detriment of his/her honour').
> (2a2æ 72, 1, p. 158)

Aquinas distinguishes between the sins of defamation and detraction, according to the motivation of the speaker, and the presence or absence of the person spoken about. He declares that

> *contumelia oritur ex ira, detractio autem ex invidia* ('defamation originates in anger but detraction originates in envy')
> (2a2æ 73, 3, p. 176)

---

[1] St Thomas Aquinas, *Summa Theologiae*, 60 vols, vol. 38 (London: Eyre and Spottiswoode, 1975), 2a2æ 72, 1, p. 156. My translations.

and asserts:

> *verbo aliquis dupliciter aliquem lædit: uno modo in manifesto, et hoc fit per contumeliam ... alio modo occulte, et hoc fit per detractionem* ('a person harms someone else by words in two ways: one way is openly, and this is through defamation ... the other way is secretly, and this is through detraction').
> (2a2æ 73, 1, p. 170)

Aquinas indicates the significance of witnesses to both these sins of language. Witnesses are also important in later medieval laws governing language use, and their role is transferred, as we shall see in Chapter 3, to the audience of biblical plays, especially those which take language and law as a theme. In Aquinas's view the presence of one or more witnesses who hear insulting remarks exacerbates the sin. He writes that one way in which words can cause harm is that:

> *homo damnificatur quantum ad detrimentum honoris sui vel reverentiæ sibi ab aliis exhibendæ. Et ideo major est contumelia, si aliquis alicui defectum suum dicat coram multis* ('a man is injured by the loss of his honour or of the respect due to him from others, and for that reason the defamation is greater if someone tells a man his failing in the presence of many people').
> (2a2æ 72, 1, p. 158)

Other definitions given by Aquinas provide possible interpretations of transgressive language in the festive context of which the biblical plays were a part. He makes the point that:

> *cum peccatum convicii vel contumeliæ ex animo dicentis dependeat, potest contingere quod sit peccatum veniale, si sit leve convicium, non multum hominem dehonestans, et proferatur ex aliqua animi levitate, vel ex levi ira absque firmo proposito aliquem dehonestandi* ('since the sin of abuse or defamation depends on the spirit in which it is said, it can happen that it is venial sin, if it is trivial abuse not dishonouring a man much, and uttered from some spirit of lightheartedness, or from slight anger without a firm intention that someone should be disgraced').
> (2a2æ 72, 3, p. 162)

Mockery may be spoken with the intention of insulting, but it is conventionally associated with laughter, and Aquinas writes that:

> *derisio ... agitur enim ludo quandoque inter amicos, unde et delusio nominatur* ('because attacking with mockery sometimes happens between friends for fun, it is also called making fun').
> (2a2æ 75, 2, p. 194)

Dramatists who use transgressive language in their plays exploit these distinctions between language intended to harm and the same language which is intended to amuse. However, Aquinas notes that mockery may not always be lighthearted and takes mockery to be *gravius quam contumelia* ('more serious than defamation') if it is aimed at belittling someone. This is because:

> *contumeliosus videtur accipere malum alterius seriose, illusor autem in ludum; et ita videtur esse major contemptus et dehonoratio* ('the person who defames another seems to take his evil seriously, but the person who makes fun of another seems to treat it as a joke, and so there seems to be greater contempt and dishonour').
> (2a2æ 75, 2, p. 196)

The use of transgressive language in drama may, however, be justified as being governed by the intention of the author to entertain and instruct rather than by the intention of a character who insults and mocks. Aquinas's careful attention to context and intention in defining what constitutes transgressive language therefore needs to be more than matched by the literary critic.

Aquinas goes on to distinguish between words and actions, defining the kind of mockery which is spoken and that which is not dependent on speech. He writes

> *subsannatio et irrisio conveniunt in fine, sed differunt in modo, quia irrisio fit ore, idest verbo et cachinnis; subsannatio autem naso rugato* ('mocking gesture and mockery are alike in their purpose, but different in performance because mockery happens orally, that is by words and laughter; while wrinkling the nose is the mocking gesture').
> (2a2æ 75, 2, p. 194)

This is a distinction which we will find is significant in the context of medieval drama, where both kinds of mockery are used.

Aquinas provides a telling justification for the use of apparently sinful language in medieval drama. He considers that:

> *revelare peccatum occultum, quod ... ad detractionem pertinet, est actus virtutis vel caritatis, dum aliquis fratris peccatum denuntiat, ejus emendationem intendens* ('to expose a secret sin, which ... is part of detraction, is an act of virtue or charity when someone denounces the sin of his brother, intending its amendment').
> (2a2æ 73, 2, p. 172)

The charitable denunciation of sin is an important justification for the use of transgressive language, which could control the way the language was interpreted, and received. Qualifications such as this, and the harmless desire to entertain, may have provided defensive contexts for a dramatist who was using mockery in a play as social satire against powerful social groups or individuals.

The definitions of defamation, detraction, and mockery given by Aquinas are found in later sermons where they are expanded by the writers, who refer to them as 'sins of the mouth'.[2] These sins are again defined according to their differing motivations, uses and consequences, and the involvement of hearers.

Medieval sermon writers do not use the words 'insult' or 'mockery'. 'Insult' is not recorded in use before 1620,[3] and the earliest use of the word 'mockery' recorded in the *Middle English Dictionary* is 1425,[4] so for many of the sermon writers and particularly for their audiences it too would have been unknown. The medieval sermons use other terms. During the second quarter of the fifteenth century Richard Rolle set out a long list of sins of the mouth, including: 'bacbitynge ... defamynge, cursynge, scornynge'.[5] The *Quattuor Sermones*, from the last quarter of the fifteenth century, lists backbiting, scorning, and cursing.[6] Sermons such as *A Myrour to Lewde Men and Wymmen*,[7] from about 1400; sermon 17 in the collection of *Middle English Sermons*,[8] dating from between 1378 and 1417; and the 1440 sermon cycle *Jacob's Well*[9] add slander to their lists. Slander and defamation appear to be used as interchangeable terms.

Since the condemnation of sins of the mouth was a social rather than a theological matter, Lollard and orthodox Catholic writers hold similar opinions. The Lollard sermon *The Lanterne of Li3t*, dated 1409–10, condemns 'bakbiters',[10] while the Lollard sermon for Quinquagesima Sunday, from the

---

[2] See, for example, Venetia Nelson, ed., *A Myrour to Lewde Men and Wymmen*, Middle English Texts 14 (Heidelberg: Carl Winter Universitätsverlag, 1981), p. 126; Arthur Brandeis, ed., *Jacob's Well*, EETS OS 115, pt. 1 (London: Kegan Paul, Trench, Trübner, 1900), p. 294. I am grateful to the Council of the Early English Text Society for permission to quote from the EETS editions of the sermons cited in this work.

[3] J.A. Simpson and E.S.C. Weiner, eds, *The Oxford English Dictionary* (Oxford: Clarendon Press, 1989).

[4] Sherman M. Kuhn and John Reidy, eds, *A Middle English Dictionary* (Ann Arbour: University of Michigan Press, 1975).

[5] S.J. Ogilvie-Thomson, ed., *Richard Rolle: Prose and Verse*, EETS 293 (Oxford: Oxford University Press, 1988), pp. 11–12.

[6] N.F. Blake, ed., *Quattuor Sermones*, Middle English Texts 2 (Heidelberg: Carl Winter Universitätsverlag, 1975), pp. 12–13, 49. I am grateful to Universitätsverlag C. Winter for permission to quote from their editions of the sermons cited in this work.

[7] Nelson, ed., *A Myrour to Lewde Men and Wymmen*, p. 25.

[8] Woodburn O. Ross, ed., *Middle English Sermons*, EETS OS 209 (London: Oxford University Press, 1940), pp. xl, 101.

[9] Brandeis, ed., *Jacob's Well*, pp. xiii, 294.

[10] Lilian M. Swinburn, ed., *The Lantern of Li3t*, EETS OS 101 (London: Kegan Paul, Trench, Trübner, 1917), pp. xiii, 98.

middle of the first half of the fifteenth century, condemns 'falce diffamynge' and the person who 'falsli sclaundreth his brother'.[11]

The sermon writers follow Aquinas in distinguishing between verbal mockery and 'making mowes', or pulling faces. The writer *A Myrour to Lewde Men and Wymmen* defines scorning:

> þat is whan a man scorneþ and despiseþ anoþer for him þinkeþ þat he haþ noght þe same vertues þat he haþ; and also scorneþ gode men for here manere of lyuyng is noght like his.(106)

The same text declares: 'synnes of þe mouth ben these: ... blerynge in scorn & despyte, [mowe makynge]' (126). Richard Rolle similarly advises his readers that they should not 'mowe on any man' (12). There are few references to 'making mowes' in either biblical or morality plays, but where they occur, they usually take the form of mocking remarks directed at Christ during his Crucifixion, such as the N-Town Quartus Judeus's derisive: 'We grete 3ou wel on þe newe gett, | And make on 3ou a mowe.'[12] However, the most significant form of mockery by action in the biblical plays is the mocking of Christ by clothing Him in white and purple during His Passion.

The sins of the mouth which are most frequently and consistently preached against in sermons are defamation, also called slander, and backbiting. The author of *Jacob's Well* declared: '3if þou clepe an-oþer "theef", or suche an-oþer name þat soundyth defame .... for malyce & for wretthe, wherby he my3te be vnworschepyd, it is dedly sinne' (99). The sermon writers place great emphasis on what Aquinas calls *detractio,* and his definition of this sin forms part of their definition of backbiting. According to the author of one of the *Quattuor Sermones*:

> The second synne is enuye and thys is when thou art sory for thy neyghbours welfare and ioyest of his euylfare. Of this wyckyd synne comyth many braunchis ... The thyrd is bacbytyng and that is to speke yuel behynde hym whiche thou mayst not ne wylt not auowe afore hym. (51)

The sins of defamation and detraction are referred to in drama, but less frequently than in the sermons. They are used in themes in a small number of biblical plays.

---

[11] Gloria Cigman, ed., *Lollard Sermons*, EETS 294 (Oxford: Oxford University Press, 1989), pp. 31, 107.
[12] Spector, ed., *The N-Town Play*, play 32 *The Crucifixion*, ll. 208–9. All quotations from N-Town plays are from this edition.

In drama the distinction between defamation and backbiting becomes apparent when, for example, in the Chester *Innocents,* the first woman calls the first knight 'stronge theiffe'.[13] This is common abuse in the context of the action, but is nevertheless defamatory. When the N-Town detractors slander Mary and Joseph at the beginning of the *Trial of Mary and Joseph* this is backbiting, because they are rejoicing in what they believe to be the couple's 'euylfare'. This rejoicing takes the form of remarks which would be familiar as gossip in any small community.

The sermons show that hearers as well as speakers could be tainted by sins of the mouth. The writer of the *Quattuor Sermones* picks up Aquinas's observations about hearers, in order to condemn them. He warns that if 'though thou speke not euyl thyself thou hast lykyng to here euylspekyng of hym ... thou synnest dedely. For not onely he that spekyth euyl but also he that wol gladly here euyl spoken are in default of synne' (51). This definition enables dramatists to position an audience in relation, for example, to the slandering of the Virgin, tempting them, and implicitly judging their willingness to participate in that act.

While dramatists make effective use of the sermon definitions of sins of the mouth, they do not use the lively, and often lurid imagery associated with those definitions. The author of *A Myrour to Lewde Men and Wymmen* provides this description: 'the ferþe branche of yuel tonge is bakbityng, and þei þat vseþ þat vice may be liknet to þe foxe taile for her trecherie ... bakbiters beþ þe deueles scolers' (214). *Jacob's Well* favours canine images for those who commit sins of the mouth and calls the backbiter 'a bocherys dogge, euermore hauyng a blody mowth full of synfull defamyges' (262). This imagistic conception of sins of the mouth is also evident in sermon descriptions of punishments awaiting those who misuse language. John Mirk warns in his homilies: 'þoo at louen to bakbyte so, hell-howndes schull gnawe hem bak and bely wythouten any lesyng, but yf þay amende er þay hethen passe'.[14] A Lollard sermon for the *Second Sunday in Lent* also uses canine imagery for backbiters when it warns that 'þe deuel huntiþ a man þat is his prey, and letiþ slip at him his grehoundis þat rennen not wiþ open mouþe, but pursuen ful stilly, and sharply rennen at þe backe, þat ben bacbiters and priue sowers of discorde' (154). The savage imagery of the sermons is not transferred directly into the extant drama, being incompatible with the biblical and allegorical topics, but it indicates that transgressive language was perceived as a form of violence, and it is commonly associated with physical violence in the biblical plays.

---

[13] R.M. Lumiansky and David Mills, eds, *The Chester Mystery Cycle*, 2 vols, EETS SS 3, 9 (London: Oxford University Press, 1974; 1986), play X *The Innocents*, l. 341. All quotations from the Chester plays are from this edition.

[14] Theodore Erbe, ed., *Mirk's Festial: A Collection of Homilies by Johannes Mirkus*, EETS ES 97 (London: Kegan Paul, Trench, Trübner, 1905), p. 284.

Both orthodox Catholic and Lollard sermons characterize backbiting as manslaughter. The Lollard author of *The Lanterne of Li3t* declares 'Þis bakbiter sleeþ þre at a strok. Þat is to seie his owne soule, his wilful heerar, & him þat þei falsli sclaundren' (98). The author of the orthodox *Myrour to Lewde Men and Wymmen* declares: 'þis comandement defendeth vs all gostliche manslaghter, as þus: whan a man hateþ anoþer dedliche, or bakbiteþ him or sclaundreþ him forto byneme him his gode los or his lifelode wherby he schulde be susteyned, he is þen gostliche a mansleer' (80). This view of defamation and backbiting is taken up by the N-Town dramatist in the *Moses* play, where he provides homiletic, rather than dramatic, elaborations on each of the Ten Commandments. Moses says of the fifth:

> Vnyrstonde þis precept þus:
>   Scle no wyght with wurd nor wyll.
> Wykkyd worde werkyth oftyntyme grett ill:
>   Bewar þerfore of wykkyd langage.
> Wyckyd spech many on doth spyll:
>   Therfore of spech beth not owtrage.
> (6: 133–8)

The imagery suggests the destructive effect of defamation and detraction upon the victim, and associates it with mortal sin. However, while sermons preached in vivid terms of the eternal punishments awaiting those who committed these sins, the punishments commonly imposed by ecclesiastical and secular courts do not reflect an association with manslaughter, but with socially disruptive offences such as fornication or selling mouldy bread.

Language and the laws

Of all the forms of sinful language condemned in medieval sermons, only defamation was actionable at law. Records of defamation cases in both ecclesiastical and secular courts indicate that the proper and respectful use of language was not just an ideal set out in sermons, but was a major concern in medieval society.[15]

As a sin, defamation came under the jurisdiction of ecclesiastical courts, unless the plaintiff 'pleaded that they had actually suffered some definite harm other than simple loss of good name',[16] in which case the action was heard in

---

[15] Carl Lindahl, *Earnest Games: Folkloric Patterns in the Canterbury Tales* (Bloomington: Indiana University Press, 1987), p. 87.

[16] R.H. Helmholz, ed., *Select Cases on Defamation to 1600*, Selden Society, vol. 101 (London: Selden Society, 1986), p. lii. I am grateful to the Selden Society for permission to quote from this work.

secular courts. Both jurisdictions required that the person claiming defamation should have been of 'good fame' before the defamation occurred,[17] malice had to be a motive, [18] there had to be witnesses,[19] and some damage had to result either to the victim's good reputation, or through financial loss,[20] otherwise the words were merely abusive. No distinction is made under either jurisdiction between defamation and detraction, since both involve damage to a person's reputation. Mockery was not actionable in law unless it damaged a person's good name, when it would be treated as defamation.

Court cases under both jurisdictions from the thirteenth to the sixteenth century indicate that many of the forms of transgressive vernacular vocabulary which occur in drama constituted defamation in society throughout the period covered by this study. The transgressiveness of this vernacular vocabulary is thus established in society, although in drama it is most commonly used simply as abuse rather than being defamatory in the legal sense.

The cases identify some of the widespread and long-lasting vocabulary of insults recognized as defamation in medieval law. The consistory court of the Diocese of York in 1381 heard that John Greenhode called John Topcliffe 'false man' and 'false lurdan'.[21] 'Lurdan', meaning 'lout' or 'scoundrel', is common abuse, but the accusation of falseness, meaning untrustworthiness, is defamatory because it could lead to economic injury by implying that the defamed person would not pay their debts or honour their obligations.

Accusations of falseness were common. Carl Lindahl suggests that 'the insult quoted most frequently in the London records is 'false man'.[22] At the consistory court in the Diocese of York in 1424–25 John Rayner was accused of defaming Thomas Robinson by calling him 'false side-glance thief'.[23] At the commissary court in the Diocese of London in 1481 Robert Faram called Thomas Thomson a 'false knave'. John Howie complained of being called a 'false harlot' in 1513, and in Norwich in 1522, Christine Crow was accused of calling William Crane 'false churl'.[24]

Despite social sensitivity to accusations of falseness such accusations are common as simple abuse in both medieval drama and literature. The Wife of

---

[17] Ibid., pp. xxi, xxxv.
[18] Ibid., pp. xxx, xxxii.
[19] Ibid., pp. xxii–iii. See also Charles Donahue Jr., 'Proof by Witnesses in the Church Courts of Medieval England: An Imperfect Reception of the Learned Law', in Morris A. Arnold et al., eds, *On The Laws and Customs of England* (Chapel Hill: University of North Carolina Press, 1981), p. 151; and J.H. Baker, *An Introduction to English Legal History*, 2nd edn (London: Butterworth, 1979), p. 64.
[20] Helmholz, *Select Cases*, pp. xxxviii, xli.
[21] Ibid., p. 4.
[22] Lindahl, *Earnest Games*, p. 77.
[23] Helmholz, *Select Cases*, p. 7.
[24] Ibid., pp. 21, 23, 15.

Bath in Chaucer's *Canterbury Tales* calls her fifth husband 'false theef' when he hits her.[25] In the Towneley *Herod* the first woman calls the first soldier 'false thefe'.[26] From the contexts in which the defamatory words are spoken the audiences would interpret them as common insults from everyday life which function simply as abusive angry responses. However, when Pilate, in the York *Resurrection*, calls the second knight 'Fals recrayed knyght',[27] this is angry abuse which is also highly defamatory because it attacks the martial status of the knight by naming him a coward as well as false.

The defamation cases show that the imputation of certain forms of low status could be very damaging. Nicholas Vernycombe complained in 1519 that Thomas Fawell 'did ... utter against...Nicholas the name and fame of servile condition, namely "bond churl" ... to the damage of the said Nicholas £20'.[28] The extent of the damage which could be caused by such defamation is illustrated by William Holdsworth, who writes that

> under cover of such a claim a powerful lord could be guilty of false imprisonment and all kinds of extortion. A petition of 1404 tells us that ... [g]ood and honest burgesses and free tenants are imprisoned till they make fine and ransom or consent to hold their lands in villeinage.[29]

Like accusations of falseness, terms signifying low status may be used in drama as simple abuse among low-status characters, but when such terms are used against Christ by figures of evil authority in biblical plays they draw attention to His supreme status and His accusers' ignorance.

Defamation in terms of servile status is associated with men in medieval records, but defamation in terms of sexual misconduct is frequently directed at women. Evidence directly from a female victim of defamatory language is provided in the Paston letters. In 1448 Margaret Paston wrote to her husband that during an altercation: 'Wymondham called my moder and me strong hores'. The women took their grievance immediately to the prior of Norwich.[30]

Men were also defamed in terms of sexual misconduct, but, as Laura Gowing observes, sexual defamation of men actually takes the form of

---

[25] Larry D. Benson, ed., *The Riverside Chaucer*, 3rd edn (Oxford: Oxford University Press, 1987), *The Wife of Bath's Prologue*, l. 800.

[26] Stevens and Cawley, eds, *The Towneley Plays*, play 16 *Herod*, l. 338. All quotations from the Towneley plays are from this edition.

[27] Beadle, ed., *The York Plays* (London: Edward Arnold, 1982), play XI *Moses and Pharaoh*, l. 229. All quotations from the York plays are from this edition.

[28] Helmholz, *Select Cases*, p. 46.

[29] William Holdsworth, *A History of English Law*, 12 vols, vol. III (London: Methuen, 1925), p. 503.

[30] Norman Davis, ed., *Paston Letters and Papers of the Fifteenth Century*, pt. 1 (Oxford: Clarendon Press, 1971), p. 224. I am grateful to Oxford University Press for permission to quote from this work.

challenges to their status rather than to their own behaviour. She writes of 'insults that are ... centred around words like "cuckold" and "whoremaster" that concern not their own sexual behaviour, but that of women over whom they are supposed to be in control'.[31] An interpretation in terms of a husband's control over the sexuality of his wife is certainly relevant to the defamation of Joseph as a cuckold in the N-Town *Trial of Mary and Joseph*, especially in view of his age and comic potential. In medieval society accusations of sexual misconduct weighed heavily on both sexes since they placed them both in the position of having to purge themselves of the accusation before the ecclesiastical court or suffer the humiliation of public penance and damage to their reputation. Mary and Joseph are both forced to purge themselves in the N-Town play as they become victims of sexually loaded backbiting and defamation, but, as with other forms of transgressive language, the drama both reflects and differs from contemporary social practice. J.A. Sharpe observes that in early modern York 'the majority of defamation cases brought before [the Church courts] was concerned with sexual matters'.[32] Sexual slander in drama often reflects the seriousness, but not the frequency, of sexual defamation in society. However, its social significance creates tension, and thus more effective drama, when it is part of the linguistic licence permitted in drama.

Defamation and witnesses

In medieval law, wherever defamation was alleged witnesses were necessary to the process of judgment, and the function of witnesses in medieval defamation trials bears significantly on the involvement of spectators at biblical plays. In defamation cases the plaintiff would claim to have been defamed 'before good and substantial persons among whom he had previously been of good fame',[33] and produce witnesses to his or her good name to disprove the defamatory accusations, a process known as compurgation.[34] Defendants would also produce witnesses to testify that what they had said was the truth, or that the offending words were spoken in anger,[35] or with charitable intention. Thomas

---

[31] Laura Gowing, 'Gender and the Language of Insult in Early Modern London', *History Workshop*, 35 (Spring 1993), p. 4.
[32] J.A. Sharpe, *Defamation and Sexual Slander in Early Modern England: The Church Courts at York*, Borthwick Papers 58 (University of York: 1981), p. 15. See also C.A. Haigh, 'Slander and the Church Courts in the Sixteenth Century', in *Transactions of the Lancashire and Cheshire Antiquarian Society*, vol. 78 (1975), p. 2.
[33] Helmholz, *Select Cases*, p. 6.
[34] Ibid., p. xxii. See also J.H. Baker, *An Introduction to English Legal History*, 2nd edn (London: Butterworth, 1979), p. 64.
[35] Helmholz, *Select Cases*, p. xxxii.

Hodgeson claimed in 1521 that he had addressed John Fyfield 'with benevolent spirit and with the intention of counselling him'.[36] A case at the commissary court for the Diocese of London in 1514 illustrates the importance of witnesses. A woman named Harmon was charged with defaming Margaret James by calling her 'strong priest's whore' and 'bawdy whore'. Harmon's accusation was liable to result in the punishment of James for fornication if she could not disprove it. James was told to appear before the court with four witnesses to purge herself. She failed to purge successfully, but Harmon failed to produce witnesses to the truth of her accusations against James. Each woman was therefore ordered to do the same penance, which was to 'march before the procession on the Sunday following with a wax candle and a rosary in her right hand, dressed in honest garb, and at the time of the priest's offertory to declare publicly to the congregation the cause for which she was undergoing penance'.[37] In the Passion plays of all the cycles dramatists use the audience's presumed Christian faith and knowledge, together with their understanding of the role of witnesses in defamation trials, to position the audience as potential witnesses to the trials of Christ dramatized in the plays.

The defamation cases referred to so far involve imputations of crime, low status, and sexual misconduct. If such imputations were proved they could result in humiliating penances for the person accused. There were, however, defamatory accusations which could have fatal consequences in medieval law for any person who was unable to prove his or her innocence.

Capital offences and the Passion plays

In the Passion plays Christ is conventionally accused of treason, witchcraft, and heresy. Richard Helmholz observes that being defamed as a traitor 'was apt to do ... serious damage to a person's reputation.... It was not a word men used in jest'.[38] John Bellamy reveals that the common penalty for treason was of the kind suffered by William Aleyn when he was sentenced 'to be drawn through the middle of Leicester to the gallows and there hanged and beheaded'.[39]

Barbara Rosen observes that: 'magic and sorcery were generally punished lightly by penance or the pillory – even after the Church had classed them as

---

[36] Ibid., p. 15.
[37] Ibid., p. 24.
[38] Ibid., p. ci.
[39] John G. Bellamy, *The Law of Treason in England in the Later Middle Ages*, Cambridge Studies in English Legal History (Cambridge: Cambridge University Press, 1970), pp. 151–3.

heresy'.[40] The accusation of witchcraft could, however, have more serious results. Rosen writes that 'the penalty for felonious witchcraft or conjuration was hanging, unless these also involved treason'.[41] The early fifteenth-century treatise *Dives and Pauper* sets out 'How wychecraft is dampnyd be þe lawe, & what pyne longith þerto';[42] the statute of 1401, *De Heretico Comburendo*, permitted the burning of heretics in England, and heresy trials continued throughout the period during which the cycles of biblical plays flourished.[43] Margery Kempe, in the first quarter of the fifteenth century, relates that when she visited York:

> þer comyn many of þe Erchebiscopys meny, despisyng hir, callyng hir "loller", & "heretyke", & sworyn many an horrybyl othe þat she xulde be brent.[44]

While the biblical plays continued to be performed in the sixteenth century, the burning of heretics gathered pace as the Catholic Church and Protestant reformers struggled for supremacy.

The original audiences would have understood the potential consequences of the accusations made against Christ in the Passion plays, and that knowledge probably added to the drama of His confrontation with secular and ecclesiastical authority in those plays. In the York plays Christ is constantly named as 'þis warlowe': in *Christ before Pilate (1): The Dream of Pilate's Wife* Caiaphas tells Pilate 'He with wicchecrafte þis wile he has wrought' (XXX: 293). Leyon, in the N-Town play *The Betrayal*, mocks Christ saying: 'Shewe forth þi wychecrafte and nygramansye' (28: 131). In the York *Remorse of Judas* and *Christ before Pilate (2): The Judgement* the priests accuse Christ of treason. In the latter play Caiaphas observes: 'To be kyng he claymeth, with croune' (XXXIII: 329), and Pilate declares: 'Sir, trulye þat touched to treasoune' (XXXIII: 333). In the Towneley *Buffetting* Christ is called 'fals tratur' (21: 171), and in the N-Town play of *The Conspiracy* Rewfyn says of Christ 'He is an eretyk and a tretour bolde' (26: 309). The

---

[40] Barbara Rosen, *Witchcraft in England 1558–1618* (Amherst: University of Massachusetts Press, 1991), p. 21.

[41] Ibid., p. 52. See also J.A.F. Thomson, *The Transformation of Medieval England 1370–1529* (London: Longman, 1983), on the trial of Eleanor Chobham who was 'accused and found guilty of involvement in sorcery' (p. 191).

[42] Priscilla Heath Barnum, ed., *Dives and Pauper*, EETS 275, vol. 1, part 1 (London: Oxford University Press, 1976), precept 34. See also Robert Bartlett, *Trial by Fire and Water: The Medieval Judicial Ordeal* (Oxford: Clarendon Press, 1986), on the use of torture for proving the guilt or innocence of a person accused of witchcraft, heresy, or treason (p. 144).

[43] John Guy, *Tudor England* (Oxford: Oxford University Press, 1988), p. 26.

[44] Sandford Brown Meech, ed., *The Book of Margery Kempe*, vol. 1 EETS OS 212 (London: Oxford University Press, 1940), p. 123.

eventual condemnation of Christ by Pilate rests on the accusations of treason. However, serious as these allegations could be in real life, Chapter 3 will demonstrate that recognition of these accusations as defamation is more important to the didactic purpose of the biblical plays than recognition of their consequences, because as defamation they situate the audience as witnesses and illustrate the ignorance of the defamers.

The laws of defamation examined so far were intended to protect the reputations of most individuals, and fell within the jurisdiction of local ecclesiastical and secular courts, but the reputations of magnates were protected by the *Scandalum magnatum* statute of 1275. We will find that major differences exist between the treatment of lords in social practice and in drama.

Transgressive language and lords

William Holdsworth writes that *Scandalum magnatum* was not enacted 'so much to guard the reputation of the magnates, as to safeguard the peace of the kingdom', and he cites a statute from the reign of Richard II which reenacted the original and records the anxiety that

> debates and slanders might arise betwixt the said lords or between the lords and the commons ... wherof great peril and mischief might come to all the realm.[45]

However, J.A. Baker suggests that 'the purpose of an action on the statute was clearly to vindicate the magnate's name'.[46] Thomas More confirms the statute's defence of the nobility in his 1531 *Confutation of Tyndale's Answer* when he writes that:

> it is not onely by the comon lawes of thys realme vppon great payne forbyden that any man sholde with any slaunderouse raylynge wordes mysse vse hym selfe toward hys prynce / but also by the playne statut *de scandalis magnatum* sore and streyghtly prohybyted, that no man shall slaunderously speke of any noble man in the realme.[47]

There seem to be few records of such cases brought before the courts. This suggests that a slandered lord may himself have dealt with his slanderer in less formal and more direct ways, if he felt the offence to be worthy of response.

---

[45] Holdsworth, *English Law*, p. 409.
[46] Baker, *English Legal History*, p. 365.
[47] Louis A. Schuster, Richard C. Marius, James P. Lusardi, and Richard J. Schoeck, eds, *The Complete Works of St. Thomas More*, vol. 8, *A Confutation of Tyndale's Answer* (London: Yale, 1973), p. 592.

The impulse to insult, abuse, and defame figures of authority, which *Scandalum magnatum* was enacted to control in society, is, however, licensed in the biblical plays where characters such as Herod, Pilate, and Caiaphas address the audience with insults and may be insulted and mocked by the audience in return. The characters are, of course, known villains, but if they are dressed as familiar figures of contemporary authority, such as noblemen and bishops, spectators are given an opportunity to express disapprobation in a way which was unlawful in everyday life, except at times when festive inversions of the hierarchy were licensed. Thus language which would be punished in society was actually encouraged within the context of the drama.

However, in both biblical and morality plays, which are concerned with the representation of divine justice and mercy, the power to punish is a significant feature. Characters who reject or subvert the norms and ideals of medieval society and Christian doctrine through their use of transgressive language are exposed to a variety of punishments which the spectators witness and at times inflict. In the case of the known biblical villains, spectators are encouraged to carry out their punishment by ridiculing them in a communal expression of disapproval which reflects everyday forms of punishment.

Transgressive language and punishment

In medieval society exhibitory punishments which exposed offenders to the insults and mockery of their neighbours were often the penalty for the use of insulting and defamatory language. Language which was punishable when used between individuals in public was permitted when it was used to express the displeasure of the community and uphold the codes of behaviour which were acceptable to both that community and the hegemony (Church and State). Mary Bateson, in *Borough Customs*, observes that 'the pillory, or the cucking-stool is the usual punishment for slander named in borough custumals',[48] and the London *Liber Albus* of 1419 declares *Judicia Pilloriae pro mendaciis, scandalis, falsitatibus, et deceptionibus*.[49] John Bellamy writes that in 1489 female scolds in Hereford were to be made to 'stand with bare feet and their hair let down, during such time as they may be seen by all passers-by upon the

---

[48] Mary Bateson, ed., *Borough Customs*, 2 vols, vol. 1, Selden Society (London: Bernard Quaritch, 1904), p. 80, n. 7. See also Arthur F. Leach, ed., *Beverley Town Documents*, Selden Society (London: Bernard Quaritch, 1900). The documents record the existence of a cucking-stool in Beverley, where a smith was identified as 'John Lorymer by the Cuckstoolpit' (p. 36).

[49] Henry Thomas Riley, ed., *Munimenta Gildhallae Londoniensis: Liber Albus, Liber Custumarum, Liber Horn*, vol. III (London: Longman, Green, Longman & Roberts, 1862), p. 531.

road'.⁵⁰ This appears to be a public sexualisation of the scold in order to deprive her of the authority she attempted to exert through her use of language. That pretended authority challenged male status and authority and so it was punished by the emphasizing of the female identity. However, this sexualization is a specific instance which is part of an exhibitory punishment, rather than an example of a comprehensive sexualizing of punishment.

A male challenge to status and authority is also punished by exhibition. Sumptuary laws from 1509 condemn farm labourers, shepherds, and common labourers who wear cloth worth more than two shillings a yard to 'imprisonment in the stokkys by thre days'.⁵¹ In towns the pillory was more common than the stocks;⁵² nevertheless, although exhibitory punishments may have taken different forms according to the ecclesiastical or secular nature of the court, the offence committed, the gender of the wrong-doer, and the rural or urban location, the intention – to humiliate the offender and reinforce the power structures of medieval society – remained the same.

The link between mockery and punishment would be well understood by a late medieval audience, so that the social and political significance of mockery as punishment could be exploited in drama. However, the examples referred to above mark an important distinction between mockery in society and that found in the biblical plays. It is evident that mockery in medieval society tended to be associated with petty crimes and misdemeanours. The frontispiece to *Munimenta Gildhallae Londoniensis* volume III shows 'a baker drawn on a Hurdle with a faulty loaf' which is hanging round his neck.⁵³ Mockery as a punishment was not only intended to shame and degrade the culprit, but was associated with low status – both that of the culprit and that of the crime. In the biblical plays mockery is directed against characters who are known villains, but who also represent authority and high status – Herod, Pilate, Caiaphas, and their soldiers. They are characterized in ways which are intended by the dramatists to incite mockery from the audience, and that mockery carries with it connotations of low status.

Mockery which is licensed and encouraged in society contributes to our understanding of the use of mockery as punishment in the biblical plays. Susan Brigden offers a late example when she writes that in 1530:

> facing their horses tails, four men ... rode ... through the City ... to be publicly shamed ... Their clothes were festooned with copies of

---

⁵⁰ John Bellamy, *Crime and Public Order in England in the Later Middle Ages* (London: Routledge and Kegan Paul, 1973), p. 185.
⁵¹ *Statutes of the Realm*, 1 Henry VIII c. 14, 6 Henry VIII c. 1.
⁵² Bellamy, *Crime and Public Order*, p. 184.
⁵³ Riley, ed., *Munimenta Gildhallae Londoniensis*.

Tyndale's forbidden Testament ... [They] were then set in the pillory'.[54]

The degradation of the reformers and their books through the streets of London served the interests of the hegemony, but medieval audiences might have been familiar with less formalized punishment of low-status offenders, such as *charivaris*, the punishment by shame and mockery, carried out by the community in which the offender lived.[55] Adam Fox, however, draws a useful distinction between licensed and unlicensed mockery when he observes that in early modern England: 'The alehouse offered a sanctuary for relative freedom of speech ... it provided the chance to ridicule in private those whom it was an offence to challenge in public.'[56] This freedom produced libels, songs, and pictures created by lower-status men and women to mock figures of local authority, but this unlicensed mockery was punished by 'large fines, whipping and branding'.[57]

While the unlicensed use of transgressive language was risky, licensed expressions of discontent which focused on the misdemeanours of members of a local community may have provided the opportunity for that community to 'let off steam'. People might have enjoyed a sense of freedom as they used sinful language without risking punishment themselves. Nevertheless, through their mocking and abusive language the pressure to conform was reasserted as they articulated, upheld, and reinforced the moral codes of the Church and society. Through the licensed use of transgressive language, therefore, hegemonic interests could maintain control over disruptive forces in society. Mockery used to condemn and punish in the biblical plays cannot, therefore, be regarded as an act of transgression by the spectators. It is rather a licensed act, in the tradition of medieval festive license which permitted the activities of Lords of Misrule and Boy Bishops.

Transgressive language used communally to punish had a counterpart in high-status performative language, and this too is found in drama. In society language as punishment was used most powerfully in excommunication, referred to in medieval sermons as the Great Curse. Excommunication was the

---

[54] Susan Brigden, *London and the Reformation* (Oxford: Clarendon Press, 1989), p. 183.
[55] Martin Ingram, 'Ridings, Rough Music and the "Reform of Popular Culture" in Early Modern England', *Past and Present*, 105 (November 1984), p. 82. The popularity and distribution of charivaris in England before the sixteenth century is open to debate, although John J. McGavin notes the existence of charivari in Scotland in 1390. See John J. McGavin, 'Robert III's "Rough Music": Charivari and Diplomacy in a Medieval Scottish Court', *The Scottish Historical Review*, vol. 74, 2: 198 (October 1995), p. 144. Colin Platt remarks on the scarcity of evidence before the early modern period, but considers that they 'undoubtedly had a much longer history'. See Colin Platt, *King Death* (London: UCL Press, 1996), p. 188.
[56] Adam Fox, 'Ballads, Libels and Popular Ridicule in Jacobean England', *Past and Present*, 145 (November 1994), p. 72.
[57] Ibid., p. 73.

Church's ultimate sanction against those who persistently committed offences which fell within its jurisdiction. When exhibitory punishments failed to correct sinners, excommunication excluded them from the Christian community.

The punishment was invested with the authority of the Church and thus required a proper and solemn form of words. *Jacob's Well* provides them: 'We denouncyn hem alle acursed, dampnyd, & departyd fro god to Sathan, þe feend, þat wyttyngly & malycyously ...' (55). Defamation is included in the long list of offences for which excommunication is the penalty. *Jacob's Well* declares:

> alle þo arn acursyd þat for malyce, or wynnyng, or fauour, or for ony oþer cause, dyffamyn or slaunderyn ony persone, & apeyryn his name among gode men & worschipfull þere he was no3t defamyd be-forn, & for þat slaundre he is put to his purgacyoun.
> (15)

Two opposite forms of language meet at this point. The power of authorized language is made explicit through the social consequences of excommunication as the sinful use of language is shown to exclude and alienate the user from society. *Jacob's Well* reveals the extent of this alienation when it also declares accursed anyone who gives excommunicants 'counseyl, fauour, or helpe' (61).

Excommunication is dramatized in the York *Cain and Abel* and the Towneley *Murder of Abel* where Cain's abusive responses to God's 'malison', or curse, challenge its power, as people in society challenged the power of the Great Curse. At a consistory court in London in 1493 Nan Hopper was accused of being 'a scorner of the court, saying "currse and blisse, I sett not a straw by the cursing ther"'.[58] In his General Prologue to *The Canterbury Tales*, Chaucer illustrates both the sinful and the orthodox views of excommunication. He includes disregard for the Great Curse among the sins and vices which characterize the Somonour, who teaches others 'to have noon awe | ... of the ercedekenes curs'.[59] However, the narrator asserts devoutly:

> ... well I woot he lyed right in dede;
> Of cursyng oghte ech gilty man him drede,
> For curs wol slee right as assoilyng savith.
> (659–61)

The Cain plays are unique in their representation of excommunication and the authority it connotes. Chapter 3 will show how they use Cain's trans-

---

[58] Paul Hair, ed., *Before the Bawdy Court* (London: Elek, 1973), p. 45.
[59] Benson, ed., *The Riverside Chaucer, General Prologue*, ll. 654–5.

gressive language to condemn challenges to the power of excommunication, while Chapter 7 will show how such a challenge becomes a virtue in the sixteenth-century morality *King Johan*, which promoted the views of Protestant reformers during the reigns of Henry VIII and Elizabeth I. However, the language of authority is less important as a punishing language in medieval drama than the licensed abuse and mockery of spectators.

The sermons and laws examined in this chapter reveal the moral and social significance of language in medieval society. The sermons establish the transgressive uses of language and begin to suggest their social significance. This is extended and emphasized by the defamation cases, which illustrate not only the words considered to constitute transgressive language, but the widespread use of such language. The court cases confirm evidence from the sermons that transgressive language was a continuing social concern, while the punishments meted out for its use show how medieval society responded to the unauthorized use of such language, and reveal that while the authoritative and formulaic language of excommunication was the ultimate punishment for defamation, many forms of linguistic transgression were punished by licensed communal ridicule and abuse.

Comparisons between the treatment of transgressive language in society and its use in drama reveal that although society and drama understand the same forms and uses of language to be transgressive, these are nevertheless exploited in drama. While there are similarities between society and drama in the perception of transgressive language, there are also important differences between society and drama in the treatment of that language and those who use it, and those differences are especially pronounced in drama's treatment of lordship, which exploits society's licence to punish socially disruptive behaviour through ridicule and abuse.

The significance of transgressive language in medieval society demonstrates that the use of such language in medieval drama is far more than just a stylistic or dramatic convention, but draws upon serious social concerns which dramatists would expect to influence an audience's reception of a play. However, while the sermons and laws define its social significance, we shall see that transgressive language as it is most widely used in medieval didactic drama takes forms which were not actionable at law, in order to perform functions which nevertheless depend upon the moral distinction between sinful and virtuous language.

Chapter 2
Transgressive language and characterization

Although the legal definitions of transgressive language provide important moral and social contexts for understanding the significance of such language when it is used in medieval drama, they are not sufficient on their own to define the many complex functions it performs there. Forms of transgressive language which were condemned in the medieval sermons, but not actionable at law, perform the primary dramatic function of characterization, upon which other social and didactic functions depend. These non-actionable forms are used to create characters who resemble members of medieval society. Biblical characters, and the personified virtues and vices of the moralities, are defined as belonging to that society by their use of the forms of transgressive language which would have been familiar to the audiences. The many forms of transgressive language create subtle shadings of character, all of which are based on the moral and social significance of language, and depend on the differences noted in Chapter 1 between medieval society's response to the use of transgressive language in society and the use of similar language in drama.

Transgressive language performs two functions when it is used as a means of creating characterizations: it indicates the spiritual status, and the social status, of the characters who use it. Spiritual status is the measure of a character's sinfulness,[1] but in didactic drama this is not simply an undifferentiated human condition which sets itself in opposition to God, but is defined, by a character's use of transgressive language, in its most extreme form as evil, and in lesser degrees, as a changeable state of sin. Evil in medieval drama may be defined as opposition to God which does not change; biblical villains such as Herod, and tempters such as Lucyfer in the morality *Wisdom* are evil. Sin, however, is opposition which is capable of change, like the shepherds in the biblical plays, and representatives of humanity such as Humanum Genus in the morality *The Castle of Perseverance*. A social distinction exists alongside this spiritual one as the difference between evil and sin is frequently linked to a character's place in the social hierarchy. The greater their social status the greater the spiritual fault represented by their use of transgressive language, and therefore the greater the degree of sin. Rulers

---

[1] Joerg O. Fichte, 'The Presentation of Sin as Verbal Action in the Moral Interludes', *Anglia*, 103 (1985), p. 41.

who abuse their power are evil, but low-status characters who use transgressive language are generally merely sinful.

These social distinctions are especially significant in the biblical plays, while social differences are less important in the fifteenth-century moralities, which dramatize the corruption of humanity in general. In both genres, however, dramatists vary their use of forms, style, and contexts associated with transgressive language to create subtle and didactically pointed characterizations.

This chapter begins with an illustration of the non-actionable forms of transgressive language which were condemned in the sermons and which contribute to characterization. It moves on to look at the association between forms and prosodic styles, and will illustrate important conventions governing the use of transgressive language as a dramatic device. It will then consider the significance of context, and will show that the complex interplay of form, intention, style, and the prior knowledge of the audience produce almost unlimited diversity in the range of transgressive language found in medieval drama. This diversity contributes to dramatically effective variations in the characterization of biblical characters, and of abstract personifications in the morality plays, defining their social and spiritual status, and making their actions and attitudes recognizable to medieval audiences.

Forms

Language in medieval didactic drama may be identified as transgressive in form (insults, abuse, oaths, curses), in intention (scorn and mockery), or in the sentiments it expresses. The most familiar forms of transgressive language used in medieval drama are those which were not actionable at law, but which are frequently defined and condemned in the sermons. Richard Rolle wrote that in addition to defamation:

> synnes of þe mouth ben these: to swere oft sithes ... sklaunrynge of Criste ... neune his name without reuerence ... bacbitynge ... cursynge, manacynge ... scornynge, unbuxomnes with word ... vayne speche, moche speche, fool speche.[2]

The *Quattuor Sermones* condemns 'auauntyng of euyl deedys',[3] while *A Myrour to Lewde Men and Wymmen* condemns 'avauntyng', and 'scornynge'.[4] *Jacob's Well* adds to these 'speche of harlotrye & rybaldrye, dy[s]honest

---

[2] Ogilvie-Thomson, ed., *Richard Rolle: Prose and Verse*, pp. 11–12.
[3] Blake, ed., *Quattuor Sermones*, p. 49.
[4] Nelson, ed., *A Myrour to Lewde Men and Wymmen*, p. 106.

woordys'.⁵ Oaths and curses of all kinds, threats, boasting, scorn, bawdy and offensive language, idle, loquacious and foolish speech are all, to varying degrees, influential in medieval drama.

Words which could constitute defamation in medieval society could also be used as common abuse, and this is the form they take most frequently in medieval drama. Insults, abuse, oaths, and curses, often of a most vituperative kind, were familiar in medieval drama and literature as a rhetorical device. Carl Lindahl refers to:

> a certain type of speech ... a language that was not taught in rhetoric books ... This folk rhetoric evolved verbally in face to face encounters.⁶

In everyday life insults, oaths, curses, and mockery are a means by which people emphasize the points they wish to make. They may be used most frequently during angry exchanges, but can occur in any social exchange. Medieval dramatists used this folk, or unofficial, rhetoric to characterize common speech. Pharaoh in the York *Moses and Pharaoh* calls Moses 'fals lurdayne' (XI: 229), but an attack on the reputation of Moses is not suggested. The insult is common abuse which emphasizes Pharaoh's anger. When the third shepherd in the Towneley *Second Shepherds' Play* calls Mak's wife, 'fals skawde' (13: 861), the insult is again common abuse associated with anger.⁷

A rich and varied vocabulary of oaths and curses contributes to transgressive language in medieval drama, and serves several purposes. Oaths and curses may be insulting in their own right, or contribute to the degree of insult being offered by one character to another, or to the audience. They may, however, simply emphasize other speech without being insulting. They are nevertheless transgressive. Orthodox sermon writers frequently preach against these sins of the mouth. In his *Homilies* John Mirk writes as if Christ Himself were preaching against swearing oaths:

> þys ... greuyth me most, þou settyst no3t by my passyon that I suffryd for þe; but by me horrybull swerus || all day, vmbraydys me sweryng by my face, by myn een, by myn armes, by myn nayles, by myn hert, by my blod ... by all my body. And soo þou marterys me by a foule vse and custom of sweryng.⁸

In the Towneley *Herod* play the King swears 'by Gottys dere nalys' (16: 116), and such oaths are common in medieval didactic drama. Equally common are minced oaths, like 'By cokkes body sakryde', used by the Worldling Nought in

---

⁵ Brandeis, ed., *Jacob's Well*, p. 262.
⁶ Carl Lindahl, *Earnest Games*, p. 87.
⁷ Helmholz, ed., *Select Cases*, pp. xxxii–iii.
⁸ Erbe, ed., *Mirk's Festial*, p. 113.

the early morality play *Mankind*.⁹ Other tempters also frequently use minced oaths. The conspirators in the late morality *Magnyfycence* swear by 'cockys armys' and by 'Cockys harte' among many other oaths, and these emphasize emotions such as surprise and pleasure, as well as irritation. The euphemistic substitution of 'cokkes' for 'God's' in such oaths will not alter the audience's understanding of their transgressiveness if the substitution is recognized, but rather emphasizes the character's determination to defy ecclesiastical teaching. Low-status characters in the biblical plays use minced oaths less frequently than high-status characters, and while this may suggest a mimetic representation of the use of transgressive language in society, it may equally represent a stylistic device used to define the spiritual difference between high- and low-status characters.

Characters in both biblical plays and moralities swear not only by the body of Christ but by the devil, and although these demonic oaths take many different forms they all suggest the speaker's allegiance to evil. In the Chester play *Balaam* King Balaack emphasizes his insults to the prophet by cursing him: 'Thou preachest, populard, as a pye; | the dyvell of hell thee destroye!' (V: 312–13). The second shepherd in the Towneley *Second Shepherds' Play* curses the sheep-stealer saying: 'Mak, the dewill in youre ee!' (13: 313). The evil character Mundus in the early morality *The Castle of Perseverance* curses his vassal saying 'Lewde losel, þe Deuel þe brenne'.¹⁰ These and many other forms of oaths and curses such as 'fie on thee' and 'ill hap on thy head' are used consistently and conventionally to add emotional emphasis to the speeches of evil characters, and simultaneously direct attention to the state of the abused character.

Other forms of transgressive language are equally important in medieval drama, although they may be less easily identified, but the ways in which they are used are always the means of defining them. Language which is neither insulting nor abusive is frequently used to express scorn or mockery by characters in both biblical and morality plays, and throughout the historical period covered by this study. Scorn and mockery are identifiable as transgressive forms of language according to the intention of the speaker. While scorn projects a serious intention to degrade, mockery degrades through laughter. These forms of linguistic transgression may include insults, abuse, and oaths but they are primarily expressed in language which is not itself transgressive. The transgressiveness of scorn and mockery in medieval drama lies in their expression of attitudes which attempt to degrade or deride Christ and Christianity in the biblical plays, or make light of virtue and vice in the moralities.

---

⁹ Mark Eccles, ed., *The Macro Plays*, EETS 262 (London: Oxford University Press, 1969). All quotations are from this edition. *Mankind*, l. 390.

¹⁰ Eccles, ed., *The Macro Plays*, *The Castle of Perseverance*, l. 1855.

In the biblical plays evil characters express scorn, and mock Christ and other virtuous characters. The first Jew in the N-Town *Crucifixion* tells the crucified Christ:

> We grete ȝou wel with a scorn
> And pray ȝou bothe evyn and morn,
> Take good eyd to oure corn,
> And chare awey þe crowe.
> (32: 210–14)

In the York *Death of Christ*, Cayphas declares: 'ȝa, late hym hyng | Full madly on þe mone for to mowe' (XXXVI: 78), mocking Christ's anguish which makes Him grimace or 'mowe'.

Virtue is mocked in the early morality *Mankind*. The character Myscheffe mocks the character Mercy, whose status as a virtue has already been established for the audience by his long aureate and homiletic opening speech. Myscheffe's language mocks that speech as he tells Mercy:

> I beseche yow hertyly, leue yowr calcacyon.
> Leue yowr chaffe, leue yowr corn, leue yowr dalyacyon.
> Yowr wytt ys lytyll, yowr hede ys mekyll, ȝe are full of predycacyon.
> (45–7)

This speech insults Mercy and his learned status by making fun of it. The internal rhyme of the last line, as much as the insult that Mercy has little wit, is reductive and challenges the learned status implied in the polysyllabic end-rhymes which mimic Mercy's speech.

All the forms of transgressive language indentified in this chapter so far are used by both high-and low-status characters in medieval drama, and where they are used by characters who represent high social status they signify low spiritual status. However, one form of transgressive language is associated with the characterization of a specific status group, and that is the 'Mahound' reference. This is common in the biblical plays as oaths and curses, and it occasionally takes the form of parodic blessings. It is rare in moralities. In whatever form it occurs the Mahound reference is a form of transgressive language because it parodies Christian references. In the biblical plays it is associated only with evil lords, their vassals, and servants. The Imperator in the Towneley *Caesar Augustus* gives his messenger the parodic blessing: 'Mahowne, he wyse the on thi way' (9: 122). In the Chester *Innocents* the first knight swears 'If anye blacke-lypped boyes be in my waye, | they shall rewe yt, by Mahound' (X: 197–8). In the York *Christ before Herod*, however, Herod swears '… be þe bloode þat Mahounde bledde' (XXXI: 207), which is doubly transgressive since it parodies oaths sworn on the blood of Christ.

There are two exceptions to the link between temporal evil authority and Mahound references. One occurs in the East Anglian morality the Croxton *Play of the Sacrament*, where one of the Jews who attacks the consecrated Host swears by Mahound but is not associated with any lord in the play.[11] The other occurs in the Chester *Harrowing of Hell* where the ale-wife confesses her wicked practices, and condemns all who cheat as she did to be 'exalted by the necke, | with my master, mightie Mahound' (XVII: 312–13). This reference is also a curse on 'Mahound'. Its association with a low-status character in a biblical play is unique to Chester, and may be a late interpolation.[12] Mahound references in other cycles are restricted to high-status characters and their vassals. Cain does not use Mahound references in any cycle, neither does Judas, because they are not part of a temporal power structure. Mahound references, in contrast to devil oaths and curses, signify a hierarchy of power and authority based on anti-Christian temporal and metaphysical allegiances which are alien to medieval society. This highly specific form of transgressive language introduces the medieval dramatists' ability to differentiate between degrees of social and spiritual status through the use of such language. The dramatists' use of prosodic style contributes to this differentiation.

Style

We have begun to discover in this chapter the variety of forms of transgressive language which occur in medieval drama, and some of the characterizing functions. Two styles are associated with this, and contribute to the subtlety of characterizations by providing conventions which dramatists were able to manipulate and adapt according to their dramatic and didactic interests. Both are particularly clear and significant in the biblical plays, but they are also used effectively in the moralities. The first style is the ranting boast and this is associated with the characterization of evil lordship. The second style is the abusive exchange, and this is commonly associated with the speeches of low-status characters. Geoff Lester has written that, in the case of the cycles of biblical plays, 'analysis of how evil is linguistically conveyed in the plays may bring to light certain recurrent features which might be regarded as aspects of an 'evil style' or 'register'.[13] The 'evil style' is a ranting boast which expresses the character's pride and vanity, and is frequently heavily alliterative, even in

---

[11] Norman Davis, ed., *Non-Cycle Plays and Fragments*, EETS SS 1 (London: Oxford University Press, 1970), *The Play of the Sacrament*, l. 453.

[12] The ale-wife is not included in the 1607 Chester ms. See the commentary to the edition: Lumiansky and Mills, eds, *The Chester Mystery Cycle*, p. 274.

[13] Geoff Lester, 'Idle Words: Stereotyping by Language in the English Mystery Plays', *Medieval English Theatre*, 11 (1989), p. 130.

plays where alliteration is not the predominant style. These boasts are associated with rulers in the biblical plays who would be already known to medieval audiences as villains. They are used in morality plays to characterize evil lordship. The boasts are set out in long, uninterrupted speeches which conventionally open plays, and which parody the high style used by God and virtuous human characters. High style used by characters who are not evil signifies their authority.[14] When it is used by evil characters that signification is present, but subverted by their use of transgressive language. High style used by evil rulers in drama accords with their apparent social status; the heavy alliteration emphasizes the transgressive sentiments expressed in the speech, which will also contain a wide vocabulary of insults, abuse, oaths, threats, and commands, and may include mockery. These elements create generic parodies of the speech with which God begins each cycle.

The bombastic speeches of evil rulers may be directed at other characters in the play, but commonly they begin with insults and threats directed at the audience, although the speaker's attention will be recalled eventually to the action of the play. Characters who use a boasting style in their opening speech conventionally continue to use insult and abuse throughout the play. This may be directed at other characters but it is also used when evil rulers address Christ, when it defines their unregenerate opposition to His ministry and divinity.

Dramatists commonly use monologues to open both biblical and morality plays, and many are the speeches of virtuous characters, but the vitality of the boastful and threatening opening speeches of evil lords would catch the attention of the audience. The commanding of peace serves a useful practical purpose amid the noise and movement which would have surrounded the playing stations in the streets and open spaces of a city, but the boastful, alliterating style is the conventional means of characterizing evil lords in medieval drama.[15]

Across the cycles evil rulers are defined and characterized by their heavily alliterating opening speeches. Herod begins the York *Christ before Herod* commanding 'Pes, ye brothellis and browlys in þis broydenesse inbrased' (XXXI:1). The Towneley Pilate opens the *Scourging* with the threat:

> Peasse at my bydyng, ye wyghtys in wold!
> Looke none be so hardy to speke a word bot I,
> Or by Mahowne, most myghty maker on mold,
> With this brande that I bere ye shall bytterly aby.
> (22: 1–4)

---

[14] P.J. Garrett Epp, 'Passion, Pomp, and Parody: Alliteration in the York Plays', *Medieval English Theatre*, 11 (1989), p. 152.
[15] Ibid., p. 151. Spector remarks on ' "Herod thirteeners" ... characterized by unusually dense alliteration'. See Spector, ed., *The N-Town Play*, p. xliii.

However, the bombastic boast may include other themes, such as the show of vanity in Herod's speech at the opening of the N-Town play *The Magi*. He declares:

> As a lord in ryalté, in non regyon so ryche,
>   And rulere of all remys, I ryde in ryal aray!
> Ther is no lord of lond in lordchep to me lyche,
>   Non lofflyere, non lofsummere, evyrlestyng is my lay!
> (18: 1–4)

The popularity and continuity of the stylistic conventions which help to create characterizations of evil lordship in drama are borne out by evidence from the very early morality *The Pride of Life*, thought to have been composed about the middle of the fourteenth century,[16] and by the morality *The Castle of Perseverance*, the manuscript of which is dated between 1400 and 1440.[17] These plays show that the verbal and stylistic conventions associated with evil lordship were in use at a date earlier than the existing manuscripts of the cycles of biblical plays, and thus constituted a familiar means of characterization which continued for more than two and a half centuries in didactic drama.

In *The Pride of Life*, although the King does not open the play, his first speech is a threatening boast:

> Pes, now, ye princis of powere so prowde,
>   3e kingis, 3e kempis, 3e kni3tis ikorne,
> 3e barons bolde, þat beith me obowte;
>   ....
>   And lestenith to my hestis, I hote 3u now her,
> Or [I] schal wirch 3u wo with werkis of wil.
> (113–19)

In *The Castle* the abstract character Mundus begins the play with a boast of his power and influence in the world.[18] He commands silence saying:

> Worthy wytys in al þis werd wyde,
>   ....
> Precyous prinse, prekyd in pride,
> Þorwe þis propyr pleyn place in pes be 3e bent!
> (1–4)

---

[16] Davis, ed., *Non-Cycle Plays and Fragments*, p. c.

[17] Mark Eccles suggests *The Castle* 'may have been composed between 1400 and 1425', *The Macro Plays*, p. xi, but Pamela M. King observes that the manuscript 'is thought to date from around 1440'. King, 'Morality Plays', in Beadle, ed., *The Cambridge Companion to Medieval English Theatre*, p. 243.

[18] Eccles, *The Macro Plays*, p. 187.

These early morality plays show that the insulting, threatening, bombastic style associated with evil lordship was an enduring convention in medieval didactic drama, although each dramatist modified it, through his choice of transgressive language, in order to construct specific characterizations and highlight a character's particular vices.

The second style associated with transgressive language in medieval didactic drama is the exchange of abuse, which is associated particularly with the characterization of low social status, and usually represents the equivalent low spiritual and social status of characters. These abusive exchanges often approach stichomythia, and they dramatize energetic interaction between characters. Speeches in this style may be alliterative because that is the predominant style of the play in which they occur, but alliteration is less influential in the definition of this style than the way in which transgressive language is exchanged.

Such abusive exchanges take place between two or more characters and may occur anywhere in a play. The characters may be given separate stanzas, as they are in the Chester *Shepherds* play, but often stanzas, and even lines, are divided between characters as they insult and abuse each other. The speakers use all the forms of transgressive language used by evil lords, except Mahound references. Although one character may assert authority over another in abusive terms, the exchange demonstrates that a degree of equality exists between the characters. Their use of transgressive language demonstrates their low social condition, but because both, or all, the speakers use similar forms of language they are generally, though not invariably, shown to be equal in their sinfulness.

Abusive exchanges take place between characters of the same sex, and between the sexes. In the Chester *Shepherds* play, for example, Trowle the boy confronts his masters in a wrestling game which is accompanied by insulting words. Trowle declares:

> ... Beginne wee this game.
> But warre lest your golyons glent.
> That were little dole to our dame,
> though in the myddest of the daye yee were drent.
> (VII: 246–9)

A sexual insult is implied in the second and third lines which the last line does not deflect. The first shepherd responds to this with an insult and curse telling Trowle: 'False lad, fye on thy face!' (VII: 250). The low social status of Trowle and his masters is defined by their occupation as shepherds, but the exchange of insults and abuse defines both characters as of equally low spiritual status.

There are, however, important exceptions to the way in which abusive exchanges define the low spiritual status of characters, and these show that the association of a prosodic style with low-status characters is a less stable measure of the characters' sinfulness than the association between ranting boasts and evil lordship. Thus abusive exchanges between low-status characters introduces the need to consider transgressive language according to the contexts in which it is used.

The biblical plays contain abusive exchanges between the sexes, such as those between Noah and his wife in all the cycles except N-Town, but these exchanges do not represent simple characterizations of sinful equality. They do, however, emphasize the importance of contexts for our understanding of the subtle uses of transgressive language. Noah's wife in the York *Flood* tells him:

> Now Noye, in faythe þe fonnes full faste,
>   This fare wille I no lenger frayne;
> Þou arte nere woode, I am agaste,
>   Farewele, I wille go home agayne.
> (IX: 89–92)

Noah responds: 'O woman, arte þou woode?' (IX: 93). In the Towneley *Noah* play Noah greets his wife civilly, saying: 'God spede, dere wife! | How fayre ye?' To which she replies 'Now, as euer myght I thryfe, | The wars I the see' (3: 274–7). As her shrewishness continues he warns her: 'We! hold thi tong, ram-skyt, | Or I shall the still' (3: 313–14). Although Noah participates in the abusive exchange, he is not being characterized as sinful in the same way as his wife, but as being adversely affected by her obstinacy, in spite of his virtuous nature. Noah's virtue is already established for the spectators by their prior knowledge of the biblical story, and by his conversation with God at the opening of the play. Noah's bad-tempered response to his shrewish wife thus dramatizes the difficulty of doing God's work in a world where conflict is an everyday occurrence.

Abusive exchanges between the knights and the mothers take place in the York, Chester, and Towneley plays of the Slaughter of the Innocents. Those in Chester and Towneley are violent and extended; the exchange in the York *Slaughter* is shorter, but still violent and dynamic, as the first knight and the first and second woman share a stanza in which the knight curses: 'Þe deuell myght spede you bothe, | False wicchis, ar 3e woode?' To which the second woman responds: 'Nay, lurdayns, 3e lye' (XIX: 220–22). The Towneley *Herod*, which contains the slaughter scene, makes plain the physical violence which attends the verbal violence of the women. The first woman tells the first knight 'Fals thefe! | Haue on loft on thy hode!' he responds: 'What, hore, art thou woode' (16: 490–92). The Chester *Innocents* lacks the stichomythic style of York and Towneley but the play is no less theatrical since it shows great variety, inventiveness, and vividness of imagery in the insults used by the mothers as they physically assault the knights. The mothers are called 'queanes' (X: 290), and 'Dame Parnell' (X: 337), and respond with conventional insults such as the first woman's: '... thou fowle harlot' (X: 353), but the dramatist uses more imaginative abuse such as the first woman's furious:

> Whom callest thou 'queane', scabde dogge?
> Thy dame, thy daystard, was never syche.
> Shee burned a kylne, eych stike:
> Yet did I never non.
> (X: 297–300)

However, the characterization of the mothers in these plays as sinful through their use of such lively transgressive language is problematic because the story of their plight as helpless defenders of their children would be known to the audience. Transgressive language and the characterizations it creates perform complex social functions in the Slaughter plays, and will be discussed further in Chapter 3.

Meanwhile, this examination of a prosodic style associated with low social and spiritual status has introduced the importance of considering contexts. When medieval drama itself actually names the kinds of abusive language discussed so far in this chapter, the need to observe contexts is highlighted, and the social distinction between high-and low-status users of transgressive language, which appears to be emphasized by prosodic styles, is eroded.

The term used in the biblical plays to define angry, quarrelsome, and abusive language is 'flyting'. Various forms of the word 'flyte' are used in all the cycles except N-Town, and may mean 'quarrel', 'argue', 'dispute with', or 'rebuke'.[19] It may also mean 'contention, a dispute, also abuse, abusive speech'.[20] The definition of 'flyting' as abuse suggests that the abusive speech of evil rulers may be defined in this way, although Priscilla Bawcutt, discussing the meanings of the term, notes that: 'In Old English *flitan* meant "to dispute or quarrel". In later centuries flyting signified noisy quarrels and arguments, carried on chiefly by the lower orders.'[21]

In the York Masons' *Herod and the Magi*, Herod insults his messenger, telling him 'Pees dastarde, in þe deueles dispite', but the messenger persists with the message he has brought, telling the king 'My lorde, now note is nere þis town', to which Herod responds: 'What, false harlott, liste þe flight?' (XVI: 130–32). 'Flight' is glossed here as 'argue', and Herod's interpretation of the messenger's language may be compared with his own 'flyting' as he abuses the messenger. Herod's 'flyting' seems to challenge Bawcutt's association of flyting with low status, but the king's abusive language subverts and degrades

---

[19] Kuhn and Reidy, eds, *A Middle English Dictionary*.
[20] Simpson and Weiner, eds, *The Oxford English Dictionary* .
[21] Priscilla Bawcutt, *Dunbar the Makar* (Oxford: Clarendon Press, 1992), p. 222.

his kingly status, so the significance of the language is defined by the conflict between the language and the character's status.

More obvious associations of abusive and quarrelsome language with low status occur in the cycles. In the Towneley *Murder of Abel* Cain curses in the devil's name the fire that would not burn his sacrifice. When Abel offers his advice Cain responds abusively:

> Com kys the dwill right in the ars!
> For the it brens bot the wars.
> I wold that it were in thi throte,
> Fyr, and shefe, and ich a sprote.
> (2: 289–92)

God intervenes, telling Cain

> Thar thou nowther flyte ne chyde.
> If thou tend right thou gettys thi mede.
> (2: 295–6)

In this instance flyting refers to the use of abusive language. In the Chester *Shepherds* play Trowle, the boy, expresses his contempt for the shepherds, saying: 'Thow fowle filth, though thow flytt, I defye thee' (VII: 197). This reference is glossed by its editors as *quarrel* or *scold*,[22] and in view of Trowle's status as a shepherd-boy, scolding is appropriate, suggesting here his contempt for the rebukes he receives from his masters, although Trowle himself can be defined as flyting since he defies the shepherds in such abusive terms. In this case, however, Trowle's defiance may be a display of bravado which is not witnessed by the shepherds.

Interpretations of 'flyte' and its various forms are clearly governed by the contexts in which they are found and used. Flyting is performed by characters representing both high and low social status; however, high-status characters indulge in one-sided abuse of their inferiors, while quarrelsome and abusive exchanges are particular to low-status characters in medieval drama. Flyting demonstrates the complex association between transgressive language and social status. Context, as much as form and style, reveals the significance of transgressive language as a means of creating varied and subtle characterizations. The next section of this chapter will focus on the way contexts define how transgressive language creates and varies characterizations, and will consider how these might alter the audiences', and our, perception of the characters who use it, and its transgressiveness.

---

[22] Lumiansky and Mills, eds, *The Chester Mystery Cycle*, glossary note.

Contexts

Many contexts govern the interpretation of language as transgressive. This chapter has already set out the most accessible, but medieval society, and drama, provide others which are perhaps less readily accessible to modern readers or audiences, or are subtler, but are nevertheless highly instructive for understanding how transgressive language creates varied characterizations, how legitimate language may be rendered transgressive, and how recognizably transgressive forms and styles of language may be legitimated by the use to which they are put.

Significant dramatic contexts which modify the interpretation of language are tone of voice; relationship between characters; the respective positions of characters within the social hierarchy; and the known virtue or viciousness of a character. Social contexts include instruction books, modes of dress, and occupations, and these contexts may conflict with the dramatic ones to highlight a character's improper use of language, by showing how it ignores codes of decorum recognized in society. This is not an exhaustive list, since the contexts governing many instances of linguistic transgression are combinations of all these in varying degrees of significance. This section sets out only to provide indications of the kinds of contexts which may be encountered, and the effects they have on transgressive language and characterization.

Social contexts

Social propriety was defined in the late Middle Ages by books such as the *Secreta Secretorum*, which instructed princes in various forms of conduct, including linguistic decorum, and Carl Lindahl observes that 'In refined circles, language was one of the most easily measured determinants of status'.[23] A mismatch between linguistic style and social status was considered indecorous. Medieval dramatists use transgressive language to create indecorousness which adds subtlety to their characterizations. The use of transgressive language by figures of authority in medieval drama is indecorous, and subverts their apparent high status. Their low language conflicts with other signs of status such as their costumes, occupations, and the respect with which other characters treat them. The use of transgressive language by low-status characters does not conflict with their social status, but signals only their sinful condition. The use of high-status language, Latin, French, or an aureate style by a character may parody the decorous use of such language, it may also reveal the ignorance, or the pretentiousness of the user.

---

[23] Lindahl, *Earnest Games*, p. 87.

The characterization of evil lords exemplifies the interaction between social propriety, transgressive language, and other ludic devices, and shows how characterizations are varied by the use of transgressive language. The verbal violence with which Herod berates his knights in the Towneley *Herod* transgresses all the rules governing language use in medieval society. Herod turns on his knights in fury when they confess to having lost the Magi, telling them sarcastically: 'Ye are knyghtys to trast! | Nay, losels ye ar, and thefys' (16: 222–3). When the knights object to his insults he repeats and increases them:

> Fy, losels and lyars!
> Lurdans ilkon!
> Tratoures and well wars!
> Knafys, bot knyghtys none.
> (16: 235–8)

The *Secreta Secretorum* advises that 'the ... thyng is that makyth a kynge to haue goode rennoune, that in spekynge he gouerne his tonge wysely, that he be not of many wordys'.[24] The *Secreta* also advises rulers that it 'nedys þat þou be tretable and curtyes' (109) to the barons, who 'er helpe and multiplicacioun of þe kyngdome, by hem ys þe court honoured and gouerned' (108). Furthermore it declares that 'mekenesse is the Seuerance and the difference betwene a kynge and a tyraunt' (180). Herod transgresses the conventions of courtly conduct by abusing his knights, but the language he uses is not only inappropriate to his status as a king, it also transgresses social conventions applying to even the lowest ranks of society. Whether or not individual spectators were aware of the codes of conduct proper to rulers, they would have understood that the character who used abuse and insulting mockery was transgressing codes of conduct which applied in everyday life.

Medieval drama provides signs which define the high social status of Herod, Pilate, Caiaphas, and Annas. They are identified as medieval lords, both temporal and ecclesiastical, by their costumes and props, such as the sword wielded by Herod in the Chester *Magi* (VIII: 200, 204 s.d.); by the titles by which they are addressed, by the deference shown to them by other characters, and by the recognizably contemporary institutional activities in which they engage, such as presiding over courts of law.

Magnificent costumes were the visual indication of high status for both secular and ecclesiastical rulers, and for virtuous and evil rulers. When these are combined with transgressive forms and styles of language that high status is subverted and degraded, and the low spiritual status of the character is

---

[24] Robert Steele, ed., *Secreta Secretorum*, vol. 1, EETS ES 74 (London: Kegan Paul, Trench, Trübner, 1898), p. 137.

revealed. Herod, in the N-Town *Magi*, boasts 'I am the comlyeste kynge clad in gleterynge golde' (18: 9). His expressions of vanity are a form of transgressive language, since vanity was condemned in sermons, and associated with Lucifer's challenge to God. As they are expressed in an opening, alliterating boast they characterize the corrupt temporal lordship of the historical evil ruler. They also combine with his rich costume to emphasize the pride and vanity of the character.

The evil kings in the fifteenth-century morality *The Castle of Perseverance* direct insults at their vassals. Belyal, for example, abuses and curses his vassals Superbia, Invidia, and Ira for letting Humanum Genus escape, telling them:

> Sey, gadelyngys – haue 3e harde grace
> And euyl deth mote 3e deye! –
> ....
> Harlottys, at onys
> From þis wonys!
> (1769–70, 1774–5)

The characters' language may appear to conflict with their costumes and subvert their apparent status, since they are dressed as kings, and Caro tells the audience: 'Behold þe Werld, þe Deuyl, and me! | ... we kyngys thre' (266–7), but it is consistent with the characterization of the vices they represent. This moral interpretation is apt for the use of transgressive language by evil rulers in biblical plays since it commonly connotes high-status vices such as pride and anger.

References to social rank in medieval drama characterize evil historical rulers in terms which made their conduct relevant to medieval audiences. They are addressed according to their apparent rank and the particular contemporary activities associated with it. In the Towneley *Buffetting* Caiaphas names himself 'a prelate, a lord in degré' (21: 154), and Annas emphasizes Caiaphas's contemporary medieval identity when he says:

> Sir, thynk ye that ye ar
> A man of holy kyrk.
> (21: 208).

Caiaphas, however, has already been raging at Christ, insulting and abusing him, ignoring the status he has assumed and which has been acknowledged by others, and thus signalling his own degraded moral and social status. Thus transgressive language is used to subvert socially accepted signs of high status and expose the corruption associated with it.

Dramatic contexts

Biblical villains are always characterized as unequivocally wicked by their unchanging use of transgressive language.[25] When confronted with Christ or other virtuous characters their language continues to be abusive or mocking. Caiaphas in the Towneley *Buffetting* tells Christ:

> Speke on in a torde,
> The dwill gif the shame,
> ....
> Fy on the fundlyng!
> (21: 215–16, 220)

Critics have, however, noted differences in the characterization of evil lords in the cycles of biblical plays,[26] and David Staines writes of Herod 'each mystery cycle chooses one approach to his presentation – the dangerous villain or the foolish and vain ruler'.[27] Close attention to a ruler's use of transgressive language reveals that changes in language may provide more dramatic impact within an individual play than this comment suggests. Herod opens the N-Town *Magi* boasting conceitedly: 'Of bewté and of boldnes I bere evermore þe belle' (18: 5), but his conceit gives way to viciousness as he is confronted with the redemptive process. When he hears news of the Nativity his tone changes as he rages: 'I xal prune þat pap-hawk and preuyn hym as a pad' (18: 88). Changes in an evil character's use of transgressive language represent emotional changes in response to external events, but while the language of evil rulers may take on a different tone, their spiritual state remains unchanged. However, their changing emotional states would probably have prompted changes in the audience's response to them, and this would contribute to the didactic purpose of the plays. The changes which take place in the language of evil rulers contrast with changes in the language of low-status characters in the biblical plays, and of human representatives in the fifteenth-century moralities, where increases or decreases in transgressiveness are used to signify changes in their spiritual condition.

Because evil rulers in medieval drama are characterized according to long-standing linguistic and stylistic conventions, there is a tendency among critics to oversimplify the characterization of biblical lords. Arnold Williams has drawn attention to the varied characterizations of Pilate in the biblical plays,

---

[25] Lester, 'Idle Words', p. 129.

[26] Lawrence M. Clopper, 'Tyrants and Villains: Characterization in the Passion Sequences of the English Cycle Plays', *Modern Language Quarterly*, 41 (1980), p. 9.

[27] David Staines, 'To Out-Herod Herod: The Development of a Dramatic Character', in Clifford Davidson, C.J. Stroupe, and C.J. Gianakaris, eds, *The Drama of the Middle Ages* (New York: AMS Press, 1982), p. 216.

writing that 'the vast majority of all Pilates in medieval drama are sympathetically treated. Rarely, however, is that characterization completely consistent'.[28] On the other hand, he observes that 'all English Pilates seem to have been ranters ... in the same manner as Herod';[29] while Lawrence Clopper observes that 'in the Chester cycle [Pilate] is a benign and philosophical ruler'.[30] In the Chester *Trial* play Pilate is not a ranter, but any benign and philosophical tendencies are subverted when he swears 'What devill of hell ys this to saye?' (XVI: 251), and calls Christ 'this losingere' (XVI: 305). Moreover, the Pilate who opens the Chester *Resurrection* does so with a display of French, and an alliterating boast, and goes on to abuse his knights, raging at them:

> Fye, theeffe; fye, traytour;
> Fye on thee, thy truth ys full bare!
> Fye, feynd; fye, feature.
> (XVIII: 266–9)

Although opening rants are a conventional sign of unregenerate evil lordship, since more than one dramatist worked on any cycle, differences in characterization should be expected. Moreover, dramatists in both biblical and morality genres vary and adapt style and vocabulary, producing individuality and variety in the representations of evil characters which are both entertaining and didactically important.

Robert Brawer, examining the characterization of Pilate in the plays of the York Passion sequence, questions 'why the York Pilate has been made intentionally complex ... The answer may be shown to lie largely in the multiple functions Pilate serves ... within the action of the York Passion'.[31] This answer helps to explain the differing representations of the same biblical evil rulers across the cycles: each serves a particular function and this is defined through modifications to the character's use of transgressive language. Moreover, the differing representations of Pilate in the same cycle reflect traditional views of the historical character in the Middle Ages, and are also governed by the sources of the plays. The sources of the Chester *Trial* are the Gospels, those of the *Resurrection* are St Matthew's Gospel and the Apocryphal Gospel of Nicodemus. Together the tradition and sources provide opportunities for dramatists to explore the forms which opposition to Christ

---

[28] Arnold Williams, *The Characterization of Pilate in the Towneley Plays* (East Lansing, Mich.: Michigan State University Press, 1950), p. 4.
[29] Ibid., p. 14.
[30] Lawrence M. Clopper, 'Tyrants and Villains', p. 13.
[31] Robert A. Brawer, 'The Characterization of Pilate in the York Cycle Play', *Studies in Philology*, 69 3 (July 1972), p. 299.

takes in the Bible, while transgressive language enables them to show how such opposition is manifested in medieval society.

This examination of various contexts which govern the use of transgressive language, and contribute to its characterizing function, has focused on high-status characters, but one important low-status character in all the cycles uses transgressive language as consistently as the evil rulers, although he does not use Mahound references. Cain the farmer, like the evil rulers, continues to use abusive language even when confronted by God. In the Towneley *Murder of Abel* God speaks to Cain, who replies insolently 'Whi, who is that hob ouer the wall? | We! who was that that piped so small?' (2: 299–300) Cain's use of transgressive language enables the dramatists to illustrate the way in which unregenerate evil is not necessarily confined to the higher social ranks but may exist at all levels, where it is again manifested through rage and violence.

The boasts and rages of evil lords and the insolence of Cain are unmistakable in their tone and impropriety, but not all transgressive language in medieval drama is spoken with equal anger, malice, or insolence. J.W. Robinson has remarked that abusive terms 'require *hauteur* or venom in their delivery'.[32] This comment provides an important insight into the relative seriousness of insult and abuse in drama, where a variety of tones may be deduced in their delivery, and these indicate the subtlety with which dramatists sought to define their characters.

Shepherds plays in all the cycles except N-Town use quarrelsome abuse to indicate sinful equality, but the significance of the insults differs according to the context in which they are spoken. Hans-Jürgen Diller suggests that when, in the Chester *Shepherds* play, the second shepherd calls Trowle 'shrew', 'in the context this is obviously intended as endearing mock-abuse'.[33] However, although the shepherd's tone of voice would control the audience's interpretation of his attitude to Trowle, it is not easy to judge that tone from the play-text in either instance where the shepherd addresses Trowle in this way

Other examples are easier to define. In the Towneley *First Shepherds' Play* insults are constantly exchanged between the shepherds. The first and second wrangle over sheep, and the first tells the second: 'Knafe, hens I byd flytt!' (12: 174) This may be only a playful display of arrogance. The third remarks mockingly 'Here ar old knafys yit | Standys in this grownde' (12: 207–8). When they all begin to quarrel over their drinking the third shepherd again declares: 'Ye be both knafys' (12: 399), but the first now responds: 'Nay, we knaues all; | Thus thynk me best, | So syr, shuld ye call' (12: 400–402). The second shepherd agrees, saying 'Furth let it rest; | We will not brall'

---

[32] J.W. Robinson, *Studies in Fifteenth-Century Stagecraft*, Early Art, Drama, and Music Series, 14 (Kalamazoo, Michigan: Medieval Institute Publications, 1991), p. 42.

[33] Hans-Jürgen Diller, 'The Composition of the Chester *Adoration of the Shepherds*', *Anglia*, 89 (1971), p. 191.

(12: 402–3). The remark defuses the petty quarrel and emphasizes the social and spiritual equality between the shepherds.[34] Thus a term which is insulting in other contexts continues to signify low status but now characterizes the humility of the shepherds, and so indicates the spiritual condition which fits them to receive news of the Nativity and accept its benefits.

Transgressive language may also be used in familiar forms of address between characters.[35] The late morality play *Magnyfycence* provides an instance of abusive language used 'in coarse jocularity'.[36] When Foly tells Crafty Conveyaunce of his sexual adventures, Crafty Conveyaunce exclaims: 'What, horson! Arte thou suche a one?' (1234). However, in the York *Christ before Pilate (1): The Dream of Pilate's Wife*, Procula uses the same abusive term when she tells the Beadle 'Why, go bette horosonne boy, when I bidde þe' (XXX: 60). The context in which it occurs defines it as neither jocular nor familiar, but abuse which emphasizes Procula's irritation and subverts her apparent social status.

Drama provides contexts in which legitimate language becomes transgressive when it is used by evil or vicious characters. In the early morality *Mankind* all the vicious characters use language to challenge authority. The devil Titivillus parodies the cultural significance of Latin when he enters and declares 'Ego sum dominancium dominus and my name ys Titivillus' (475). 'Ego sum' is the declaration with which God opens all the cycles of biblical plays except N-Town; 'dominancium dominus' is an epithet traditionally associated with Christ.[37] Titivillus's declaration becomes a form of transgressive language as it parodies the theological signification of the vocabulary, while his use of language conventionally associated with God characterizes the extent of his sinful pride and presumption.

This chapter has so far illustrated many forms of transgressive language, and many contexts which govern the way those forms create varied characterizations. Noah's wife provides a useful example of the contextual forces bearing on characterization. Martin Stevens has written that in the Towneley play she becomes 'the first, if unlikely tyrant figure ... She has all the attributes: she challenges right order, she boasts and rants'.[38] While Noah's wife certainly challenges her husband's authority in all the cycles except N-Town, she cannot be described as behaving like a tyrant in any of them, nor

---

[34] William F. Munson, 'Audience and Meaning in Two Medieval Dramatic Realisms', in Davidson, Stroupe, and Gianakaris, eds, *The Drama of the Middle Ages*, p. 220.
[35] Geoffrey Hughes, *Swearing: A History of Foul Language, Oaths and Profanity in English* (Oxford: Basil Blackwell, 1991), p. 89.
[36] John Scattergood, ed., *John Skelton: The Complete English Poems* (London: Penguin, 1983), p. 546.
[37] Eccles, ed., *The Macro Plays, Mankind*, n. to l. 475.
[38] Martin Stevens, 'Language as Theme in the Wakefield Plays', *Speculum*, 55 (1977), p. 110.

would she have been mistaken for one by a medieval audience. Her complaints and threats do not constitute boasts or rants. Her female identity, and thus her sexual inferiority in the medieval hierarchy, is shown by her female clothing, by the 'rock', or spindle, which she carries and wields in the Towneley *Noah*, and by her concern for her 'gossips' in the York and Chester plays. This identity precludes any possibility of her being understood as a tyrant by the original audience, since tyrants, or figures of evil authority, are always men in positions of power which they abuse in some way. Noah's wife does, however, behave improperly as a wife, according to the ideals of quiet, submissive womanhood laid down in all forms of authoritative medieval literature.[39] So although the character may have been played by a man, she can only be interpreted as an archwife. This example highlights the way in which many contexts must be considered in order to distinguish the significance of transgressive forms and styles of language as they are used by different characters and create characterizations.

The characterization of low status in didactic drama, by means of transgressive language, is usually entertaining; however, the most significant dramatic function of transgressive language when it is used to characterize low status is to illustrate and define the process of spiritual change. The language of low-status characters in the biblical plays, and of human representatives in the fifteenth-century moralities, increases or decreases in transgressiveness to show changes in their spiritual condition.

Spiritual change

Evil characters in medieval drama are unchanging in their resistance to God's will, but good characters are not always constant in their goodness. Many low-status biblical characters are introduced in biblical plays as sinful, although they later achieve goodness, while representatives of humanity in the moralities begin as virtuous characters, fall into sin, and only regain their virtue by divine intervention. Like evil rulers, low-status characters are created to resemble members of medieval society through their use of transgressive language, while their social status is defined by the work they are seen to do, and by their costumes. Transgressive language adds individuality to the representation of well-known biblical figures, and emphasizes the human qualities of personifications in the moralities. Unlike transgressive language used by evil lords, however, such language used by low-status characters is not generally entertaining so much through its extreme excess, as through its apparently

---

[39] See Alcuin Blamires, ed., *Woman Defamed and Woman Defended* (Oxford: Clarendon Press, 1992), p. 123. See also Robert P. Miller, ed., *Chaucer Sources and Background* (New York: Oxford University Press, 1977), p. 406.

close representation of everyday life. Nevertheless, it defines spiritual status, and its change, in both genres.

Noah, in the Chester *Noah*, loses patience with his wife when she refuses to enter the Ark, and curses: 'Come in, wiffe, in twentye devylles waye' (III: 219). Although Noah uses a devil oath his momentary sinful lapse, which the oath signifies, does not render him irredeemable, and this is dramatized by his return to devotional language during the flood.

The medieval setting and low spiritual and social status of the shepherds in both Towneley *Shepherds* plays, and the Chester *Shepherds* play are characterized through their use of transgressive language at the start of each play, and by their references to physical activities. In the Towneley *First Shepherds' Play* the shepherds drink together and quarrel. The third shepherd complains: 'Thou has dronken a quart, | Therfor choke the the deyll!', but the first responds:

> Thou rafys:
> And it were for a sogh
> Ther is drynk enogh.
> (12: 393–7)

After the appearance of the angel, the shepherds' vocabulary changes as they discuss the biblical prophecies they recall. The third shepherd declares:

> Trust it now we may,
> He is borne this day:
> *Exiet virga*
> *De radice Iesse.*
> (12: 500–503)

The fragment of Latin, the language of theology, indicates the shepherd's increasing spirituality, and wisdom. However, the change is not straightforward: it is interrupted as the shepherds quarrel over their attempt to recreate the angel's song:

1 Pastor	Breke outt youre voce!
	....
3 Pastor	I may not for the pose,
	Bot I haue help.
2 Pastor	A, thy hart is in thy hose!
1 Pastor	Now, in payn of a skelp,
	This sang thou not lose!
3 Pastor	Thou art an yll qwelp
	For angre!
	(12: 608, 610–16)

They do sing, however, and their song completes their transition into virtue as its harmonies characterize their integration into the Christian faith. That completed state is represented by their use of devotional and ritualistic language as they worship the infant Christ.

The characters change hesitantly from sinfulness to virtue in the Shepherds' plays, but the development of their Christian faith and devotion has an existing foundation in their acts of virtue – peacemaking and charity in the *First Shepherds' Play*, generosity and mercy in the *Second Shepherds' Play*, as the shepherds offer sixpence to Mak's 'baby', and only toss him in a blanket when they discover the 'baby' is the sheep he has stolen from them.

Transgressive language in these plays characterizes and dramatizes everyday human activity, and characterizes the kinds of humans who may achieve redemption: they are sinful but already capable of virtue. In the moralities the representatives of humanity are also virtuous when the plays open, but become corrupted, and this corruption is swift. Mankynde, in the morality *Mankind*, displays his virtue in his gratitude to his spiritual guide Mercy, which he expresses in aureate language: 'Now blyssyde be Jhesu! My soull ys well sacyatt | Wyth þe mellyfluose doctryne of þis worschyppfull man' (311–12). His corruption is characterized by his insulting dismissal of Mercy, when he says: 'I xall speke wyth þe anoþer tyme, to-morn, or þe next day' (727), and his recuperation begins when he acknowledges his fault, again in aureate language, saying: 'Yt ys so abhominabyll to rehers my iterat transgrescion, | I am not worthy to hawe mercy be no possibilite' (821–2).

The change from virtuous language to transgressive language generally signifies a change in the spiritual status of a character towards increasing sinfulness, and the constant use of transgressive language by a character generally signifies an unchanging state of sin or evil, but in a few important contexts language which is transgressive, and therefore characteristic of viciousness in one context, may be understood as the language of virtue in another.

Punishing language

The sixteenth-century morality *Magnyfycence* provides an unambiguous and important example of the way in which familiar insults lose their customary transgressiveness when they are used by a virtuous character to punish or enlighten a corrupted character. When the prince, Magnificence, has been morally, and financially, ruined by the tempters he is confronted by God's messenger who tells him:

> I am Adversyte, that for thy mysdede
> From God am sente to quyte the thy mede,

> Vyle velyarde, thou must not nowe my dynt withstande;
> ....
> Ly there, losell, for all thy pompe and pryde.
> (1878–80)

Adversyte has been sent to punish the prince who has rejected virtue. As Magnificence lies degraded, Adversyte then addresses the audience, telling them: 'Thys losyll was a lorde and lyvyd at his lust; | And nowe lyke a lurdan he lyeth in the dust' (1886–7). The vocabulary of abuse: 'Vyle velyarde', 'losell', 'lurdan' are, in this instance, accurate descriptions of the prince's wretched state, and degraded status. He has behaved like a losell, or scoundrel, and now he lies on the ground like a beggar or vagabond. Priscilla Bawcutt has noted that in the stylized 'flyting' poems of William Dunbar in which he set out to abuse his opponents, 'the poem itself is the punishment' because it causes humiliation.[40] Adversyte's language likewise punishes Magnificence as it humiliates him. That humiliation is increased by being witnessed by the audience.

The York cycle uses a similar technique to condemn Judas. The Janitor's use of abusive words to Judas in the *Conspiracy* is another instance of language which is transgressive in other contexts being used to punish. The Janitor tells Judas: 'Go hense þou glorand gedlyng, God geue þe ille grace, | Thy glyfftyng is so grymly þou gars my harte growe' (XXVI: 157–8). The insults are varied, and emphasized by means of alliteration, in a display which functions as a statement of disgust. Familiar terms of abuse allow contemporary society to express through an ahistoric dramatic character its revulsion at the historical character, as it might abuse one of its own criminals. In this instance, the reputation of Judas governs the interpretation of the Janitor's abusive language, although he is part of Pilate's unregenerate court. The alliteration, and the Janitor's repetition of prophetic insults to Judas's physical appearance, such as: ' ... I fele by a figure in youre fals face | It is but foly to feste affeccioun in 3ou' (XXVI: 161–2), also provide an additional context as they denote authorial control underlying the Janitor's colloquial abuse. This is not just a forceful display of revulsion by the Janitor, which the audience may participate in, but a highly crafted and authorized use of transgressive language which clearly asserts a theological judgement.

Transgressive language which is used to punish does not primarily characterize the sinful condition of the speaker, although this function may be appropriate, as it is in the case of the Janitor. More importantly, it defines the wickedness of the character who is punished. This function of transgressive language has to be interpreted according to the known or perceived conduct of the character who is abused, and, as we will see in Chapter 3, is helpful for

---

[40] Priscilla Bawcutt, *Dunbar the Makar*, p. 244.

interpreting the flyting between the mothers and the knights in the Slaughter plays of the biblical cycles.

Language in medieval drama may thus be understood to be transgressive because it is already familiar as such, or it may be interpreted according to the reputation of the character or the way that language is used. Transgressive language was a conventional but highly flexible dramatic device, taking many different forms, which define the social and spiritual status, and individual vices, of characters in both the biblical and the morality genres, throughout the historical period covered by this study, and as a means of characterization it does not appear to be governed by the genre in which it was used.

Verbal style, as well as linguistic transgression contributes to characterization. The same forms of transgressive language may be used by high- and low-status characters, but prosodic style, and the ability to change, defines characters as sinful rather than evil, while the use of transgressive language by characters assuming high social status characterizes their low spiritual status. These generalizations form a basic framework for understanding the function of transgressive language as a means of characterization.

However, the significance of transgressive language as a means of creating characterizations is defined by the contexts in which it is used, and these may be social as well as dramatic. (Social contexts become increasingly important hermeneutic devices in the sixteenth-century moralities.) From the forms, styles, and contexts which are defined as, and associated with, transgressive language, dramatists create a wide variety of dramatically significant characterizations. In the biblical plays these are evil lords and low-status characters, in the fifteenth-century moralities they are the tempters and representatives of humanity. Chapter 4 will illustrate in detail the variations in the forms of transgressive language which are specific to the fifteenth-century moralities, and create characterizations in these plays.

In both genres evil is characterized as unregenerate in its opposition to the will of God when a character's use of transgressive language does not change. In the morality plays evil characterized by unchanging transgressive language is associated with tempters, but in the cycles of biblical plays it is especially associated with evil rulers. The N-Town Herod's vanity and vicious determination to retain power, the Towneley Caiaphas's uncontrolled rage, the general abusing of vassals, servants, and Christ (blasphemy in everyday life), illustrate the diverse representations of unregenerate evil, created through the use of transgressive language, in the biblical plays.

Transgressive language also creates diverse low-status characterizations. However, its most significant dramatic function in characterizing low status is to chart the achievement or loss of virtue by characters whose use of that language defines them as of low social and spiritual status. A decrease in that use, and increasing use of devotional and aureate language, indicates a change towards virtue. Change in the opposite direction, as transgressive language is used more frequently by a character, indicates a loss of virtue and increasing corruption. The process of spiritual change moves from sinfulness to virtue in the biblical plays and from virtue through corruption to recuperation in the fifteenth-century moralities.

Characterizations in the late moralities are often more complex than those in the biblical and earlier morality plays, and will be discussed in detail in Chapters 5, 6, and 7, which examine the sixteenth-century moralities *Magnyfycence, The Play of the Wether*, and *King Johan* individually. Nevertheless, in both genres, and throughout the period covered by this study, transgressive language creates characterizations which, besides providing entertaining diversity, dramatize degrees of resistance to God's will, reveal the forms that resistance takes in medieval society, and signal dramatic development, including spiritual change. It is used in a few significant instances to punish wickedness, and to dramatize the loss of virtue, but it does not then indicate the sinfulness of the user but that of the person abused. When transgressive language is used in this way it directs an audience's attention to the actions of the abused characters, and the punishment which these actions provoke. We have begun to see that variations in characterization, created by the contexts in which transgressive language is used, perform instructive functions in medieval drama, and as the next chapter will show, those functions extend into areas of social as well as religious instruction.

Chapter 3

Social comment, religious dissent, and audience response in the biblical plays

Transgressive language in the biblical plays not only defines the characters who use it, but in doing so prompts responses to those characters from the audiences. These responses serve the social and religious purposes of the plays and direct attention to areas of social and religious dissent in medieval society. This chapter looks first at the way transgressive language prompts audience responses which challenge socially disruptive conduct; and second, at how that language prompts responses which challenge the audience as a whole to reflect upon its orientation towards sin, guilt, and its Christian faith. It will, however, become apparent that the functions of transgressive language in many biblical plays are so complex that they seldom fit neatly into these groupings.

In the biblical plays the responses of spectators to transgressive language would act as challenges to social misconduct, which is differentiated according to social status. Certain forms of misconduct recur as topics in the plays: the abuse of secular and ecclesiastical lordship, perversions of the law, the violence of knights, conflicts between masters and men, and discord between husbands and wives. The transgressive language used by evil biblical lords and their vassals would prompt ridicule and abuse from the audience which challenged the conduct of the characters, and members of society who behaved like them. Social subversion expressed through the transgressive language of lower-status characters might provoke audience responses which challenged it, but more probably reminded spectators of society's ideals and norms without prompting their condemnation of subversion.

Social misconduct of both high- and low-status characters is always linked to some form of religious dissent or doubt, but when transgressive language directs audience attention specifically to religious dissent, doubt, and ignorance, it addresses all levels of society and challenges the faith and virtue of all spectators, without regard for social status.

Transgressive language would have been expected by audiences as part of their experience of watching certain plays and particular characters in the cycles. The entertainment inherent in transgression, the liveliness of the language, and its traditional association with festival all contributed to capturing the attention of spectators. In the biblical plays transgressive language returned to its place of origin when performances took place in the streets and public spaces, where the very familiarity of such language would influence an audience's reception of the play in which it is used.

Although dramatists were writing ostensibly in the service of theological doctrine, the growing confidence of urban communities may have prompted entertaining authorial comments and complaints about the socio-political conditions which affected those communities. Michael Camille suggests the importance of sustaining a sense of community when he writes: 'polysemous and multicoded, the city was the seat of exchange, of money, goods and people, creating a shifting nexus rather than a stable hierarchy'.[1]

The cycles of biblical plays purported to assert such a hierarchy against the process of change. They also provided a means of bonding an unstable population through an act of celebration which took the form most familiar to illiterate and literate spectators. Where communities may have been able to afford only a single biblical play as part of an act of celebration, the familiar doctrinal themes would serve the same bonding purpose. A spectator's condemnation of characters who committed familiar acts of injustice and social misdemeanours confirmed that spectator's integration into the medieval Christian community. At the same time, however, the dramatization of discord in the plays reveals potential challenges and sites of disruption within the community. The containment of challenge and disruption by the didactic, ludic, and celebratory contexts of the cycles cannot be taken for granted. As James C. Scott observes of carnival:

> the view that [it] is a mechanism of social control authorized by elites ...
> is seriously misleading. It risks confusing the intentions of elites with the
> results they are able to achieve.[2]

Thus unresolvable tensions may have existed between the ostensible intention of the cycles to reassert the medieval hierarchy of authority, an author's desire to highlight social abuses, and an audience's appreciation of the entertainment provided by transgressive language.

Evil lords and mocking audiences

As we saw in Chapter 2, biblical evil lords are characterized by their use of transgressive language. Many spectators would have been familiar with this convention, which was intended to incite an audience to ridicule the characters. The laughter and abuse of the audience served two purposes: the religious purpose was the charitable correction of the sins of real lords, the ostensible

---

[1] Michael Camille, *Images on the Edge: The Margins of Medieval Art* (London: Reaktion, 1992), p. 130.
[2] James C. Scott, *Domination and the Arts of Resistance* (New Haven: Yale University Press, 1990), p. 178.

socio-political purpose may have been to defuse popular discontent with local abuses of power.[3]

Reactions to biblical evil lords would have varied among the heterogeneous audiences who attended the plays, and were probably controlled by the episodic structure of the cycles, which does not permit prolonged confrontation between evil characters and the audience. Individual plays often dramatize attitudes associated with contemporary complaints about bad lordship and then juxtapose them to the overall redemptive theme in a way which generalizes them once more. Nevertheless, it was the audience itself, rather than a distant figure of authority, which challenged socially unacceptable or disruptive lordly behaviour.

While the linguistic excesses of evil rulers such as Herod, Pilate, and Caiaphas make their authority laughable, these characters frequently display sensitivity to being insulted or mocked. This draws attention to the way the audience seems to be encouraged to react to them. Herod in the N-Town *Trial before Herod* demands of Christ: 'Hast þu skorne to speke onto þi kyng?' (30: 222); Caiaphas, in the York *Christ before Annas and Caiaphas*, complains of Christ '3itt hadde I neuere such hething of a harlott as hee' (XXIX: 325). The sensitivity of these characters enhances the degree to which the audience's ridicule functioned as an assault on false pride and arrogant authority, and contrasts vividly with the same characters' abuse and mockery of Christ.

The boasts with which evil characters open biblical plays, or make their first appearances, all involve the audience by addressing them directly, often with insults and threats. In the York *Herod and the Magi*, Herod tells his knights: 'Arest 3e þo rebaldes þat vnrewly are rownand, | Be they kyngis or knyghtis, in care 3e thaim cast' (XVI: 35–6). Here rather than being passive onlookers, anyone in the audience who continued to chatter became part of the action. The command might provoke laughter and ridicule among the rest of the audience, focusing not only on their noisy companions but on the character who is assuming an authority over them. Spectators would have been drawn into a relationship with the character which narrowed the distance between them and the opening action of the play. However, the authority which the evil ruler assumes over the audience would probably have been rejected and laughed at in spite of the threats, because the ludic context assured them that it was part of the entertainment.

It is important to notice that the opening relationship set up through the use of transgressive language between an evil ruler and the audience does not last

---

[3] William Tydeman, 'Satiric Strategies in the English Mystery Cycle Plays', in Flemming G. Anderson et al., eds, *Popular Drama in Northern Europe: A Symposium* (Odense: Odense University Press, 1988), p. 23. See also John Gardner, *The Construction of the Wakefield Cycle* (Carbondale and Edwardsville: Southern Illinois University Press, 1974), p. 6.

throughout any play. Although the audience may become involved again, it is always in a different relationship. The Towneley *Conspiracy and Capture* begins with a boast from Pilate in which he calls for silence, insulting the audience as he cries:

> Peas, carles, I commaunde!
> Vnconand I call you!
> I say stynt and stande,
> Or foull myght befall you,
> Fro this burnyshyd brande.
> (20: 1–5)

These threats might unite the audience in opposition to him, but towards the end of his speech his tone becomes insecure as he says:

> He prechys the pepyll here
> That fature fals, Iesus,
> That if he lyf a yere,
> Dystroy oure law must vs.
> (20: 53–6)

Pilate's relationship with the audience changes, mediated by their Christian knowledge as his speech moves from direct address into historical references which include the insulting accusation that Jesus is 'fature fals' or a false deceiver. The spectators become distanced. They might ridicule Pilate for his ignorance and thus their knowledge of Christianity confirms their place in the Christian community. Simultaneously they would be removed to the position of passive rather than interactive witnesses. It is, however, more usual for other characters to address the ruler, drawing his attention away from the audience to the action of the play, and repositioning the audience as passive witnesses once again.

The York *Christ before Annas and Caiaphas* uses the style and vocabulary consistent with evil secular rulers as a means of challenging clerical encroachment on secular authority. The play begins with Caiaphas making a conventional call for silence:

> Pees bewshers, I bid no jangelyng 3e make,
> And sese sone of youre sawes and se what I saye.
> (XXIX: 1–2)

The character goes on to boast of his learning and power until in the fifth stanza he declares:

> I haue þe renke and þe rewle of all þe ryall,
>   To rewle it by right als reasoune it is.

All domesmen on dese awe for to dowte me
That hase thaym in bandome in bale or in blis.
(XXIX: 18–21)

Caiaphas's boast illustrates the way poetic style is used for its conventional connotations in order to extend the significance of a speech. Pretensions to secular power are shown to be at issue in this speech by the style the York dramatist has chosen, and the speech addresses a real political concern through the characterization of the high priest.

The political implications of extended and corrupt ecclesiastical power were addressed in the second half of the fourteenth century by John Wyclif. Although he writes metonymically of the 'materialle swerd', he is explicit about the danger he perceives, and warns:

> þis swerde ... may be drawe so fer owte of his place þat it wille be vnpossible to brynge it a3en. For þus it stondiþ of þis swerde in fulle many londis, wher clerkis han fully þe seculer lordeschipis in her power; & it is ful like for to stonde in þe same wise wiþ-in a few 3eris in ynglonde .... Ande wete lordis well þat, if þe clergi gete þis swerde oonys fully in her power, þe seculer party may go pipe wiþ an yuy lefe for eny lordeschipis þat þe clerkis wille 3eue hem a3en.[4]

The political and ecclesiastical significance of the characterization of Caiaphas would have depended on the audience's knowledge of the abuses of ecclesiastical power in medieval society. The characterization would have been based first upon the reputation of the character, the Jew who sought Christ's death, and secondly upon a pejorative opinion of the power of prelates which was so widespread that it was safe to express it in civic drama.

However, the characterization of Caiaphas would always have remained open to interpretation. Any didactic significance derived from it would have depended upon the individual spectator's experience of bad ecclesiastical lordship, and upon a spectator's orientation towards the religious changes which took place during the period when the plays flourished. With the advent of the Reformation the characterization of Caiaphas may have served as anti-Catholic condemnation of the power of the Catholic episcopate. The Protestant polemicist John Bale, writing towards the middle of the sixteenth century, refers to 'the Annas of London' and 'the Cayphas of Wynchestre'.[5]

The relationship between ecclesiastical and secular lords and their subjects is represented in medieval drama as being deeply troubled, and historical

---

[4] F.D. Matthews, ed., *The English Works of Wyclif Hitherto Unprinted*, EETS OS 74 (London: Trübner, 1880), p. 372. See also Richard Helmholz, *Canon Law and the Law of England* (London: Hambledon Press, 1987), pp. 77–8.

[5] Thora Balslev Blatt, *The Plays of John Bale: A Study of Ideas, Technique and Style* (Copenhagen: G.E.C. Gad, 1968), p. 220.

records bear this out. The Beverley Town Documents, for instance, record that between 1515 and 1529 the Duke of Buckingham 'imprisoned five of his tenants, who had been successful in litigation with him'.[6] Lordship was a problem for communities as well as individuals. Sarah Beckwith notes that in the fifteenth century

> in Bury, the urban traders had long demanded the legal status of incorporation against the powers of abbatorial control of the markets.[7]

However, while oppressive lordship clearly caused discontent in medieval society, the relationship between lords and subjects was more complex than the drama suggests. Michael Hicks observes that:

> lords were important customers, seekers of credit, sources of patronage and mediation with other authorities ... and the dominant local context within which towns plied their trade.[8]

Lorraine Attreed writes that although 'York's citizens possessed as keen awareness of their liberties and privileges', nevertheless,

> The nobility resident in the area ... were called upon ... to exercise that vague but all-encompassing notion of 'good lordship' which saw men such as Henry Percy earl of Northumberland consulted about local riots.[9]

The Paston Letters provide further evidence of the complex relationship between lords and citizens. In 1484 John Paston complained that his uncle had forced him

> to lende on-to the reuerende fadere in God George, late Archeb[i]sschop of York, m^l mark, which was nat payed ageyn by the summa of c li.[10]

The financial relationship between the archbishop and the wealthy, but not aristocratic, landowner suggests that the lord's authority would be modified by his obligations, altering the respect and reverence which his status otherwise commanded.

---

[6] I.S. Leadam, ed., *Court of Requests 1497–1569*, Selden Society, vol. XII (London: Bernard Quaritch, 1900), p. lxix, n. 3.
[7] Sarah Beckwith, 'Ritual, Church and Theatre: Medieval Dramas of the Sacramental Body', in David Aers, ed., *Culture and History 1350–1600* (Hemel Hempstead: Harvester Wheatsheaf, 1992), p. 70.
[8] Michael Hicks, *Bastard Feudalism* (London: Longman, 1995), p. 81.
[9] Lorraine C. Attreed, ed., *The York House Books*, vol. 1, *House Books One and Two/Four* (Gloucester: Alan Sutton, 1991), p. xx.
[10] Norman Davis, ed., *Paston Letters*, part 1, p. 626.

None of the biblical plays represents such everyday relationships between lords and citizens because lordship in them polarizes around acceptance of, or opposition to, the Christian message. Only those forms of misconduct and evil especially associated with medieval lordship are used to dramatize the corrupt power of biblical evil lords in terms familiar to the audiences.

Social and dramatic conventions would have combined with a modified perception of lordly status particular to the local urban auspices of the biblical plays to influence the presentation and reception of transgressive language which characterized and thus challenged bad lordship. Pejorative characterizations of lordship may have been interpreted by medieval spectators as criticism of their local oppressive lord, if they happened to be suffering under one, but they may equally represent attacks made against *types* of bad lords.[11] The exact significance of the dramatic representations created by transgressive language would depend upon the relationship of the audience to a particular local lord at a particular time, and this would be subject to change.

The opportunity to ridicule evil lordship in the form of conventional, historical villains or evil types may nevertheless have fulfilled useful functions. The audience's mockery was intended to release anger or fear *before* it caused civil unrest and a challenge to legitimate authority. It was an expression of disapproval at the 'discord and disharmony'[12] caused by those who ignored the rules of conduct for figures of authority, and it may be related to other forms of social mockery such as those discussed in Chapter 1. The mocking of rulers, especially at their most vicious, is thus a dramatic device which functions within the ludic context, with the intention of degrading the transgressive conduct of the character. That conduct is treated as if it were common and socially unpopular misbehaviour of the kind punished in society by the exhibition of the offender to the ridicule of the community, rather than being privileged as deeply serious and disruptive.

The dramatist's attempts to control audience response and defuse discontent may not always have been successful. Historical records show a link between civic disorder and religious celebrations which encouraged large gatherings of people and thus provided opportunities for tensions between social groups to erupt into violence.[13]

Disorder is associated with Corpus Christi drama in a Proclamation for the York Plays which commands that: 'no man go armed in þis Citee with swerdes,

---

[11] Douglas Gray, 'Rough Music: Some Early Invectives and Flytings', in Claude Rawson, ed., *English Satire and the Satiric Tradition* (Oxford: Basil Blackwell, 1984), p. 30.
[12] Ibid., p. 25.
[13] Thomas Pettitt, '"Here Comes I, Jack Strawe": English Folk Drama and Social Revolt', *Folklore*, 95 (1984), part 1, p. 5. See also Mervyn James, 'Ritual, Drama, and Social Body in the Late Medieval English Town', *Past and Present*, 98 (February 1983), p. 28; and Margaret Aston, 'Corpus Christi and Corpus Regni: Heresy and the Peasants' Revolt', *Past and Present*, 143 (May 1994), p. 10.

ne with carlill axes, ne none othir defences in distourbaunce of þe kynges pees & þe play'.[14] William Munson refers to a preacher who complained of the York plays in 1426: 'although they are laudable, they are accompanied by feastings, drunkenness, shouts, songs and other insolences'.[15] However, these examples of disorder are not obviously directed at lordship; and only some festive disorder focused on the drama. Richard Holt and Gervase Rosser note that 'squabbles over precedence disrupted many a Corpus Christi procession'.[16] Disorder is often associated with these processions, but again it does not focus on lordship.

Complaints concerning lordship and government do not seem to be particularly associated with Corpus Christi. Antony Gash notes that the Yule king's procession in Norwich in 1443 was accompanied by a riot against the local abbot,[17] and elections in York, Leicester and Northampton in the fifteenth and sixteenth centuries led to riots.[18] Religious drama was, therefore, only one of many opportunities for disorderly behaviour which might have included the airing of grievances, and riots were not the only means of expressing those grievances. Jennifer I. Kermode notes that

> dissatisfaction became more sophisticated in York during the fifteenth century, as the commons tempered their mass protests with detailed petitions.[19]

Any attempt by dramatists to defuse discontent by offering the people a figure of authority to ridicule should thus be seen in the context of widespread festive disorder, of historical and economic change, and increasing popular sophistication. The representation of evil authority in the cycles by means of transgressive language would have been perceived by spectators according to their ambivalent and fluctuating relationship with local lords. Serious discontent would not be defused.

---

[14] Beadle, ed., *The York Plays*, p. 35.
[15] William F. Munson, 'Audience and Meaning in Two Medieval Dramatic Realisms', in Davidson, Stroupe, and Gianakaris, eds, *The Drama of the Middle Ages*, p. 187.
[16] Richard Holt and Gervase Rosser, eds, *The Medieval Town: A Reader in English Urban History 1200–1540* (London: Longman, 1990), p. 15. See also Miri Rubin, *Corpus Christi: The Eucharist in Late Medieval Culture* (Cambridge: Cambridge University Press, 1991), p. 263, and Margaret Aston 'Corpus Christi and Corpus Regni', p. 10.
[17] Antony Gash, 'Carnival against Lent', in David Aers, ed., *Medieval Literature Criticism, Ideology and Literature* (Brighton: Harvester, 1986), p. 85.
[18] S.H. Rigby, *English Society in the Later Middle Ages* (Basingstoke: Macmillan, 1995), p. 175.
[19] Jennifer I. Kermode, 'Obvious Observations on the Formation of Oligarchies in Late Medieval English Towns', in J.A.F. Thomson, ed., *Towns and Townspeople in the Fifteenth Century* (Gloucester: Sutton, 1988), p. 102.

The audience's mockery of biblical villains nevertheless provided theatrical *exempla* for contemporary rulers. Julian Pitt-Rivers writes that 'the dishonourable conduct of one reflects upon the honour of all .... Honour pertains to social groups of social groups possess a collective honour in which their members participate; any size.'[20]

The audience's mockery of a biblical ruler thus had social implications, and the character's shame was intended to reflect upon rulers generally if they were guilty of behaving like the characters in the plays. The drama, and particularly audience reaction to it, advised local lords forcefully that their pride, threats, violence, and corruption generated discontent among their subjects which was manifested in the ludic context by the audience's ridicule, but in society by riots and disputes.

The mocking of evil lords could, however, have been interpreted as the charitable correction of sin. This was considered a Christian duty which, by pointing out sinful conduct, enabled the sinner to repent and live more virtuously. However, although the criticizing of evil lordship was regarded as a Christian duty, prudence in the correction of lordly sins was undoubtedly necessary during the later Middle Ages. It was not always safe to claim that displaying the sinfulness of a lord was an act of Christian charity. Wyclif wrote that 'þo men þat reprouen bi charite & by discrecion here open synnes helpen to amenden here synnes', but he complains:

> prelatis ... seyn þat in here absence men may not speke a3enst here open cursed synnes for synne of bacbitynge and schlaundrynge; & þei ben so malicious and my3tti in worldly power þat þei wolen suffre no man to speke a3enst her synnes in here presence.[21]

Lines were obviously drawn about who could say what, and in what way. The connection with heresy made the criticisms of Lollard preachers unacceptable, but their complaints may be compared with the frequent and accepted preaching in orthodox sermons against sins attributed to lordship. Criticism of lordship in the biblical plays was acceptable, because they upheld the major tenets of the Christian faith, and because the highly entertaining forms of transgressive language through which they were expressed constantly suggested the festive and ludic context. However, the plays were civic in their auspices and criticism in them may indicate growing self-confidence among an urban oligarchy made up of wealthy and influential merchants and officers of the craft guilds.

The audience's freedom to ridicule the type of a corrupt ruler, while it may have provided a safe opportunity to vent their anger if they had been suffering

---

[20] Julian Pitt-Rivers, 'Honour and Social Status', in J.G. Peristiany, ed., *Honour and Shame* (London: Weidenfeld and Nicolson, 1965), p. 35.
[21] Matthews, ed., *The Works of Wyclif*, p. 101.

under an oppressive lord, depended on the recognition of a set of contexts. If a biblical ruler and his knights bore a strong resemblance to a contemporary magnate and his vassals who were known for their violence, recollections of real fear would be juxtaposed to the conventional and recognizably ludic aspect of the action, creating excitement for some spectators, but apprehension for others who may have been intimidated by even the ludic representation of familiar violence. Others of a more defiant nature might look for confrontation. Tension between the ludic contexts in which violence is portrayed, and the individual's experience of violence in real life, would have created complex audience responses. This tension reaches its height in the plays of the slaughter of the Innocents.

Vassals, violence, and audience reactions

In everyday life the medieval magnates caused great unease by retaining knights who supported their causes against other landowners. Legislation against this practice was frequent, but wholly ineffective during the later Middle Ages.[22] In all the cycles of biblical plays, knights or soldiers in the service of evil lords carry out acts of violence which are accompanied by transgressive language. In the plays of the slaughter of the Innocents that language would have prompted complex audience responses.

Attention is drawn to the status and violence of the knights in all *Slaughter of the Innocents* plays. In the York *Slaughter* the second woman cries: 'þe knyght vppon his knyffe | Hath slayne my sone so swette' (XIX: 212–13). The first woman in the Chester *Innocents* rages: 'Have thou this, thou fowle harlott | and thou knight, to make a knott' (X: 353–4). In the same play the first knight protests to his companions:

> A villanye yt weare, iwys,
> for my fellowe and mee
> to sley a shitten-arsed shrowe.
> (X: 155–7)

It is not killing which concerns him, but the low status of his victim.

Acts of martial violence are commonly left unresolved in biblical plays where they contribute an anachronistic comedy, and simultaneously provide disturbing images of brutality. In the Chester, Towneley, and York Slaughter plays the abusive language of the knights is entirely in keeping with their callous and violent conduct. The mothers are historically incapable of defending their infants and as the action is played out their insults are reactions

---

[22] John G. Bellamy, *Bastard Feudalism and the Law* (London: Routledge, 1989), pp. 85–6.

to extreme violence, and compatible with their desperation, but they also provide comedy as the mothers vehemently abuse and beat the knights.[23]

The male actors playing the mothers switch rapidly from stereotypically female roles, impotently bewailing the loss of their infants, to resembling Noah's wife in their use of violence and transgressive language. During the flyting in the Chester *Innocents*, the liveliest insults are given to the mothers. The second woman confronts the second knight saying: 'Saye, rotten hunter with thy gode, | stytton stallon, styck-tode' (X: 313). The uniqueness of these insults suggests the Chester dramatist's imaginative flexibility and willingness to depart from conventional insults in order to hold his audience's interest, but this comic element creates tension as moments of comedy are rapidly juxtaposed with moments of anguish. In the Towneley *Herod* the second soldier begins: 'Com hedyr, thou old stry | That lad of thyne shall dy' (16: 504–5), and an exchange of insults follows with the second woman exclaiming:

> Haue at thy tabard,
> Harlot and holard:
> ....
> Outt! morder-man, I say,
> Strang tratoure and thefe!
> Out, alas and waloway!
> My chyld that was me lefe!
> My luf, my blood, my play,
> That neuer dyd man grefe!
> (16: 517–18, 512–26)

The insults are gendered, and gendered conflict is foregrounded in the entertainment, but not resolved, as it is in the Noah plays. The transgressive language of the mothers, like that of the knights, lends reality to the historical situation. In the context of the biblical story, however, medieval audiences might have understood the insults of the mothers not as a sign of their place in sinful medieval society, but as a form of punishing language which is directed at the knights.[24] The conduct of the mothers thus represents a violent condemnation of this manifestation of evil authority. On the other hand, where the mothers' language becomes comic in its extravagance it may have contributed to a sense of 'game' which distances the horrific action from reality, and defuses any potential aggressive reaction in the audience. That sense of 'game' nevertheless conflicts with the known theme of the play, intensifying the violence by apparently making light of it.

---

[23] T.W. Craik, 'Violence in the English Miracle Plays', in Neville Denny, ed., *Medieval Drama*, Stratford-upon-Avon Studies, 16 (London: Edward Arnold, 1973), p. 180.
[24] See Chapter 2 above.

The abundance of contemporary medieval complaints and sermons against knightly misconduct suggests that the knights in the Slaughter plays represent the type of evil knighthood, rather than specific instances, although locally notorious thugs and bullies might have been identifiable to a particular audience, in which case the resistance of the mothers, emphasized by their use of insults, may have been gratifying to the victims.

The physical relationship of the audience to the action is significant in determining the impact of transgressive language in the Slaughter plays. If part or all of the action was played at ground level, in front of and around a standing audience, the flyting would enhance the sense of reality, being couched in the familiar language of conflict. If some spectators were viewing from scaffolds set up 'for the accommodation of the audience',[25] or from upper rooms overlooking the playing space, they would be less involved in the action and the flyting would be part of the entertainment. If, however, as Eileen White has suggested of York, scaffolds were erected for paying spectators, and those who could not or would not pay were left to find themselves space on the margins of the playing area, physical distance from the action would have inhibited their appreciation of the entertainment and the didactic purpose of the play.[26] It would have emphasized their marginalization in relation to the devotional and unifying context of the performance, reinforcing their exclusion from other wealth and status-related areas of contemporary society, such as the guilds.

Audience reaction, therefore, would not have been consistent. Those closest to the action might have laughed at the flyting and the beating of the knights by the mothers. They might have laughed at the spearing of a dummy infant if proximity enhanced the sense of artifice, or because the 'killings' safely recreated a deeply transgressive act, or because they enjoyed the horror. Others might have been distressed by this. Some of the audience might have reacted against the knights in spite of, or because of, the ludic context. A real-life grievance might be safely expressed in the celebratory context of the cycle. This range of reactions would create tensions within an audience, as laughter conflicted with anger, or expressions of pity. The rapid juxtaposition of horror and comedy might also create tension within an individual as their laughter was confronted suddenly with another killing; the individual might even find her or himself laughing at the act, caught up in a communal festive light-heartedness which did not take the performance seriously.

If the Slaughter plays with their apparently paradoxical blend of comedy and horror provoked mixed reactions among an audience, this would be at odds

---

[25] Richard Beadle and Pamela King, eds, *York Mystery Plays: A Selection in Modern Spelling* (Oxford: Clarendon Press, 1984), p. xvii.

[26] Eileen White, 'Places for Hearing the Corpus Christi Play in York', *Medieval English Theatre*, 9:1 (1987), p. 25.

with any sense of community and integration which the civic celebration of a cycle performance might bring about. The flyting contributes to the sense of a 'game', but its usefulness as a dramatic device for controlling the reactions of an audience depends upon their acceptance of a single interpretation or range of interpretations of both the individual play, and its place in the cycle. Among an eclectic audience such acceptance could not be guaranteed, especially when the content of the play and the device used appear to be at odds. However, by turning the subject into a comedy the oppressive activities of knights and retainers could be exposed to the reductive power of laughter; but laughter itself could be problematic and may have served a didactic purpose by illustrating through laughter a lack of compassion which leads to people standing aside while others are victimized. This is condemned in sermons, such as *Jacob's Well*, which teaches that it is a sin of omission to have 'no sorwe' of other people's 'euyll-fare', and counsels 'enioyeth no3t of operes harm ... beth sory of here dyssese' (296, 83).

The lack of unified audience reaction to the Slaughter plays illustrates the complexity of potential audience responses to representations of high-status violence. Transgressive language used by biblical evil rulers and their vassals could involve audiences in varying relationships with the drama, and these could address a number of social and ethical issues. The language might have prompted ridicule from spectators and simultaneously challenged the conduct of real rulers. It might have provoked audiences to express anger at familiar acts of oppression and violence, and thus defused potential unrest. It might also have prompted laughter which was a release of social tension, or a culpable display of callousness; and all these responses could have been present simultaneously in any audience. Audience response to transgressive language used by biblical evil rulers and their vassals would thus have been extremely complex. Transgressive language which defines the misconduct of low-status characters prompts a different range of responses.

Social subversion and audience responses

Authors in each cycle use transgressive language to focus attention on certain subversive challenges to the hierarchy which recur as topics in the biblical plays: challenges to social norms and ecclesiastical authority, conflict between masters and men, and discord between husbands and wives. These are always linked to some extent with religious dissent. Many spectators might well have been sympathetic to these challenges, and although the playwrights place differing degrees of emphasis on the forms of subversion, the individual choice of transgressive language signals a playwright's concern. It also allows different kinds of audience response according to a play's biblical and social topic.

The representation of social subversion in the plays draws on festive inversions of the hierarchy which were licensed in medieval society.[27] These festive inversions took various forms,[28] but were, in all cases, limited by the duration of the religious festival with which they were associated. Nevertheless, a strong tradition of subversion associated with religious festivals existed in medieval society, and is mirrored in the biblical plays, where all the forms, which were individually licensed at specific times during the first half of the year, are gathered together in one act of celebration framed by the themes of redemption and integration into the Christian community. The representation of subversion in the cycles defines its place within the redemptive process, but also exploits the freedom associated with the licensed challenges in order to enliven the biblical episodes and explore the extent of discord and dissent in society.

Temporal and divine authority

Early in each cycle a Cain and Abel play introduces the temporal subversion of authority. Cain's evil nature is characterized through his use of transgressive language and his rejection of the social and religious norms which were familiar to medieval audiences. His disregard for these norms defines him, and more importantly, anyone who behaves like him, as 'other' in that society. In all the cycles, Cain's abusive language dramatizes his defiance of God, and his scorn for social obligations.

In the N-Town *Cain and Abel*, Cain remarks scornfully to Abel 'Thow my fadyr I nevyr se, | I 3yf not þerof an hawe' (3: 21–2). His disrespect for the temporal authority represented by his father is a prologue to his contempt for God which occurs only in the N-Town play, but in all the cycles Cain objects to making his sacrifice and expresses his defiance of God. In the Chester *Cain* he declares: 'Hit weare pittye, by my panne, | those fayre eares for to brenne' (II: 537–8). In the incomplete York *Cain and Abel*, an angel comes to Cain after he has killed Abel and tells him: 'God hais sent the his malyson' (VII: 91), to which Cain replies: '... he that sent that gretyng downe, | The devyll myght speyd both hym and the. | Fowll myght thowe fall' (VII: 93–7). Cain's disrespect for his father, for the obligation to make sacrifice, and for God's curse dramatize challenges to the hierarchy of authority, towards tithing, and

---

[27] Charles Phythian-Adams, 'Ceremony and the Citizen: The Communal Year at Coventry 1450–1550', in Holt and Rosser, eds, *The Medieval Town*, pp. 248–50. See also Ronald Hutton, *The Rise and Fall of Merry England: The Ritual Year, 1400–1700* (Oxford: Oxford University Press, 1994), p. 45, and *The Stations of the Sun* (Oxford: Oxford University Press, 1996), pp. 100–108; also Robert Wright, 'Community Theatre in Late Medieval East Anglia', *Theatre Notebook*, 28:1 (1974), pp. 26–7.

[28] The *Records of Early English Drama* volumes testify to many such festive inversions.

towards excommunication, which might be entertaining in the plays, but those members of medieval society, perhaps in the audience, who exhibited similar disrespect for their social obligations, or who treated excommunication with contempt, are implicitly condemned as being like Cain.

The Towneley *Murder of Abel* includes an important variation on the conventional challenge to authority in Cain and Abel plays. Similar challenges are represented in the York *Cain and Abel*, and in Shepherds' plays from Towneley and Chester.

Masters and men

The Towneley *Murder of Abel* recalls inversions of authority associated with Christmas festivities as Cain's apprentice Pikeharnes fights with his master. Cain hits him saying, 'That shall bi thi fals chekys!' Pikeharnes retorts: 'And haue agane as right!' (2: 50–51). The dramatized challenge would have been entertaining, especially to apprentices in the audience, while masters would have recognized the harmlessness of the festive game, and the implicit re-assertion of the norms which are being transgressed. However, Cain is a familiar biblical villain characterized in the play by his constant use of transgressive language and his challenge to God, therefore Pikeharnes's challenge to Cain's authority must be weighed against his transgression. The author of *The Murder of Abel* thus problematizes the challenge to masters by proposing that, like Cain, a master may be a villain.

The flyting and wrestling between Trowle the boy and the shepherds in the Chester *Shepherds* play in which Trowle is the more aggressive and successful, shows similar signs of subversion, although the shepherds are not villains, but kindly men. However, Trowle refuses the food they offer him, telling the second shepherd rudely:

> Nay, the dyrte is soe deepe,
> stopped therin for to steepe,
> and the grubbes theron do creepe
> at whom at thy howse.
> (VII: 214–17)

As he wrestles with the third shepherd he warns him: 'Keepe well thy score | for feare of a fart' (VII: 278–9). The entertainment provided by this inversion of the hierarchy serves the didactic purpose of the play, which is to illustrate the shepherds' transition from disunity, depicted by the flyting and wrestling, to Christian fellowship after the angel's appearance. Spectators might enjoy Trowle's insulting language, but they would notice that the insults cease after the angel's appearance.

The Cain plays, and more obviously the Noah plays, introduce festive challenges into the Chester, Towneley, and York cycles at an early stage in order to represent the discord which characterizes post-lapsarian society. The inclusion of these ludic challenges in the cycles suggests an intention to exert continuing control over the forms of social discord which they playfully represent; however, individual dramatists use transgressive language in ways which subvert that intention.

Husbands and wives

Verbal abuse and physical violence dramatize the inversion of the domestic hierarchy in the Chester, Towneley, and York Noah plays. The flyting between Noah and his wife in the Towneley *Noah* provides lively entertainment.[29] Noah threatens his wife: 'In fayth, and for youre long taryyng | Ye shal lik on the whyp.' She is unimpressed, replying: 'Spare me not, I pray the | ... | Thise grete wordys shall not flay me'. Noah asks as he hits her 'Ar strokys good? say me', but she mocks him, asking: 'What say ye, Wat Wynk?' (3: 545–54).

The defiant language of Noah's wife would have been received with pleasure and approval by those women in the audience who did not accept the patriarchal ideal of subservient womanhood, finding it inappropriate in the context of their own experience. In letters to her husband, Margaret Paston illustrates the variety of tasks she undertakes. She begins one letter: 'I ... prey 3ow to gete som crosse bowis, and wyndacis to bynd þem wyth, and quarell'. She ends the letter: 'As for the childeris gwnys, and I haue cloth I xal do hem maken.' The next in the collection begins 'I commawndyd Herry Goneld to gon to Gunore to have copys of þe pleyntys in þe hundrede.'[30] Such historical evidence reveals that during the later Middle Ages women had responsibility and were active in ways which didactic drama largely chose to ignore, or represented as comic inversion.[31]

Men watching the Noah plays might have found pleasure in the comic representation of the arch-wife. They might have identified with Noah's conventional complaints about the hard lives of married men, and appreciated the chance to criticize the shrewish wife. They might also have enjoyed seeing domestic conflict projected and distanced from them, or simply have enjoyed the fight. Individual women might, of course, have criticized Noah's wife, or enjoyed the representation of domestic violence. However, the representation of Noah's wife, acted by a man, could have been so obviously a burlesque that both male and female spectators would have enjoyed the performance purely for its comedy.

---

[29] Gash, 'Carnival against Lent', p. 79.
[30] Norman Davis, ed., *Paston Letters and Papers*, p. 227.
[31] P.J.P. Goldberg, 'Women in Fifteenth-Century Town Life', in Thomson, ed., *Towns and Townspeople*, p. 115. See also A.G. Dickens, *The English Reformation*, 2nd edn (London: Batsford, 1989), p. 33.

Audience reaction to the Noah plays may, therefore, have polarized around conventional representations of gender roles, but Edgar Schell observes: 'What is striking about the Wakefield Master's treatment of Noah and his wife ... throughout the play, is its evenhandedness'.[32] Other Noah plays also maintain that evenhandedness. Any polarization brought about by transgressive language and conduct therefore continually reflects two sides of a convention in a festive context so that the audience's laughter remains good-natured. The festive context and convention restrict the interpretation of any serious challenge to the patriarchal hierarchy.

The comic inversion of the domestic hierarchy, together with the wife's resistance to the will of God, is resolved during the Flood. Noah's wife is characterized by her use of transgressive language as the kind of person who is sinful and only capable of change when she is confronted with disaster. She does not change in response to hearing about God's intervention on earth, but defies it. The alteration in the wife's language from confrontational to supportive and devout emphasizes for the audience the social and doctrinal points that she has become absorbed into the whole hierarchy of authority.[33]

However, the author of the York *Flood*, who characterizes Noah's wife as similarly recalcitrant, provides an insight into the reason for her challenge to authority. She rounds on Noah, saying:

> Noye, þou myght haue leteyn me wete;
>   Erly and late þou wente þeroutte,
> And ay at home þou lete me sytte
>   To loke þat nowhere were wele aboutte.
> (IX: 113–6)

The wife's angry insults have arisen from Noah's lack of consultation with her, and some spectators might have interpreted this as a wife's desire to pry into her husband's business. However, as the York dramatist traces the source of the conflict in the personal relationship, rather than characterizing it simply in terms of conventional female disobedience he shows how the wife's marginalized status in relation to the hierarchy provokes her challenge.

Social and religious alienation

All the characters in the cycles who subvert social and religious norms are, to some extent, shown to be excluded or alienated from medieval Christian society. Unregenerate evil rulers are never integrated into that society, but, apart from Cain, low-status characters are commonly integrated through the

---

[32] Edgar Schell, 'The Limits of Typology and the Wakefield Master's *Processus Noe*', *Comparative Drama*, 25 (1991), p. 180.

[33] R.D.S. Jack, *Patterns of Divine Comedy* (Cambridge: D.S. Brewer, 1989), p. 119.

process of spiritual change. However, one unique low-status character remains steadfastly excluded through his use of transgressive language, although he does not confront authority as Cain does. Mak, in the Towneley *Second Shepherds' Play*, not only uses common forms of transgressive language, but supplements this with the language of magic.

Mak's transgressive language suggests his 'otherness' in comparison to the shepherds. His pretensions to status and difference are characterized in the language he uses to address them. He tells them:

> What! Ich be a yoman,
> I tell you, of the kyng,
> ....
> Fy on you! Goyth hence
> Out of my presence!
> I must haue reuerence.
> (13: 292–8)

Mak's assertions of superiority unite the shepherds in anger against him. To his airs and insulting 'Fy on you', the first shepherd tells him:

> Now take outt that Sothren tothe,
> And sett in a torde!
> (13: 215–16)

The scatological insult to Mak characterizes the shepherd as sinful, but challenges Mak's pretension, echoing other instances of transgressive language used to punish. The reference to Mak's 'sothren tothe' shows that he is affecting a language separate from that of the northern community where the play was performed. The dramatist has used an unfamiliar dialect, together with Mak's haughty and insulting language to characterize him as 'other' in the community represented by the shepherds, although they are also sinful.

The forms of Mak's 'otherness' are part of his fascination and significance. He appears to draw a magic circle around the sleeping shepherds while speaking a spell over them,[34] saying:

> ... abowte you a serkyll
> As rownde as a moyn,
> To I haue done that I wyll,
> ....
> And I shall say thertyll
> ....
> On hight,

---

[34] David Mills, 'Approaches to Medieval Drama', in Peter Happé, ed., *Medieval English Drama*, Casebook Series (London: Macmillan, 1984), p. 47.

Ouer youre heydys, my hand I lyft.
Outt go youre een! Fordo youre syght!
(13: 408–10)

He has already offered a parodic prayer: '*Manus tuas commendo, | Poncio Pilato*' ('I commend your hands to Pontius Pilate') (13: 384–5). This may be interpreted as a sign of his allegiance to evil, although it may simply represent his misunderstanding of the Latin liturgy, but however Mak's prayer is interpreted, both it and his occult language are a sign of his marginal condition.

Mak's association with magic, his ignorant or transgressive use of liturgical Latin, and his arrogance do not incite absolute condemnation in the play, although he is not redeemed in it. The marginal world he represents seems to be observed and dramatized by the playwright, but not damned, because it was a world which continued to exist around the contemporary audience.

The social purpose of the plays, which is always underpinned by a religious didactic purpose, was to heal divisions and assert hierarchical authority by challenging low-status subversion, but audience responses and the dramatists' observations may have subverted those purposes. Transgressive language used by low-status characters in the biblical plays characterizes people and defines attitudes which challenge the hierarchy of authority, and draw attention to the existence of discord in medieval society.

While abuses of power by lords and vassals are challenged by audience responses, and social subversion is hardly challenged in the biblical plays, the religious didactic purpose of the plays is foregrounded as the faith and virtue of spectators themselves are challenged in plays which use transgressive language to position them as witnesses to defamation, violence, and the Passion of Christ.

Audiences challenged

The defamation of Christ

It is conventional to see legal corruption represented in the plays of the trials of Christ. Through references to the medieval laws of defamation, dramatists challenge real or notional legal corruption by characterizing it as part of the persecution of Christ. It also serves the cause of affective piety by presenting that persecution in ways which directly involve the audience as potential witnesses.[35]

---

[35] John F. Plummer, 'The Logomachy of the N-Town Passion Play 1', *Journal of English and Germanic Philology*, 88 (1989), p. 326.

Accusations of witchcraft, necromancy, and sorcery are made against Christ in the Passion plays of all the cycles, except Chester. Although the accusations are made more frequently and insistently in the York trial plays than in the other cycles, in all instances the accusations constitute defamation and lead to injustice.

In the N-Town *Conspiracy* the Primus Doctor blames Cayphas for permitting Christ 'With his fals wichcraft þe pepyl to blynde' (26: 228). This takes place in Christ's absence, but in the other cycles the defamatory accusation of witchcraft is made in His presence. The torturers in the Towneley *Buffeting* bring Christ before the priests and tell Cayphas of the raising of Lazarus, complaining of Christ: 'All men hym prase; ... | Such wychcraft he mase' (21: 148–50). A similar accusation is made in the York *Christ before Pilate (1)*, when Cayphas tells Pilate:

> Sir, halte men and hurte he helid in haste,
>   The deffe and þe dome he delyuered fro doole
> By wicchecrafte.
> (XXX: 441–3)

While the accusation of witchcraft alone represents a misunderstanding, on the part of Christ's accusers, of the physical manifestations of His divinity, the accusation of heresy which is made against Him represents the misinterpretation of Christ's teaching, and a denial of its truth. In the N-Town *Betrayal*, the character Gamalyel addresses Christ saying: 'Lo, Jesus, þu mayst not þe cace refuse: | Bothe treson and eresye in þe is fownde' (28: 113–4).

The accusations are not only culpable theological misinterpretations, in the medieval legal context they are all defamatory. This is tacitly recognized in the York *Christ before Pilate (1)*, when Pilate challenges Annas and Caiaphas, declaring: 'Ye meve all þe malice ye may | With youre wrenchis and wiles to wrythe hym away' (XXX: 483–4). Malice was the formulaic motivation in the medieval legal definition of defamation, and since the audience would be in no doubt that the trials of Christ are based in medieval legal practice, the refusal to allow witnesses to be called, besides accurately representing the treatment of Christ in the Gospels,[36] would have been understood as a perversion of justice relevant to medieval society.[37] The denial of this right is the means by which

---

[36] The Gospels of Matthew, Mark, and Luke all include this injustice. See for example Matt. 26: 65 *Tunc princeps sacerdotum scidit vestimenta sua dicens blasphemavit quid adhuc egemus testibus ecce nunc audistis blasphemam* ('Then the high priest tore his clothes, saying, He has blasphemed. Why do we need witnesses now you have heard the blasphemy?'). Robert Weber, ed., *Biblia sacra iuxta vulgatam versionem*, 4th edn (Stuttgart: Deutsche Bibelgesellschaft, 1969). All references are to this edition. My translations.

[37] R.H. Nicholson describes the work of tribunals 'formed from the membership of the [King's] Council', and notes that they could, 'like the Inquisition, both accuse and bring down judgement upon the accused'. Nicholson comments: 'This is exactly what happens in the case

the playwrights dramatize the injustice of Christ's trial in terms having both theological and social impact.

In each trial play, in each cycle, the defamatory accusations made against Christ are such that the Christian audience could, in theory at least, act as His compurgators. However, in each cycle persecutors declare, as Cayphas does in the Towneley *Buffeting*: 'We nede no wytnes: | Hysself says expres' (21:375–6), and Cayphas again in the N-Town *Trial before Annas and Cayphas*: 'What nedyth us to haue more wytness? | Here 3e han herd all his owyn word' (29: 175–6). In the York *Christ before Annas and Caiaphas*, Caiaphas tells Christ 'Yf þou be Criste, Goddis sonne, telle till vs two' (XXIX: 292). Christ replies: 'Sir, þou says it þiselffe, and sothly I saye | Þat I schall go to my fadir þat I come froo' (XXIX: 293–4). Annas then declares: 'Nowe nedis nowdir wittenesse ne counsaille to call, | But take his sawes as he saieth in þe same stede' (XXIX: 300–301). Christ objects that He has been wrongly denounced, telling Cayphas 'Sire, sen þou with wrong so me wreyes, | Go spere thame þat herde of my spekyng' (XXIX: 323). The high priest ignores the suggestion that other testimony should be sought.[38]

The Chester *Trial* does not use defamatory accusations of witchcraft, heresy, and treason, but Cayphas actually calls on the audience to act as witnesses to the falseness of Christ when He declares Himself to be the Son of God who will 'justefye' (XVI: 50) or judge humanity. Cayphas exclaims:

'Justifie!' Marye, fye, fye on thee, fye!
Wytnes of all this compenye
that falsely lyes hee!
(XVI: 51-3)

---

of Christ the sorcerer in the York cycle'. R.H. Nicholson, 'The Trial of Christ the Sorcerer in the York Cycle', *Journal of Medieval and Renaissance Studies*, 16 (1986), p. 154. I am not convinced that medieval spectators would generally be familiar with this legal process. I believe most spectators would, however, understand the injustice of the trials in the context of local consistory courts, and the process of compurgation (see Chapter 1 above).

[38] In *c*.1486 the authors of the manual of the Inquisition, the *Malleus Maleficarum*, observed that in cases of witchcraft and heresy 'in a charge of this kind two witnesses do not seem sufficient to ensure an equitable judgement, on account of the heinousness of the crime in question. For the proof of an accusation ought to be clearer than daylight; and especially ... in the case of ... heresy'. Heinrich Kramer and James Sprenger, *Malleus Maleficarum*, trans. Montague Summers (New York: Dover, 1971), p. 208. English law, however, accepted the evidence of only two witnesses, *particularly* for heinous crimes such as heresy, as Sir Thomas More asserted in his 1531 *Dialogue Concerning Heresies*. He also declared that in the specific case of Thomas Bilney's trial for heresy 'whan he was so clerely conuycted by so many / so honest & so farr from all suspycyon of corrupcyon / yt were ... a thyng not conuenyent / to bryng proves a fresshe'. See Thomas M.C. Lawler, Germain Marc'Hadour, and Richard C. Marius, eds, *The Complete Works of St. Thomas More*, vol. 6, *A Dialogue Concerning Heresies* (New Haven: Yale University Press, 1981), pp. 260–65. The drama thus represents the bias in English law which disadvantaged defendants, and which acquired a political significance during the 1530s.

While the priest is anxious to have witnesses of his own, he denies them to Christ, saying: 'Ye hearen all that he sayes here. | Of wytnes nowe what neede were?' (XVI: 54–5). Thus Christ is given no opportunity to purge Himself of the accusation of being false. The Chester dramatist increases the tension for the audience by having the evil priest assign them the role of his witnesses against Christ.

The primary function of defamatory accusations of witchcraft and heresy in the trial plays is to illustrate the speakers' misunderstanding of Christ's ministry. That not only excludes the speaker from the Christian community which is present as the audience, it also reflects upon members of the audience who may themselves doubt the miraculous nature of Christ's works, consigning the doubters to the margins of medieval society, along with the historical tormentors of Christ.

In all the trial plays the audience *could* act as witnesses to the divine nature of Christ and His miracles, but they are denied the opportunity. They must watch, helplessly, the inevitable course of the trials, which they would already know will lead to His torture and death. Though the outcome of the trials is already known, the contemporary medieval legal framework nevertheless provided spectators with a reminder of their ability to testify on Christ's behalf, and therefore to testify to their own belief. Doubting or spiritually ignorant individuals would, on the other hand, be drawn to the story as they recognized familiar forms of legal corruption being played out before them.

One cycle, N-Town, includes two plays which use medieval defamation laws to challenge the audience's faith, and its acceptance of the sins of defamation and detraction. Transgressive language in *The Trial of Mary and Joseph* challenges religious doubt while in *The Woman Taken in Adultery* it challenges the audience's vicarious delight in sin.

Defamation, doubt, and sin

The N-Town *Trial of Mary and Joseph* exploits the audience's familiarity with the law of defamation, the sin of detraction, and the role of witnesses in both, as it dramatizes and condemns doubts concerning the Incarnation and the virginity of Mary. The audience witnesses the slandering of Mary and Joseph by the aptly named characters Bakbytere (14: 62) and Reysesclaundyr (14: 66) whose speeches illustrate the attitudes which lie behind their slander. Reysesclaundyr tells Bakbytere:

> Within a shorte whyle a thynge befelle,
>   I trowe þu wylt lawh3 ryght wel þerate:
> For, be trowth, right mekyl hate,
>   If it be wyst, þerof wyl growe.
> (14: 68–71)

To which Bakbytere responds: 'If I may reyse þerwith debate, | I xal not spare þe seyd to sowe' (14: 72–3). The intention to provoke trouble, rather than to know the truth, is put forward by the dramatist as the motivation behind doubts concerning Mary's pregnancy.

Rather than simply condemning the act of detraction and its motivation, as the sermons do, the play provides lively illustrations of those forms of language which constitute detraction and the attitudes underlying it. The sin imputed to Mary is based on the kind of gossip and innuendo which has always had a place in society. Reysesclaundyr declares: 'Sum fresch 3onge galaunt she lovyth wel more | þat his leggys to here hath leyd!' (14: 87–8), and Bakbytere adds:

> Such a 3onge damesel of bewté bryght,
>   And of schap so comely also,
> Of her tayle ofte-tyme be lyght
>   And rygh tekyl vndyr þe too.
> (14: 94–7)

The character of the Bishop overhears the last speech and warns the detractors: '3e be acursyd so hire for to defame' (14: 108). The contents of the speeches may, however, be defined either as backbiting or detraction, so the Bishop's speech draws attention to the fact that defamation is taking place, thereby focusing the audience's interest and emphasizing the legal framework. This emphasis suggests the importance of the play's topic, and authorial concern that such defamatory remarks about Mary might be taken lightly by the medieval audience. The comic potential of the transgressive language in the ludic context is being controlled so as to define scepticism as sinful rather than trivial.

The audience would understand the sinfulness of the detractors' remarks, and this is crucial to the didactic purpose of the play. The detractors express their doubts, the Bishop warns them against defaming Mary, but they then make their accusations to the Bishop. This formal act of 'presenting' leads to the trial itself, during which Mary and Joseph are obliged to purge themselves of the accusations made against them openly before the Bishop's court.

In court the detractors accuse Joseph to his face of being a cuckold, and mock Mary for maintaining her innocence. However, the play departs from contemporary medieval legal process and introduces a tone of divine mystery as Mary and Joseph purge themselves. Rather than calling witnesses, the Bishop presents Joseph with a bottle from which he and Mary must drink the 'drynge of vengeawns' (14: 233). They do so without ill effect. Although trial by ordeal had long been superseded in English law by other methods of proving guilt and innocence, a biblical source provides for the inclusion of this ordeal. Robert Bartlett draws attention to this source when he remarks that: 'in the Book of Numbers a procedure is described in which a wife suspected of infidelity is subjected to the ordeal of bitter waters'.³⁹

In the biblical account the drink is a vehicle for a curse which will fall upon the wife if she is guilty of infidelity. Although the curse is missing from *The Trial of Mary and Joseph* the effects of the drink as proof of guilt and innocence are the same as the biblical drink of bitter waters. No harm comes to Mary or Joseph because Mary is innocent.

Because Mary successfully passes the ordeal, the accusations made against her are proved to be defamation. The play then returns to the tenets of medieval law which punished defamers for their uncharitable words. Bakbytere himself is forced to take the ordeal. The Bishop tells him:

> ... for þu dedyst hem fyrst defame,
> Þu xalt ryght here, magré þin heed,
> Beforn all þis pepyl drynk of þe same.
> (14: 359–61)

As he dies, Bakbytere cries: '... I do me repent | Of my cursyd and fals langage' (14: 366–7). As he acknowledges that his expressions of doubt are false, medieval society's potential scepticism is characterized as an act of defamation.

The Trial of Mary and Joseph uses contemporary medieval laws on language to dramatize the common topos of doubts about Mary's virginity. By including the biblical reference to the trial appointed by God for infidelity, the dramatist proves Mary's purity by divine law, acting through the medium of temporal law. This retains and emphasizes the mystical nature of the Incarnation, and contrasts the power of divine law with the common and uncharitable acts of defamation and detraction.

The spectators here are not passive witnesses of the drama. At the beginning of the play they are put in the position of hearers of detraction. The dialogue between Reysesclaundyr and Bakbytere is full of lively and familiar sexual innuendo. The Bishop's intervention would remind the spectators that what they heard was not harmless and entertaining gossip, and while it was sinful to speak in that way, it was equally sinful to listen. During the trial the spectators

---

³⁹ Robert Bartlett, *Trial by Fire and Water: The Medieval Judicial Ordeal* (Oxford: Clarendon Press, 1986), p. 84. Numbers 5: 12–31 details the ritual appointed by God in the case of a wife's infidelity: *vir cuius uxor erravit ... adducet eam ad sacerdotem. ... aquam sanctam in vase fictilii et pauxillum terrae de pavimento tabernaculi mittet in eam. adiurabitque eam et dicet si non dormivit vir alienus tecum et si non polluta es ... non te nocebunt aquae istae amarissimae ... et dabit ei bibere.* ('The husband of a wife who has gone astray ... will lead her to a priest. In a clay vessel he [the priest] will put holy water, and a very little of the earth from the floor of the tabernacle into it, and he will adjure her, saying: if a strange man has not slept with you, and you are not defiled ... these bitter waters ... will not harm you ... and he will give it to her to drink').Weber, ed., *Biblia sacra*. My translation.

are positioned as witnesses. By hearing Mary defamed they would be reminded of what they had been taught concerning the doctrine of the virgin birth. However, the use of contemporary medieval legal proceedings allows the dramatist to 'prove' the doctrine of virginity to anyone in the audience who doubted, or simply did not know it.

Given the heterogeneous nature of audiences for biblical plays the most effective drama would address the widest range of interest and levels of religious knowledge. Those who could not be reached because of their doubts or ignorance might have been influenced by the contemporary legal process played out before them in *The Trial of Mary and Joseph*. The early fifteenth-century Wycliffite *Tretise of Miraclis Pleyinge* provides the orthodox view of the biblical plays even as it condemns them. The author writes: 'they seyen that siche pleyinge doith more good than the word of God whanne it is prechid to the puple'.[40]

In *The Trial of Mary and Joseph* the sins of defamation and detraction characterize doubts concerning the Incarnation, and provide a contemporary framework within which those doubts can be attacked and disproved. The same sins are used in another N-Town play, *The Woman Taken in Adultery*, where the most scurrilous sexual insults are a means of challenging the sins of backbiting and defamation while illustrating Christ's merciful forgiveness of sinners.

In *The Woman Taken in Adultery* the Scribe, Pharisee, and Accusator present a woman who is known to be promiscuous to Christ to be judged. Prior knowledge of the woman's moral status has important implications for the judgement, and her reputation is never in doubt. If the audience have forgotten, or never knew, the story it is set before them in words, and in lively action as her lover escapes from the conspirators with his breeches unlaced and his boots in his hand.

The play is remarkable for the violence and obscenity of the sexual abuse used by the conspirators to address the woman. The Scribe tells her:

> Come forth, þu stotte, com forth, þu scowte!
> Com forth, þu bysmare and brothel bolde!
> Com forth, þu hore and stynkynge bych clowte![41]
> (24: 145–7)

The Pharisee joins in the abuse, adding:

---

[40] Clifford Davidson, ed., *A Tretise of Miraclis Pleyinge*, Early Drama, Art, and Music Monograph Series 19 (Kalamazoo, Mich.: Medieval Institute Publications, 1993), l. 631.

[41] This unusual gendered insult is glossed by the editor as 'rag of a whore', or perhaps 'cursed rag'; see Spector, ed., *The N-Town Play*, vol. 2, p. 486. It may, however, be derived from a contemporary medieval form of menstrual dressing.

> Com forth, þu quene, com forth, þu scolde!
>   Com forth, þu sloveyn, com forth, þu slutte!
> We xall the teche with carys colde
>   A lytyl bettyr to kepe þi kutte.[42]
> (24: 149–52)

Because the woman already has a reputation as a whore these insults do not constitute defamation in the medieval legal sense. The woman cannot purge herself of the accusations, and is only concerned to spare her friends shame. She begs her accusers in terms relevant to medieval society:

> If I be sclaundryd opynly,
>   To all my frendys it xul be shame.
> I pray 3ow, kylle me here in þis place
> Lete not þe pepyl know my defame.
> (24: 173–6)

A similar view that shame extends beyond the person defamed is expressed in *The Trial of Mary and Joseph*, when the Secundus Doctor Legis tells Mary: 'If God with vengeauns set on þe his syse, | Not only þu but all þi kin is schamyd' (14: 318–19).

If the audience had recently watched the trial of innocence in *The Trial of Mary and Joseph* they are now presented with the judgement of guilt in *The Woman Taken in Adultery* as the woman is taken before Christ and begs Him for mercy, saying:

> Now, holy prophete, be mercyable!
>   Vpon me, wrecch, take no vengeaunce.
> For my synnys abhomynable
>   In hert I haue grett repentaunce.
> (24: 209–12)

The woman's penitent words are answered by words of mercy and forgiveness from Christ. He tells her:

> For me þu xalt nat condempnyd be;
>   Go hom ageyn and walk at large.
> Loke þat þu leve in honesté,
> And wyl no more to synne, I þe charge.
> (24: 276–80)

---

[42] The editor glosses 'kutte' as 'private parts', but in view of the tone of the speech the modern English offensive slang term 'slit' maintains an appropriate level of humiliating vilification.

Christ's merciful forgiveness of the guilty woman contrasts not only with the abusive malice of the conspirators towards her, but also with the ordeal to which His innocent mother was subjected in *The Trial of Mary and Joseph*. Under Christ's merciful law the most vilified sinner, having repented and asked, receives forgiveness for the very sin of which Christ's mother had earlier been accused. The temporal law which demands vengeance and is corruptible by malice is in both plays characterized through the use of transgressive language. The thematic links between the two N-Town plays are not surprising even though the cycle is known to be a compilation, since both plays are found in the Proclamation Play, the source of much of the cycle,[43] and are in keeping with its Marian emphasis.

In response to the conspirators' vengeful desire to have the woman stoned, Christ writes their sins in the dust, which dismays them. The presentation of this action on any stage would not achieve the impact it has in the biblical story, but the dramatist overcomes this by a more impressive representation of words which reveal guilt. These are the terms of sexual abuse used by the conspirators. Their fluent use of this abuse reveals their familiarity with sexual misconduct. The spoken words are a sign of the conspirators' own prurient interest in the subject, as well as a sign of their malicious desire to punish the woman, and trap Christ.

However, the language of sexual abuse does not only give the play a contemporary relevance, or characterize the corruption of temporal law which is based on vengeance and malice, or condemn those who use such language in society, although all these are possible concurrent interpretations of its use in the play. There is also a rhetorical pleasure in the construction of the accusers' speeches for both the dramatist and the audience. The rhetoric briefly privileges the dramatist's skill over the dramatic effect, and over the moral significance. That rhetorical pleasure may, however, be sinful if it becomes pleasure in hearing language which is overtly sexual and recalls sexual sin. The sins of the conspirators would then become the sins of individual spectators. Similarly, Christ's judgement against the conspirators becomes His judgement against people in contemporary medieval society who both condemn and delight in the sexual misconduct of others.

These N-Town plays use sinful, legally actionable, and plain abusive language to dramatize religious scepticism, and characterize the vicious impulses underlying both scepticism and the sins of defamation and detraction. The process of judgement in *The Trial of Mary and Joseph* 'proves' Mary's innocence to the audience. In *The Woman Taken in Adultery* a different process of judgement reinforces the message of Christ's mercy. In both plays trangressive language in the form of defamation involves the audience as

---

[43] Fletcher, 'The N-Town Plays,' p. 168.

witnesses, and as sexual abuse it challenges their acceptance or vicarious enjoyment of sinful language and behaviour.

Transgressive language which induces an audience to become involved in dramatizations of sin, but is not presented as defamation, is exploited in both biblical and morality plays. The sin is created in the audience as it is played out before them, and the technique is observed in the *Tretise of Miraclis Pleyinge*, which records the orthodox view that:

> ofte sithes by siche miraclis pleyinge ben men commited to gode livinge, as men and wymmen seing in miraclis pleyinge that the devul by ther aray ... makith hem his servauntis ... wherthoru they leeven ther pride and taken to hem afterward the meke conversacion of Crist.[44]

A similar technique, using relatively little transgressive language, is used in the York *Crucifixion* to involve the audience in guilt.

Guilt and affective piety

The York *Crucifixion* uses less direct abuse than the other Passion plays which precede it, and less than many other biblical plays, but again language, action, and staging combine to question the attitudes of an audience. The third soldier tells Christ: 'Come forthe þou cursed knave' (XXXV: 45), as he sets to work with three others to crucify Him. They discuss what they are doing, and their stichomythic exchanges are not deeply abusive, but indicate their unity, and give the play a lively, colloquial atmosphere. This may have distracted the spectators' concentration from the act of crucifixion, especially if Christ was not always visible to them. The soldiers chatter like workmen:

IV Miles	I hope þat marke amisse be bored.
	....
I Miles	Why carpe 3e so? Faste on a corde
	And tugge hym to, by toppe and taile.
III Miles	3a, þou comaundis lightly as a lorde;
	Come helpe to haale, with ille haile.
I Miles	Now certis þat schall I doo –
	Full snelly as a snayle.
	(XXXV: 109, 114–8)

The insults between them, and disregard for their victim, indicate the evil nature of the soldiers, and their exclusion from the Christian community which surrounded them. However, their colloquial chatter situates them in that community, and it is likely that they wore the costume of medieval soldiers to

---

[44] Davidson, ed., *A Tretise of Miraclis Pleyinge*, l. 150.

reinforce the sense of immediacy. Thus they represent evil which is not distanced by time from the audience.

Torturers appear to have been so familiar in drama that *The Simonie*, an early fourteenth-century poem, could use them as a convention to condemn fashionable young men, complaining: 'Hii ben degised as turmentours þat comen from clerkis plei'.[45] The audience's familiarity with these characters and their role would have influenced its reception of their language and actions. However, the physical position of the audience in relation to the soldiers is important for understanding the impact of this play, as it was for the Slaughter plays. If the spectators were standing at street level they would not see the action on the pageant wagon clearly, and what they would hear would be more significant. Even if they were seated on raised scaffolds, or in the windows of houses overlooking the playing station, the spectators would see more of the soldiers than of Christ, who would be lying down on the Cross, and surrounded by them as they worked. The soldiers' complaints that the work is too hard, and gruesome details such as the second soldier's '3aa, assondir are bothe synnous and veynis' (XXXV: 147) may, for some spectators, have been shocking and deeply moving. The *Tretise of Myraclis Pleyinge* records that

> men and wymmen, seinge the passioun of Christ ... ben movyd to compassion and devocion, wepinge bitere teris.[46]

For other spectators the stichomythic exclamations of the soldiers as they lift the Cross would be detached from the Christian significance, becoming comic and gratifying a taste for horror and violence as the play takes on the aspect of a contemporary execution, until the moment when the Cross achieves its final and familiar iconographic position.

Tension between comedy and affective piety in plays which include martial violence may have been resolved through the structure of the plays and the cycles, as transgressive language in one play or part of a play is followed by a vividly presented aspect of the redemptive process in which familiar iconography is combined with decorous modes of speech.[47] However, this process is modified in the York *Crucifixion*, which does not end with devotional language but with mockery, although it is followed immediately by *The Death of Christ*, which is conservative and iconic. This play opens with

---

[45] Dan Embree and Elizabeth Urquhart, eds, *The Simonie: A Parallel-Text Edition* (Heidelberg: Carl Winter Universitätsverlag, 1991), p. 86, A 283. John Bale also uses the convention as a pejorative reference in his *Image of Both Churches*, published in 1545. See Henry Christmas, ed. *Selected Works of John Bale*, Parker Society (Cambridge: Cambridge University Press, 1849), p. 433.
[46] Davidson, ed., *A Tretise of Miraclis Pleyinge*, l. 162.
[47] Margery M. Morgan, ' "High Fraud" in the Shepherds' Plays: Paradox and Double-Plot in the English Shepherds Plays', *Speculum*, 39 (1944), p. 688.

Pilate's boast and conversation with Caiaphas and Annas, and in this instance the chain of dramatic action increases the tension of the Passion sequence, by dramatizing the unremitting evil opposed to Christ.[48]

The *Crucifixion* comes to a climax as the soldiers raise the Cross, but the first and fourth soldiers mock Christ's agony at this point, asking: 'Say sir, howe likis you nowe, | Þis werke þat we haue wrought?' (XXXV: 249–50) and the fourth asks: 'We praye youe sais vs howe | 3e fele, or faynte 3e ought?' (XXXV: 251–2). Christ responds with a conventional complaint from the Cross, addressing 'Al men þat walkis by waye or strete' (XXXV: 253), but the play ends with soldiers mocking him. The first remarks: 'We, harke, he jangelis like a jay', the second adds: 'Methynke he patris like a py', while the third observes: 'He has been doand all þis day' (XXXV: 265–7). The raising of the Cross changes the context of the soldiers' mockery. While the audience would have expected, and perhaps relished, the violence of the evil characters, expressed in both language and action, the didactic intention is that those who have enjoyed the play for its comedy and horror will now realize that by their reactions they share in what they have seen and heard, and consequently share the guilt of the Crucifixion.

The audience which laughed at the Crucifixion may, however, have been less culpable than this interpretation suggests. In medieval drama laughter was licensed, encouraged, and served the didactic purpose.[49] Dramatists set out to control audience response by using laughter to condemn behaviour and attitudes which were unacceptable to society, or by demonstrating that spectators were themselves sinning as they enjoyed the entertainment. Where unlicensed laughter occurred it was rejected. The York A/Y Memorandum Book records the complaint by the Masons about their pageant *The Funeral of the Virgin*, also known as *Fergus*: *ubi ffergus flagellatus erat ... magis risum & clamorem causabat quam deuocionem* ('when Fergus was flogged ... it caused more laughter and shouting than devotion').[50]

Mikhail Bakhtin suggests a further dimension to laughter at the *Crucifixion* when he writes of 'the grotesque imagery' of death[51] in the Middle Ages which 'can be understood only within the unity of folk and carnival spirit'.[52] Bakhtin

---

[48] Peter Happé draws attention to a potential problem here when he notes: 'the practice of authorship for the cycles is more than a little incoherent'; Peter Happé, *English Drama before Shakespeare* (London: Longman, 1999), p. 67. The technique for resolving tension seems to be widely used in the cycles by many different authors, and may be suspended until the end of a Passion sequence. Subject matter rather than authorship seems to define the moment when tension is defused.

[49] Jack, *Patterns of Divine Comedy*, p. 71.

[50] Alexandra F. Johnson and Margaret Rogerson, eds, *Records of Early English Drama: York*, 2 vols (Manchester: Manchester University Press, 1979), vol. 1, p. 47.

[51] Mikhail Bakhtin, *Rabelais and His World*, trans. Hélène Iswolsky (Cambridge, Mass.: MIT Press, 1968), p. 50.

[52] Ibid., p. 52.

interprets grotesque imagery in the context of this unity so that 'death is not a negation of life ... but part of life as a whole – its indispensable component, the condition of its constant renewal and rejuvenation'.[53] As such, Bakhtin asserts that it is a cause for festive laughter. Although this view appears to conflict with the medieval Church's emphasis on the suffering of Christ, festive laughter at the Crucifixion is not inappropriate to the redemptive theme of the cycle, since it is only by Christ's death that humanity can be redeemed. However, those spectators who laughed at the soldiers during the *Crucifixion* are unlikely to have noticed any degree of appropriateness, but might have enjoyed the freedom of festive laughter and their own transgression against affective piety.

In all the biblical plays which use transgressive language to position the audience as witnesses, and/or involve them in sin, that language also has a mnemonic effect: it reminds the audience of the Christian doctrine they had been taught. In some plays, such as the York *Crucifixion*, recollection is less important than promoting affective piety and remembrance of culpability among the audience, and to this end the mocking of Christ emphasizes His suffering. Other Passion plays use the mocking of Christ to remind spectators of His divinity and majesty.

Mnemonic mockery and abuse

Marcia Colish observes that in St Augustine's epistemology 'the Word may make the subject remember God if he is already a believer, or orient the subject towards God if he is not'.[54] In the biblical plays, abuse and mockery directed at Christ function as mnemonic devices which remind the audience of what they *should* already know. When Caiaphas in the Towneley *Buffetting* ridicules Christ, saying: 'What, nawder bowted ne spurd, | And a lord of name?' (21: 213–14), the dramatist intends that Caiaphas's remark would remind the audience of the nature of Christ's spiritual lordship by the contrast with the reference to boots and spurs, which were familiar outward signs of temporal lordship in medieval society. Since boots and spurs were also associated with university training, Caiaphas's mocking challenge may also suggest that he recognizes Christ as a teacher, but dismisses His lack of formal qualifications![55] Other evil lords, and their vassals, mock Christ's kingship,

---

[53] Ibid., p. 50.

[54] Marcia L. Colish, *The Mirror of Language*, rev. edn (Lincoln, Nebr.: University of Nebraska Press, 1983), p. 43.

[55] The association of boots and spurs with secular medieval lords need not be elaborated here, but a footnote to William Tyndale's *Obedience of a Christian Man* provides an insight into the significance of boots and spurs as associated with theological distinction and therefore (potential) ecclesiastical lordship. It refers to a seventeenth-century tract which asked 'Whether it be not a pretty foundation for the Oxford doctors to stand booted and spurred', and

innocence, and divinity, but in each case the religious scepticism their mockery represents is condemned as the attitude of villains.

In the plays of the trials of Christ insults and abusive language directed at Christ function in several ways, all of which are influenced by His rhetorically significant silence. The speaker of insults and abuse in these plays assumes power and status which is subverted by the audience's prior knowledge of Christ's divinity. The speaker is degraded in his use of transgressive language because it expresses his ignorance or rejection of Christ's supreme status. Transgressive language in this context once again dramatizes attitudes which exclude the character, and consequently individuals who behave like him, from the community of Christian belief to which the audience nominally belong. When, in the N-Town *Trial before Herod*, the king calls Christ 'þu onhangyd harlot' (30: 221), his words function in all these ways.

Caiaphas, in the York *Christ before Pilate (1)*, tells Pilate 'we haue brought here a lorell – he lokis like a lambe' (XXX: 274). The priest insults Christ when he names Him 'lorell', or scoundrel, but when he observes that Christ looks like a lamb, Caiaphas is suggesting that Christ's meek appearance disguises a wicked nature. However, for Christian spectators the word 'lamb' should recall Christ's name as the Lamb of God.

Understanding the allusions signifies knowledge of the Christian faith. This would not only unite spectators but would afford even the lowest in social status a spiritual status higher than that of the evil characters. Thus all social levels might be united in a sense of community by their Christian knowledge, which is opposed to the ignorance of the historical villains. Such unity provides a framework for judging the significance of transgressive language, although that judgement may be disrupted at times by festive and ludic contexts.

Insults are a form of naming, and characters who name Christ abusively may do so to His face, or to a third character. Abusing a person in their presence but to a third party, as Caiaphas names Christ 'lorell' before Pilate, is more insulting than direct abuse, since it disregards the presence of the abused. The power to change a person's status by naming them would have been familiar to medieval spectators. A man was elevated by being dubbed knight, and contemporary medieval defamation cases demonstrate the power of naming to degrade a person's status in society. Abusive names are also associated with the punishment of socially unacceptable misdemeanours. However, when historical villains name Christ they cannot alter His status, but rather draw the audience's attention to His passive innocence. Their abusive

---

therefore (potential) ecclesiastical lordship. It refers to a seventeenth-century tract which asked 'Whether it be not a pretty foundation for the Oxford doctors to stand booted and spurred', and notes that '[b]oots were introduced by the Benedictines [at Oxford] and were worn by masters of arts ... till the doctors appropriated them'. See William Tyndale, *The Obedience of a Christian Man*, ed. Richard Lovett, Christian Classics Series V (London: Religious Tract Society, n. d.), p. 164.

naming not only reminds the faithful of this, but emphasizes to the ignorant the evil of the persecutors and the humility of Christ.

Though the evil rulers assume power when they attempt to name Christ, that power is subverted by their inability to control the abusive and mocking language they use. Language is shown to be unstable in the mouths of the unredeemed, who are free to use language as they choose, but cannot control its meaning, as perceived by the audience, which constantly evades their intention. This instability contrasts with Christ's use of language and confirms the power and stability of the Word of God, and the Word made Flesh.

Christ is mockingly addressed as King by the torturers in the Passion plays of all the cycles. The mockery directs attention to the mockers' ignorance, but more importantly to the true nature of Christ. After He has been crowned with thorns, the second torturer in the Towneley *Scourging* mocks Him saying:

> Hayll, kyng! Where was thou borne,
> Sich worship for to wyn?
> (22: 317–18)

The fourth Jew in the N-Town *Crucifixion* addresses Christ before the Cross has been raised, saying: '... I trowe þu art a worthy kyng' (32: 78). The mockery should remind the audience that Christ's kingship transcends His degradation and humiliation. This transcendence may be compared with the fragility of temporal lordship which is dramatized in all the cycles as the historical evil lords' need to assert their power through bombast and threats.

Mockery of Christ's transcendent kingship is given visual form when the torturers crown Him with thorns. In the N-Town Passion sequence Christ is also clothed in purple to mock His kingship, in the other cycles He is clothed in white robes associated in medieval society with both natural fools and the state of holiness. The clothing of Christ in white invokes social and symbolic interpretations which add new dimensions to the verbal mockery.[56]

Herod in the Chester *Trial* commands: 'Cloth him in white' (XVI: 195), and the second Jew ridicules Christ when this is done saying: 'Nowe thou art in thy royaltie!' (XVI: 208). The references to kingship are used ironically by the evil characters, but the authorial intention is to draw the audience's attention to the aptness of robing Christ in white and hailing Him as king, since, although the characters intend this as a mocking insult, the whiteness may be interpreted as signifying His purity and the spiritual form of His kingship.

The First Duke in the York *Christ before Herod* explains the significance of the white robe, saying: 'fooles þat are fonde þei falle such a fee' (XXXI: 342).

---

[56] Mary H. Marshall, 'Aesthetic Values in Liturgical Drama', in Jerome Taylor and Alan H. Nelson, eds, *Medieval English Drama* (Chicago: University of Chicago Press, 1972), p. 37.

Christ's silence is interpreted by Herod and his court in this play as a sign of the witlessness of a natural fool, and for this reason they clothe Him in white, rather than the motley of an artificial fool who was in control of his wits.[57] However, holiness was also associated with white clothing in medieval society. Margery Kempe notes the sensitivity which existed towards such clothing when she relates that she 'suffryd ... schamys & repreuyngs for weryng of hir white clothys'.[58] The clothing of Christ in a fool's garment may also have recalled to a spectator's mind St Paul's First Epistle to the Corinthians: *spectaculum facti sumus mundo et angelis et hominibus nos stulti propter Christum* ('we are made a spectacle for the world, and angels, and men. We are fools on account of Christ').[59] The visual mocking of Christ as a fool therefore extends the significance of the mocking insults, and would permit a variety of interpretations, depending upon the knowledge of the audience.

Christ's apparent powerlessness and degradation at the hands of His tormentors not only enhance the pathos of the Passion plays but remind the audience of the greatness of His sacrifice as He submits to the violence and laughter of His tormentors. Nowhere in the biblical plays does Aquinas's condemnation of ridicule as being worse than defamation or detraction register more clearly. It is more degrading than verbal insults, but nowhere is a speaker's intention to degrade more surely undermined, most impressively by Christ's passive demeanour, and also by the prior knowledge of the audience.

The language used by Christ's enemies to mock and abuse Him is intended by the dramatists to prompt recollection of Christian doctrine among spectators. That language frequently takes on the form of references which focus on Christ's divinity and kingship. This non-abusive but mocking language reminds or teaches spectators about the spiritual kingship of Christ which is opposed to corrupt temporal authority. At the same time that authority, and all those who mock and challenge the divinity of Christ and the significance of His Passion, are defined as alienated from the Christian community.

Although the use of transgressive language might be expected to be constrained by the biblical sources of the plays, dramatists used many forms to entertain, comment, and instruct, and were able to reach all levels of society, and all levels of intellectual and religious understanding. The forms of transgressive language they chose create changing relationships between spectators and dramatic action which were intended to serve the didactic purposes of the plays. However, that language frequently exists in a context of conflicting interpretations which reveal the diversity of outlook and opinion in medieval

---

[57] Sandra Billington points out the distinction between artificial and natural fools. See Sandra Billington, *A Social History of the Fool* (Brighton: Harvester, 1984), p. 48.
[58] Meech, ed., *The Book of Margery Kempe*, p. 105.
[59] Weber, ed., *Biblia sacra*, Cor. 1, 4: 9–10.

society, or exists to create one, in order to explore or challenge important social and theological topics.

The transgressive language used by evil lords at the start of plays involves spectators in the condemnation of evil lordship. The sinful language of those same lords, acting as judges, reveals the association of evil lords with injustice, but may also challenge spectators to recall what they know of Christian doctrine, or to understand the Christian message. Transgressive language also characterizes social subversion in the form of challenges to the hierarchy by low-status characters. These subversive challenges are used by the dramatists to illustrate how people may be absorbed into the hierarchy through faith, and this is dramatized by changes in the language of recalcitrant characters. However, representations of subversion, like representations of bad lordship, may not necessarily defuse discontent, but inevitably draw attention to its presence in society.

We may distinguish an apparent imbalance between the treatment of bad lordship and the treatment of low-status subversion in the plays which, in part, demonstrates the constraints imposed by their biblical sources, where the opposition of evil lords to the Christian message is thematic. However, the imbalance suggests that low-status social subversion was regarded by dramatists as less problematic than bad lordship. All the cycles characterize bad lordship, but they do not uniformly characterize low-status subversion, except that of Cain.

Transgressive language in some biblical plays positions audiences as witnesses to defamation, detraction, and the injustice of evil lords, and dramatists exploit the laws governing the use of sinful language in society as a means of challenging religious scepticism. However, while transgressive language is used to remind spectators of their Christian beliefs and thus confirm their integration into the Christian community, in some plays it also challenges their willingness to be drawn into the sinful enjoyment of both verbal and physical violence. Offering audiences the temptation to enjoy sin may seem to conflict with the Christian didacticism of the biblical plays but it is a powerful means of confronting spectators with their own culpable attitudes, and is a technique also exploited in morality plays.

Chapter 4

Transgressive language in fifteenth-century morality plays

Transgressive language, which creates such complex audience responses in the biblical plays, also directs the responses of spectators to the three fifteenth-century morality plays *The Castle of Perseverance, Wisdom,* and *Mankind,* known as the Macro plays. These plays use transgressive language as one means by which they instruct audiences to recognize and avoid temptation, as this is manifested in the world around them, in order to live a virtuous Christian life. However, each morality play dramatizes in a different way the conflict between vice and virtue which is their common theme, and although the moralities are free of the constraints imposed on cycle plays by their biblical sources, they are subject to other constraints which influence each dramatist's choice of transgressive language, and the functions it performs. This chapter illustrates further the diversity and complexity of transgressive language in medieval didactic drama as it reveals striking differences between the forms and functions of transgressive language in the Macro plays and its forms and functions in the biblical plays.

The extant texts of the Macro plays represent a small amount of dramatic material in comparison to the texts of the cycles of biblical plays. The lack of performance records may indicate that each play was only briefly popular, or pertinent, to its audience. However, the plays may have been performed many times, over many years, since the social topics addressed in them, as well as their moral themes, would have been pertinent to audiences throughout the period covered by this study. In spite of the paucity of texts and records, the three existing moralities, individually and as a genre, make important contributions to our understanding of the variety and significance of trangressive language in fifteenth- and sixteenth-century didactic drama. Indeed these plays use forms of transgressive language, and assign it functions, which are not found in the biblical plays, as well as showing variations on what appear to be conventions shared by both genres, and variation within the morality genre of generically specific conventions.

There are areas of similarity between the use of transgressive language in the cycles of biblical plays and in the Macro plays, but the similarities are few. We saw in Chapter 2 that *The Castle of Perseverance* uses a style similar to that used in the biblical plays to characterize evil authority. It also uses transgressive vocabulary similar to that found in the N-Town plays *The Fall of Lucifer, The Trial of Mary and Joseph,* and *The Woman Taken in Adultery* as part of the characterization of evil. Some of the similarities in the vocabulary used in *The Castle* and in the N-Town plays may indicate that their authors, or scribes, used conventions of transgressive language which were particular to East Anglia, or to East Anglian drama, since the N-Town plays, like the Macro plays, have been assigned an East Anglian provenance.¹ However, similarities in vocabulary exist between these plays and other biblical and morality plays which indicate the use of widespread rather than localized transgressive expressions, and although *Wisdom* does not share in a common transgressive vocabulary, it shares a topic with many biblical plays as it comments on the association between corrupt authority and perversion of the law. *Mankind* shares a topic with the Chester *Shepherds'* Play and the Towneley *Second Shepherds' Play*, as they all address the problem of elite language.

Although these similarities show that biblical and morality plays addressed common interests, there are radical differences between the genres, and between the moralities themselves, in the forms of transgressive language they use and the ways in which they use them to create characterizations, to address differing social topics, and to direct audience attention to the specific moral topic of each play. The differences between the biblical plays and the moralities are governed by several factors. First, the moralities have allegorical rather than biblical frameworks. Second, the characters in them are personified abstractions and generalized representatives of humanity, rather than known biblical characters. Third, the plays instruct audiences to avoid moral dangers such as avarice and idleness, rather than instructing them in aspects of religious doctrine such as the virgin birth. Fourth, they address different audiences. Only *The Castle* appears to have been intended for an audience as large and eclectic as that which might have attended an urban biblical play. The courtly romance allegory and the socio-political topic of *Wisdom* suggests a smaller and more generally literate audience, while *Mankind* may have been intended for a smaller audience than *The Castle*, but a more eclectic audience than *Wisdom*.² These differences affect the ways in which transgressive language is used to create characterization, to direct socio-political comment, and for moral instruction. Nevertheless, the particular didactic intention of each play is given dramatic impact through the author's use of transgressive language.

Features such as allegory and audience composition, which differentiate the moralities from the biblical plays, also contribute to the differences between the moralities themselves. Thus similarities between the forms and functions of transgressive language which are used in the Macro plays may only be expressed as broad generalizations: each play uses transgressive language to characterize the specific forms of evil or vice which are appropriate to the

---

[1] Spector, ed., *The N-Town Play*, p. xxix. Fletcher, 'The N-Town Plays', pp. 164–7, and King, 'Morality Plays', p. 243. See also Eccles, ed., *The Macro Plays*, pp. xi, xxxi, xxxviii.

[2] King, 'Morality Plays', p. 248.

allegorical framework and the play's didactic purpose. In all three plays, homiletic speeches show that the moral life is understood by the representatives of humanity before their temptations begin, and remind the audience of the difference between virtue and vice. Entertaining displays of transgressive language by evil and corrupted characters follow, and may set up tensions for the audience as their awareness of vice conflicts with their enjoyment of the verbal transgression. Each morality uses linguistic change to show the moral decline and recuperation of the representative of humanity.

This chapter begins by looking at areas of apparent similarity between the Macro plays and the biblical plays before discussing differences between the moralities: first, in the way transgressive language is used in them to create characterizations and signal spiritual change; second, the use of that language to address their specific social topics; and third, the contribution transgressive language makes to the didactic purpose of each play.

Similarities and variation

Transgressive language in *The Castle* performs a limited function in characterizing evil. Although there are similarities between the use of transgressive vocabulary for this purpose in *The Castle* and its use in other plays, in *The Castle* its most important function is to represent the relationship between forms of evil and vice in terms of medieval allegiance. This function is discussed below under Didactic Intention.

The play shares a few gendered abusive terms with some N-Town plays, and in all the plays the abuse contributes to the characterization of the user as evil. In *The Castle* Belyal names the Virtues 'skallyd skoutys' (1907). His name defines his evil status, and this is demonstrated by his use of transgressive language. Similarly, when Malus Angelus tells Wrethe: 'prefe Paciens, þe skallyd scowte' (1975), and Invidia calls Charyte 'þu hore clowte'[3] (2150), the personified abstractions who are speaking are characterized as evil in recognizably human terms through their abuse of the equally abstract personifications of the virtues Patience and Charity.[4] In the N-Town *Trial of Mary and Joseph* Mary is insulted with the insinuation 'on þis wyse excusyth here every scowte' (14: 181), and the same abusive term is used in *The Woman Taken in Adultery* (24: 145), from that cycle. In the morality, the abuse characterizes the opposition of vice to virtue, but in the biblical plays, although it serves this function, it also connotes doctrinal doubt, and tempts the audience to become involved in the sins of defamation and backbiting. While some

---
[3] The form 'byche clowte' occurs in N-Town play 24 *The Woman Taken in Adultery* l. 147. See Chapter 3 above.
[4] Malus Angelus may not have been regarded as an abstraction in the Middle Ages.

spectators at the morality performance might enjoy hearing the virtues abused, that abuse is not as prolonged and intense and it is in the biblical plays, because its function in *The Castle* is to characterize the opposition of vice to virtue, rather than to emphasize such doctrinal points as Mary's virginity, and the mercy of Christ, which is its function in the N-Town plays.

Like *The Castle*, *Wisdom* and *Mankind* are also East Anglian, but *Wisdom* does not resemble other morality or biblical plays in the use of gendered insults, or other forms of abuse, since these are inappropriate to its allegorical framework. *Mankind*, however, includes a gendered insult similar to that used in the N-Town compilation, but not found in *The Castle*.[5] Thus the vocabulary of gendered insults may represent the use of an East Anglian dialect, or a dramatic convention, common to the morality and N-Town playwrights. However, although the N-Town compilation is dated between twenty and sixty years later than *The Castle*, and is roughly contemporaneous with *Mankind*,[6] it is possible that the gendered insults in all these plays represent a more general convention which the N-Town and morality dramatists drew on independently.

The variations on scatological references which are found in *The Castle*, and in biblical plays and moralities throughout the fifteenth and sixteenth centuries, do not suggest the use of particular East Anglian conventions of transgressive language, but the use of widespread social or dramatic conventions. Malus Angelus, in *The Castle*, uses forms of scatological language which are recognizable in other plays. His insult to Bonus Angelus, 'goode boy, cum blow | At my neþer end!' (813–14), is echoed in *Mankind*, when the Worldling Nowadays tells his companion Nought 'Go and do þat longyth to þin offyce: Osculare fundamentum' (141–2); and in the Towneley *Murder of Abel* when Pikeharnes tells the audience rudely 'who that ianglis any more, | He must blaw my black hoill bore' (2: 6–7). Variant forms occur in the sixteenth-century moralities *The Play of the Wether* and *King Johan*, and in each case these scatological insults suggest a convention for expressing contempt which was common to both genres, wherever they were performed, and through which the abuser attempted to assert his superiority by degrading the victim and his, or her, use of language. While it is used in all the moralities by vices or devils, and Pikeharnes in the biblical play is a human character, nevertheless, as Cain's apprentice, he appears to be characterized in terms which suggest a link with personifications of vice, and thus closes the gap between the genres.

---

[5] Compare 'statte' in *Mankind*, l. 729, and 'stott' in N-Town play 24 *The Woman Taken in Adultery*, l. 145.

[6] Eccles dates *The Castle* 1400–25, *Wisdom* and *Mankind* 1465–70. However, King dates *The Castle* 1440 and *Wisdom* 1460–65; 'Morality plays', p. 243. Spector dates the N-Town compilation to 'the second half of the fifteenth century and perhaps the earlier part of the sixteenth'; *The N-Town Play* p. xxxviii; but Fletcher shows that the Proclamation Play, from which *The Trial of Mary and Joseph* and *The Woman taken in Adultery* are derived, is before 1468; 'The N-Town Plays', pp. 164, 168.

Scatological language is also used in both genres to express fear. Malus Angelus in *The Castle* declares 'I frete, I fart, I fesyl fowle' (2408), after the forces of evil have been vanquished. Invidia similarly complains: 'Al myn enmyte is not worth a fart; | I schyte and shake al in my shete' (2208). These expressions resemble Lucyfere's complaint in the N-Town *Fall of Lucifer*: 'For fere of fyre a fart I crake!' (1: 80). The association of fear and farting illustrates the existence of similar conventions of expression in both morality and biblical genres, some of which may indicate that plays shared a similar provenance. It also reveals that dramatists adapted the convention in their characterizations of evil.

Although some similarities exist between the biblical plays and the moralities in the forms of transgressive vocabulary they use, these are few and often tenuous. Gendered abuse in *The Castle* and plays from the N-Town compilation may represent the use of a dialect, or a set of dramatic conventions, common to East Anglian authors or scribes; or it may indicate a widespread conventional vocabulary of gendered insults which is incidentally found in East Anglian drama. Scatological forms of transgressive language in the Macro plays suggest that both biblical plays and moralities used common social or dramatic linguistic conventions by which contempt could be expressed. In all instances the forms of transgressive language are adapted to the dramatic context in which they are used.

Difference and variation

Characterization

While differences could be expected between the biblical and morality genres in the use of transgressive language, there are important differences between the Macro plays themselves. Although all the plays present audiences with characters who are personifications of evil and vice, and with representatives of humanity who are personifications of human qualities, each morality uses a different form of transgressive language to define and distinguish its tempters and its human characters.

Tempters in moralities are related to Satan in the cycles of biblical plays through their temptation of human representatives, but temptation, as it takes place in the moralities, differs from the temptation of Adam and Eve and Christ in the biblical plays. Not all tempters in the moralities are devils: each play uses one or more tempters who incite the human character(s) to reject virtue; and this is followed by a return to virtue.

The tempters in each play use distinctive forms of persuasive language. Language which incites sin is unequivocally transgressive, and is used by Malus Angelus and the vices to tempt Humanum Genus in *The Castle*. Lucyfer, in *Wisdom*, however, tempts the Mights with sophistic arguments which may have had an intellectual appeal to that play's more literate audience. When Mynde defends the contemplative life, Lucyfer replies:

> Contemplatyff lyff for to sewe
>   Yt ys grett drede, and se cause why:
> They must fast, wake, and prey, euer new,
> Wse harde lywynge and goynge wyth dyscyplyne dew,
> Kepe sylence, wepe, and surphettys eschewe,
>   Ande yff þey fayll of thys þey offende Gode hyghly.
> (431–6)

The tempters' language in *Mankind* may have appealed to literate and illiterate spectators alike as it is both highly entertaining and obviously transgressive. The devil Titivillus completes the corruption of Mankind by the use of a lie when he declares:

> Alasse, Mankynde, alasse! Mercy stown a mere!
>   ....
> But ȝet I herde sey he brake hys neke as he rode in Fraunce;
> But I thynke he rydyth on þe galouse, to lern for to daunce.
> (594, 597–8)

However, the Worldlings make the first assault on Mankynde, using scatological mockery in their attempt to distract him from his virtuous labour. Nought remarks:

> Here xall be goode corn, he may not mysse yt;
> Yf he will haue reyn he may ouerpysse yt;
> Ande yf he wyll haue compasse he may ouerblysse yt
>   A lytyll wyth hys ars lyke.
> (372–5)

The forms of language associated with tempters bring about the corruption of the human representatives, and represent the aggressive power of temptation in the world.[7] Each morality offers a different aspect of transgressive language with its own persuasive force to characterize that power. The attacks of the world, the flesh, the devil, and the vices associated with them are dramatized in *The Castle* as repeated incitements to sin. The power of corrupt but reasoned argument is dramatized in *Wisdom*, and this becomes a form of transgressive language; while *Mankind* reveals that the whispered lies of the devil may be more dangerous than the open mockery of the world. Thus morality dramatists

---

[7] Kathleen Ashley, 'Titivillus and the Battle of Words in *Mankind*', *Annuale Medievale*, 16 (1975), p. 131.

offer varying conceptualizations of the relationship between the human character and the experience of vice and virtue, but the result of that character's free choice between vice and virtue is represented in all three plays as a fall into sin.

Spiritual change

Forms of transgressive language which are not found in the biblical plays are associated in the moralities with the spiritual change which takes place in the representatives of humanity after their moral corruption. Spiritual change from vice to virtue in the biblical plays is easily observed through the loss of transgressive language from the changed character's speech. Since the moralities trace the corruption of innocent or virtuous characters, an increase in their use of transgressive language might be expected as an indicator of their moral corruption. While this does take place, it is only in the sixteenth-century morality *Magnyfycence* that the corrupted character increasingly uses abusive language. In the Macro plays the forms of transgressive language are less obvious than the insults and oaths which characterize spiritual imperfection in the biblical plays. Pamela M. King has suggested that in the Macro plays 'fall into sin is characterized by fragmented lines, blasphemy and nonsense'.[8] However, although the style and vocabulary of human characters' speech do change, it nevertheless remains wholly intelligible as the morality dramatists use linguistic change to signal spiritual change, and illustrate how the corrupted state of fallen characters can be recognized in the everyday medieval world.

Apart from a brief exchange of insults between the corrupted Mights, *Wisdom* appears at first sight to lack transgressive language. The only insulting exchange takes place as Wyll tells Wndyrstondynge 'I sett þe at nought!' (764). Mynde insults Wyll's dancers crying: 'Hurle hens thes harlottys!' (767), while Wndyrstondynge curses: 'Ill spede þe' (769), and 'ewyll be þou thryvande' (778). This simple abuse confirms the corrupt moral state of the characters. However, the medieval sermons show that other forms of language in the play are transgressive, and the same sources show that all the Macro plays use forms of transgressive language which differ from those examined in previous chapters.

The sermon collection *A Myrour to Lewde Men and Wymmen* condemns the 'forsakyng of resoun & good teching, [for som men þere beþ þat wil knowe good teching]'. The consequence of this rejection of reason is revealed through a sin of the mouth as people 'voydeþ & defendeþ þe good vndyrstondyng and maynteyneþ þerwith wrong, so þat þei falleþ in erroures and in false

---

[8] King, 'Morality Plays', pp. 242–3, 249.

opynyouns.'[9] This definition sheds light on the way language is used in all the Macro plays.

The change which takes place in Humanum Genus's language in *The Castle* takes the form of speeches in which he expresses his acceptance of sinfulness. In a state of innocence, he is confronted with good and bad angels, and chooses to follow the bad. He tells his bad angel '... þou I be fals, I ne recke, | Wyth so þat I be lordlyche' (440–1). His declaration of desire for worldly power, and his lack of concern over the methods used to achieve it, are sinful because they indicate his rejection, or forsaking, of the good angel's teaching and his acceptance of sin. His corruption develops as he accepts other forms of sinfulness. He responds to Avaricia's temptation with an uncharitable expression of greed:

> I schal neuere begger bede
> ....
> Rather or I schulde hym cloþe or fede
> He schulde sterue and stynke iwys.
> (871, 873–4)

Humanum Genus's response to Luxuria's seductive offer: 'Mankynd, my leue lemman, | I my cunte þou schalt crepe' (1189–90), is not so obviously transgressive. He merely replies 'Lechery, cum syt be me' (1197). This is not transgressive language on the scale of the insults, abuse, and cursing which are so abundantly used by corrupt and sinful characters in the biblical plays, but, as the sermon cited above goes on to explain, it constitutes a sin of the mouth 'for hit may moche greue þeigh parauenture hit be faire polisshed'.[10] Humanum Genus's reply to Luxuria expresses his acceptance of sin which endangers his soul, it thus constitutes a form of transgressive language.

Mankynde, in the play named after him, accepts sin in more lively and explicit terms than Humanum Genus. As soon as he hears the lie that Mercy has been hanged as a horse thief, Mankynde tells the audience:

> Adew, fayer masters! I wyll hast me to þe ale-house
> ....
> And geett me a lemman wyth a smattrynge face.
> (609–11)

Later, in the parodic court scene he swears formally to rob, steal, kill, and go to the ale-house instead of Mass (700–717).

The significant forms of transgressive language used by the corrupted Mights in *Wisdom* are shamelessness and boasting of sin. These forms are once

---

[9] Nelson, ed., *A Myrour to Lewde Men and Wymmen*, p. 220.
[10] Ibid., p. 211.

again identifiable as sins from the sermons. The forms identified in *A Myrour to Lewde Men and Wymmen* are supplemented in *Jacob's Well*, which condemns 'unschamfulnes; þat is, whan þou hast no schame of þi synne, & whanne þou auauntyst þe of þi wyckydnes, and spekyst of þin harlotrye opynly to þe peple, for dely3t, and leuyst for no schame of god ne of þe world'.[11] These are forms of transgressive language which express the rejection of virtue and boast of corruption. They are the means by which the *Wisdom* dramatist makes socio-political comments, and links his didactic point to the everyday life of his audience.

The language of the Mights is sinful according to the sermon definitions as soon as they reject the virtues they have acknowledged during their encounter with Wisdom and declare their delight in sin. Mynde announces 'Farwell perfeccyon' (553); Wndyrstondynge declares 'Farewell consyens' (563) and 'Truthe on syde I lett hym slyppe' (565); while Wyll announces 'I haue atastyde lust: farwell chastyte!' (568). By bidding farewell to these virtues they indicate their rejection of the goodness which they have earlier shown that they understand and accept in their speeches before Wisdom. This may be compared with Humanum Genus's choice, from a state of innocence, between goodness and sin which are external to him. Mankynde's rejection of the virtue which he seems devoutly to rejoice in at the start of *Mankind*, is, however, so gleeful it suggests how easily humanity may be corrupted.

Language which is not abusive or insulting but expresses a willingness to accept sin is the basic form of transgressive language used to characterize the corruption of the representatives of humanity in all the Macro plays. The change back from corruption to repentance and virtue which takes place in all the plays is signaled by the human character's realization of its sinfulness, and this realization takes the form of expressions of sorrow and pleas for mercy. However, these changes are not presented in the same way in each play.

One significant aspect of spiritual change in the Macro plays is apparently absent from the biblical plays, and this is the association of changes in a human representative's language with changes in costume. Unlike the biblical plays, the moralities do not rely on the signifying power of transgressive language alone. Spiritual change, the most essential, but abstract, aspect of morality drama, is emphasized in all the Macro plays by visual as well as verbal devices,[12] as a cultural delight in display is simultaneously exploited for its dramatic effect and challenged as a sign of moral corruption. Each morality presents costume change differently. In *The Castle* and *Mankind* it is simple, and explicit only in textual references. In *Wisdom* it is complex, and clearly

---

[11] Brandeis, ed., *Jacob's Well*, p. 77.
[12] Paula Neuss, 'Active and Idle Language: Dramatic Images in *Mankind*', in Neville Denny, ed., *Medieval Drama*, Stratford-upon-Avon Studies 16 (London: Edward Arnold, 1973) p. 44.

defined in stage directions. These draw attention to its significance as a dramatic device in the play, but the association of linguistic and costume change as a means of signifying spiritual change is important in all the moralities.

Costume change in *The Castle* is less clearly defined that in the other Macro plays. Humanum Genus appears first wearing only a 'crysme' (294), or christening cloth, symbolizing his innocence.[13] When he declares his acceptance of the sinful patronage of Mundus, he is clothed in fine robes. There may be a change to penitential dress when he encounters Confescio and confesses his sinfulness, but this is not indicated in the play. In *Wisdom* the Mights' changed moral state is represented verbally, and visual by changes in their costumes as they discard their respectable 'syde aray' (509) for more fashionable clothes. In *Mankind* the process is more entertaining and dramatic as Mankynde gives his respectable long gown to the Worldlings who progressively shorten it during the 'court session'. It is given back to him, much altered, after he has sworn to commit sin.

Only in *Wisdom* is the change back from vice to virtue clearly accompanied by changes in costume. This does not involve the costumes of the Mights, but changes to Anima's costume. She appears first dressed in a white gown over which she wears a black mantle. This costume symbolizes the pure soul covered in corrupt flesh. The corruption of the Mights (which 'belong' to Anima as her faculties of Mind, Will, and Understanding), is lamented by Wisdom, and after this Anima reappears dressed 'in þe most horrybull wyse, fowlere þan a fende' (s. d. 902). The Mights recognize their faults and repent, as does Anima herself, who later re-enters clothed in her first costume. The fashionable costumes of the corrupted Mights indicate worldly folly; the effect of that folly on the soul is represented visually by Anima's horrible costume, while repentance restores the pure soul although the flesh remains corrupted.

Anima does not use transgressive language at any time, because she – the Soul – is not corrupt, but, like the Mights, she does use the language of repentance. By limiting the use of transgressive language to the Mights, but altering Anima's costume, the dramatist shows how temptation which focuses on these faculties leads to the corruption of the inherently virtuous soul.

The similarities in the way the Macro plays use transgressive language distinguish them from the biblical plays. In contrast to the insults, abuse, oaths, and curses which characterize evil and sin in the biblical plays, the forms of transgressive language which characterize the tempters, vices, and corrupted representatives of humanity in the Macro plays are less obvious to modern readers than those found in the biblical plays, but medieval sermons identify

---

[13] Ann Eljenholm Nichols, 'Costume in the Moralities: The Evidence of East Anglian Art', in Clifford Davidson and John H. Stroupe, eds., *Drama in the Middle Ages*, 2nd series (New York: AMS, 1991), p. 286.

those forms as sinful. Thus the moralities differ from the biblical plays in the forms of transgressive language they use.

While spiritual change in the biblical plays is associated with a few characters who would be familiar to most spectators, the moralities present the corruption and recuperation of abstract characters who represent humanity. The change in their spiritual condition caused by their moral corruption must be clearly defined, since the forms of transgressive language which accompany that corruption do not necessarily include obvious forms such as abuse. Although contemporary medieval spectators would have been familiar with the forms of transgressive language used in both biblical and morality plays, the verbal signs of change in the moralities are nevertheless given visual expression in a way not apparently employed by the biblical plays, making spiritual change in the abstract characters unmistakable. The conventional association in the moralities of linguistic and costume change signifying changed spiritual and moral status is later adapted to great effect in the sixteenth-century moralities, and will be discussed in subsequent chapters.

In all the Macro plays transgressive language creates drama as it conflicts with virtuous language and traces the process by which the human character becomes corrupted. The language of the tempters is juxtaposed with the virtuous language which the human characters use at the start of the plays so that spectators are always aware of the danger to the human character. This creates tension as spectators witness the human character's temptation and eventual rejection of virtue. The character's transgressive expressions of delight in sin are then abruptly juxtaposed with the warnings and lamentations of virtuous characters, emphasizing the disunity between the corrupt human character and its virtuous guide.

While similarities exist, and could be expected within the morality genre, in the functions of transgressive language, the Macro plays differ among themselves as each play uses distinctive forms of transgressive language to characterize its tempter(s), and the corrupted state of its human representative(s). Although all the plays characterize that corruption through forms of language which express the character's willingness to commit sin, the forms of language and aspects of sin are particular to each play. Joerg O. Fichte suggests that sins of the mouth were used in morality drama to avoid 'overemphasizing the negative aspects of human behaviour'.[14] I would argue that sins of the mouth (transgressive language) were used by morality dramatists precisely in order to impress upon spectators the ease with which humanity succumbs to temptation, and its subsequent delight in sinfulness. This language also represents the variety of forms temptation may take, and the

---

[14] Fichte, 'The Presentation of Sin as Verbal Action', pp. 31–2, 41.

effect they have in the real world, as each dramatist presents temptation in a different verbal form.

Social comment

Transgressive language in the Macro plays does not always contribute to social comment as it does in the biblical cycles. In *The Castle* scatological conventions and common insults which characterize evil contribute to the play's didactic purpose but seem to have no substantial social or political relevance. However, in *Wisdom* shamelessness, or boasting of evil deeds, follows the Mights' rejections of goodness as they boast of the parts they play in various forms of legal corruption. These boasts are not like those of evil rulers in the biblical plays, who boast of personal attributes and their power to command, but they do serve a socio-political purpose.

The corrupted Mights vaunt their association with the social and legal evils of maintenance, perjury, and lechery. Mynde as Mayntennance declares:

> Men sew to my frendeschyppe
> For meyntnance of her schendeschyppe.
>   I support hem by lordeschyppe.
> (633–5)

The practice of maintenance – a mutually supportive arrangement in which men supported their lord's interests, especially in legal cases; exerted pressure on plaintiffs and jurors; and gained protection and status in return – was a medieval practice much complained of and legislated against, but never eradicated. John Bellamy writes: 'statute 1 Richard II c.7 (1377) was directed against those who gave livery and made covenants with the recipients so that they should maintain each other in their quarrels'. He also notes: 'Act 8 Henry VI c. 4 (1430) said that [earlier acts] were not being operated because of lack of indictments on account of maintenance.'[15]

Maintenance was a serious problem in medieval society, and the first shepherd in the Towneley *Second Shepherd's Play* provides an illuminating description of the problems it caused to ordinary working men. He complains:

> These men that ar lord-fest,
> Thay cause the ploghe tary;
>   ....
> Thus ar husbandys opprest,
> On ponte to myscary
> On lyfe.

---

[15] John G. Bellamy, *Bastard Feudalism and the Law*, pp. 19–20.

For may he gett a paynt slefe
Or a broche now-on-dayes
....
Dar no man hym reprefe,
....
And all is thrugh mantenance
Of men that ar gretter.
(13: 29–52)

Mynde's boast, on the other hand, draws attention to the power structure which supported and continued this perversion of justice.

By its very nature a complaint about maintenance would have implied a complaint about corrupt lordship, its network of alliances, and the part it played in the perversion of justice.[16] Maintenance was geographically so widespread and continued for so long that the satirizing of the practice in *Wisdom* could be understood simply as a pertinent, but conventional, generalization. John Marshall, however, has suggested that the play includes a protest against an identifiable lord, and proposes that costume served to identify that lord.[17] After his corruption and change of costume, Mynde is joined by six dancers who are 'dysgysyde in þe sute of MYNDE, wyth rede berdys, and lyouns rampaunt on here crestys' (s. d. 692). Marshall suggests that the play's local East Anglian audience would have interpreted the costume in terms of heraldic devices, such as the red beards used by the De La Pole family who were Dukes of Suffolk at a time consistent with the date of *Wisdom*.

Mynde's change of costume, from the respectable 'syde aray' condemned by Lucyfer (510), to 'a new aray' (551), shows that he has become Lucyfer's maintained man, illustrates his spiritual corruption, and thus, by implication, would condemn the Duke as spiritually corrupt. The character's boastful declaration of his corruption condemns the Duke specifically for his part in the corrupt practice of maintenance.

Other forms of corruption are associated with maintenance in *Wisdom*, as Mynde's companions Wndyrstondynge and Wyll boast of their support for other perversions of the law. Wndyrstondynge as Perjury announces: 'Be þe cause neuer so try, | I preue yt fals, I swere, I lye' (641–2), and Wyll as Lechery justifies his sinfulness because 'It ys holde but a nysyte. | Lust ys now comun as þe way' (651–2). Perjury's announcement is a shameless confession of his use of recognizable sins of the mouth: false witness and lying, in support of unjust

---

[16] Olga Horner suggests that in the York Passion plays and the *Resurrection* the problem of maintenance is again thematic. See Olga Horner, 'Us Must Make Lies: Witness, Evidence and Proof in the York *Resurrection*', *Medieval English Theatre*, 20 (1998), pp. 36–53.

[17] John Marshall, ' "Fortune in Worldys Worschyppe": The Satirising of the Suffolks in *Wisdom*', *Medieval English Theatre*, 14 (1992), pp. 44–6.

causes.[18] Lechery's justification of sin is, however, just as much a sin of the mouth.

The sin of lechery is the motivation behind Perjury's sins of the mouth when Wyll, as Lechery, expresses his desire to be rid of his sexual rival. Mynde as Mayntennance offers to intimidate the rival, but Perjury advises:

> Arest hym fyrst to pes for fyght,
> Than in another schere hym endyght,
> ....
> A preuenire facias than haue as tyght,
>   Ande þou xalt hurle hym so þat he xall haue inow.
> (850–6)

Perversions of the law such as false accusations and 'fals endytyng' are sins of the mouth particular to injustice.[19] Thus *Wisdom* not only uses transgressive language to characterize the corrupt practices of lords, but draws attention to the ways in which language is misused in society in order to pervert justice.

In *Mankind* legal procedure is parodied as the Worldlings Nought and Nowadays join Myscheff in the 'trial' of Mankynde. Nowadays proclaims the session shouting: 'Oyyt! Oy3yt! Oyet! All manere of men and comun women | To þe cort of Myschyff othere cum or sen!' (667–8). Myscheff reads the document Nought gives him, announcing: 'Here is blottybus in blottis, | Blottorum blottibus istis' (680–1). The 'trial' does not represent a serious comment on legal corruption, but the mock Latin is part of a series of mocking challenges, made by the tempters in the play, to learned language, and especially to Latin as the language of learning and authority. The challenges begin with Myscheff's parody of Mercy's sermon:

> ... 3e sayde þe corn xulde be sauyde and þe chaff xulde be feryde,
> Ande he prouyth nay, as yt schewth be þis werse:
>   'Corn seruit bredibus, chaffe horsibus, straw fyrybusque'.
> (55–7)

The Worldling New Guise ridicules the use of Latinate terms when he asks Mercy's name and is told: 'Mercy ys my name by denomynacyon. | I conseyue 3e haue but a lytyll fauour in my communycacyon' (122–3). New Guise responds: 'Ey, ey! yowr body is full of Englysch Laten, | I am aferde yt wyll brest' (124–5). His companion Nought responds to Mankynde's assertion; '... Nec in hasta nec in gladio saluat Dominus' with the parodic Latin: 'No,

---

[18] Brandeis, ed., *Jacob's Well*, 'þe synnes of þi mowth arn þise ... beryng a fals wytnesse ... to seyn a3ens truthe ... excusyng & defendyng of synne', pp. 294–5.
[19] Ibid.

mary, I beschrew yow, yt ys in spadibus. | Therfor Crystys curse cum on yowr hedybus' (397–9).

The mocking and parodic use of Latin in *Mankind*, like the corrupt Latin used in some biblical plays, reflects discontent in medieval society over the use of Latin. Problems caused by the Latin liturgy were not only recognized by the Lollards,[20] but had been considered by the Catholic Church at the Fourth Lateran Council, and official steps taken to redress them are reflected in John Mirk's sermon in which he tells his congregation: '3e schull know wele þat ych curatour ys holden by all þe lawe yn holy chyrche, forto expowne þe 'Pater Noster' to his paryschons ones oþyr twyse yn þe 3ere'. Mirk goes on to show that Latin was misunderstood and therefore incorrectly spoken when he remarks:

> hit ys moch more spedfull & meritabull to you to say your 'Pater Noster' yn Englysche þen yn suche Lateyn, as 3e doþe. For when 3e spekyth yn Englysche, þen 3e knowen and vndyrstondyn wele what 3e sayn.[21]

The first shepherd's prayer in the Towneley *Second Shepherd's Play* illustrates the problem caused by the use of the Latin liturgy when he prays: 'Ressurex a mortruus ... | Iudas carnas dominus' (13: 504–6). His use of Latin is not simply corrupt and nonsensical, the words themselves have a value which subverts the shepherd's attempt at Christian devotion. This dramatization of the problem may be no more than a festive parody, but while the character may think his words signify his inclusion in a community of Christian faith, they are a sign, not just of his ignorance, but of his marginalization which is caused by misunderstanding liturgical language.

This social comment cannot be applied to the misuse of Latin by Myscheff and the Worldlings in *Mankind*. Their parodic use of the language is an intentional challenge to its status, and the status of those who use it, not a sign of disadvantage as it is in *The Second Shepherds' Play*. The challenge may recall to the minds of spectators Lollard complaints concerning the use of Latin by the Catholic Church, but since the tempters in *Mankind* are clearly opposed to all virtue, Lollard criticisms are implicitly condemned. However, the audience may have enjoyed the temporary degradation of learning and authority, and that enjoyment contributes to the self-corrective didactic intention of the play.

Wisdom and *Mankind*, then, both comment on social concerns which were also addressed in biblical plays. *Wisdom*, like the Passion plays of all the cycles, addresses the problem of corrupt lordship and its connection with

---

[20] For a detailed discussion of the relationship between *Mankind* and the Lollard demands for a vernacular Bible see Janette Dillon, *Language and Stage in Medieval and Renaissance England* (Cambridge: Cambridge University Press, 1998), pp. 56–7.
[21] Erbe, ed., *Mirk's Festial*, p. 282.

perversions of the law. *Mankind*, like the Towneley *Second Shepherds' Play*, focuses on the use of Latin in medieval society. However, while these moralities each share a topic with one or more biblical plays, they each use transgressive language to address that topic in a unique way.

The forms of corruption referred to in *Wisdom*: corrupt lordship and its association with corruption of the law, were endemic in medieval England. When they occur in biblical plays they are characterized by unmistakably transgressive language, which provides a medieval context for the biblical action, as well as condemning the character who uses that language. In *Wisdom*, however, the problem is characterized through less obvious forms of transgressive language, is grounded entirely in medieval society, and may focus on the corruption of an identifiable local lord.

Mankind differs from *The Second Shepherds' Play* in the way transgressive language is used to problematize the use of Latin. In the biblical play the first shepherd's prayer is an unintentional parody which illustrates the results of the ignorance caused by the use of the Latin liturgy. *Mankind*, however, uses mockery and parody by evil characters to condemn the disparagement of learned language and confirm the propriety of its use. The difference between the biblical play and *Mankind* in their use of parodic Latin defines differing attitudes to learned language which are addressed to different audiences.

The appearance of the same social topics in both biblical and morality plays shows the degree to which these topics constituted a problem in medieval society. Transgressive language used by authors in both genres enables them to present different aspects of these social problems in ways which were relevant to differing audiences and differing auspices. It also contributes to the particular didactic purpose of each Macro play.

Didactic intention

The composition of the audience, which influences each morality dramatist's choice of allegory, and social topic, also influences the way transgressive language is used to represent the dangers of sin. In *The Castle* transgressive language characterizes the structure and power of evil; in *Wisdom* it represents the connection between spiritual corruption and social evils, while in *Mankind* it involves the audience in using sinful language, and highlights the distinction between virtuous and sinful language.

Although *The Castle* includes a form of the bombastic boasting characteristic of evil lords in drama, this does not have the socio-political force of the same convention used in the biblical plays. Instead, it initiates the martial allegory. The costuming of the evil kings Mundus, Belyal, and Caro might have suggested real evil rulers to the medieval audience, although any comment on the connection between corrupt lordship and the vices represented by the characters could be understood in the most general terms. However, all the evil characterizations created by means of transgressive language serve the play's didactic purpose as they personify the number of vices which tempt humanity.

The martial allegory makes use of conventional dramatic representations of the conduct of medieval magnates and their vassals. The characterization of three of the vices as kings who have other vices as their vassals dramatizes evil in terms which would be familiar to medieval audiences, as a great and structured force which is ready to assault humanity. In this way the power and number of the abstract forces of evil, and the apparent inequality of the confrontation between them and a single human, may have been readily understood by an eclectic audience.

The forms and didactic function of transgressive language in *Wisdom* are subtler than those in *The Castle*, and suggest a more elite and learned audience.[22] The way transgressive language functions in *Wisdom* to link the socio-political and moral issues within a courtly romance allegory is consistent with such an audience, although the social topic addressed in the play could also appeal to less educated, lower-status spectators.

As the corrupted Mights express their support for contemporary legal corruption their comments direct attention to important socio-political problems. The corruption of the Mights expressed in this way also serves the didactic intention of the play as it parodies a human spiritual condition which willfully disregards the possibility of its own perfect relationship with God. The devotion of the corrupted Mights to perversions of the law parodies the courtly romance allegory in the first scene of the play, in which Anima, the Soul, declares her devotion to Wisdom, who is Christ the King, and therefore the supreme judge. The corruption of the Mights leads to the transformation of Wyll into Lechery, which degrades the ideal loving relationship between the Soul and Justice to its most corrupt and socially divisive form.

As the Mights boast of their participation in perversions of the law they mock both earthly and divine justice, but this highlights the difference between the forms of justice: while earthly justice is open to corruption, divine justice is not. Thus, like the mockery of Christ by figures of evil authority in the biblical plays, the Mights' boastful mockery reveals theological truth.

The corruption of the Mights takes forms which illustrate that the corruption of the soul is not merely a theological, or dramatic, concept detached from real life. *Wisdom* shows that rejection of the love of God and the corruption of souls

---

[22] Milla Cozart Riggio, ed., *The Wisdom Symposium* (New York: AMS, 1986), p. 14. John Marshall, however, has suggested that the play may have been intended for performance before the St Edmund's guild in Bishop's Lynn [modern King's Lynn]. John Marshall, ' "O 3e Souerens þat Sytt and 3e Brothern þat Stonde Ryght Wppe": Addressing the Audience of *Mankind*', *European Medieval Drama 1* (Turnhout: Brepols, 1997), p. 192.

are manifested in the everyday world as the familiar forms of legal and social corruption which may affect the spectators' own lives and prosperity.

Social comment in *Wisdom* directs the audience's attention to the ways in which the abstract concept of the corruption of souls may be observed in society, and has social relevance. In *Mankind* transgressive language associated with social comment – the parodic use of Latin by the tempters – provides entertainment which begins the process of encouraging spectators to participate in the sin of using transgressive language. The play draws attention to the power of language and reveals the moral significance of transgressive language by focusing on the effects it produces. The effects of that language are contrasted with the effects of aureate language in the play.

As part of the process of involving the audience, *Mankind* includes scatological references which are unlike those used in *The Castle*. The entertaining transgressiveness of this language, together with the parodic challenges to learned language, are intended to involve the audience in committing the sin of taking transgressive language lightly, and so experience the power of temptation, rather than having it expounded to them, or demonstrated before them. This form of audience involvement, created through the use of transgressive language, is more immediate than that created by the biblical plays and complained of in *The Tretise of Myraclis Pleyinge*.[23] Although the York *Crucifixion* may have involved spectators in guilt, if they enjoyed the colloquial exchanges and violence of that play, it does not prompt them to participate; and the forms and functions of transgressive language in that play cannot be compared with those in *Mankind*. Similarly, the N-Town *Woman Taken in Adultery* does not encourage active participation in using sinful language, but questions spectators' attitudes to hearing it.

Mankind's spectators, however, are quickly encouraged to participate in linguistic transgression. Nowadays announces: 'Make rom, sers, for we haue be longe! | We wyll cum gyf yow a Crystemes songe', and Nought adds: 'Now I prey all þe yemandry þat ys here | To synge wyth ws wyth a mery chere' (331–4). At this point the Worldlings sing the outrageously scatological, and therefore highly entertaining and transgressive, song.

Jacob's Well condemns the use of such 'dyhonest woordys', saying: 'þou þat spekyst so faryst as a sowe or as an hogge, for þou art no3t aschamyd to puttyn þi mowth in as foul fylthe as þou puttyst þy fete'.[24] If the audience join in the Christmas song then they succumb to temptation more easily, in fact, than Mankynde does. It requires the trickery of Titivillus, the devil traditionally associated with the improper use of words, to accomplish Mankynde's temptation. However, the didactic intention of the scatological references in the play may be subverted.

---

[23] Davidson, ed., *A Tretise of Miraclis Pleyinge*, p. 150.
[24] Brandeis, ed., *Jacob's Well*, p. 262.

The willingness of the spectators to join in would signal their rejection of linguistic constraints. The ludic context permits this rejection, which would always be likely as an individual response, to emerge as a group activity. The scatological language may have performed a unifying function which operated against the didactic intention. As Mikhail Bakhtin notes:

> the bodily element is deeply positive. It is presented ... as something universal, representing all the people ... a people who are continually growing and renewed.[25]

Thus the scatological song may have promoted a sense among the spectators of a unified challenge to the official ideology.

Much of the entertainment in *Mankind* is provided by scatological references. Only the sixteenth-century morality *The Play of the Wether* uses scatology in a comparable way (although for different didactic purposes). Bakhtin links scatological language with festive expressions of resistance to authority, and refers to laughter's 'indissoluble and essential relation to freedom'.[26] Although festive laughter is appropriated into the official rhetoric in *Mankind*, nevertheless, even as it serves the play's didactic purpose, the laughter prompted by scatological references and all other forms of transgressive language may have escaped authorial control. This highlights the constant problem posed by the use of transgressive language in didactic drama, since its reception by, and effect upon, an audience could not be entirely controlled.

However, the spectators' freedom to use and enjoy transgressive language does not go unchecked in *Mankind*. Changes of context alter the impact of that language in the play, creating tension between the freedom associated with entertainment and the didactic purpose of that entertainment so that the freedom signified, and encouraged, by transgressive language is diminished.

The transgressively liberating scatological song is problematized during the temptation of Mankynde by Titivillus, who involves the spectators directly in the downfall of Mankynde by addressing them. The emphasis is on the action of the play as a game in which the spectators are participating. Titivillus draws attention to the effect of that 'game' on Mankynde when he asks the audience: 'Wethere ys he, trow 3e? ... | I haue sent hym forth to shyte lesynges' (567-8). In his corrupted state what Mankynde produces is no longer the Word of God, represented in the image of the corn he had intended to sow, but verbal filth, and this is a sign of his corruption which reflects on the audience's earlier use of verbal filth. When Titivillus defines corrupted language as excrement, this

---

[25] Bakhtin, *Rabelais and His World*, p. 19.
[26] Ibid., p. 89.

reflects back on the Christmas song, and the audience's willingness to sing it is illuminated as the effect of temptation upon them.

While the forms of transgressive language in *Mankind* are unmistakable, virtuous language is more problematic, but it can be identified according to the contexts in which it occurs, and the effects it has. Mercy's reappearance after Mankynde's corruption provides a series of contexts which focus on the effects of language. Mercy's dramatic demonstration of grief sets a tone which pervades the scene, creating tension as it conflicts with the subsequent speeches of Myscheff and the Worldlings. They again offer the temptation of mockery and scatological language, but, in this changed context, do not quite recover the comedy. Myscheff and New Guise mock Mercy's language. Nowadays mocks him with the complexities of the law, but Nought adds scatological remarks which reflect on the Worldlings' speech and actions. He tells Nowadays:

> I am doynge of my nedyngys; be ware how 3e schott!
> Fy, fy, fy! I haue fowll arayde my fote.
> Be wyse for schotynge wyth yowr takyllys, for Gode wott
>   My fote ys fowly ouerschett.
> (783–6)

As Nowadays fouls his own foot, and warns his companions against doing likewise, the speech connotes the effects of the tempters' mocking language, which are now degrading to them, rather than to the virtue of Mercy, Mankynde, or the audience.

Changes in context focus the audience's attention on the effects of transgressive language, and these provide an instructive contrast with the effect of virtuous language in *Mankind*. Virtuous language is problematized in the play by the forms it takes in Mercy's remarkable Latinate homiletic speeches, which seem to invite mockery.[27] However, the beneficial effects of this extravagant language, rather than its form, define it as virtuous. The effect of the entertaining scatological Christmas song is to lure the audience into joining in and thus committing the sin over which Titivillus has jurisdiction. On the other hand, although Mercy's language is at times excessively aureate, as long as Mankynde shares this aureate diction he remains virtuous. When he adopts the vernacular speech of the tempters he falls increasingly into temptation.

---

[27] Janette Dillon refers to this as a 'priestly dialect' in her detailed discussion of *Mankind*. Dillon, *Language and Stage*, p. 61; but H. Leith Spencer observes that 'three elaborate, probably monastic, sermons for Passion Sunday and Lent 4 in MS Worcester F. 10 (c. 1389–1404) display not merely profuse preaching jargon but a number of loan-words ... Yet ... they certainly do not dominate these three sermons like the aureation favoured by Mercy'. See H. Leith Spencer, *English Preaching in the Late Middle Ages* (Oxford: Clarendon Press, 1993), pp. 119–20.

Thus *Mankind* suggests that it is not the form of language which is important, but the effect it produces.

Mankind shares this interest in the beneficial effects of unfamiliar language with the Chester *Shepherds'* play, in which the shepherds try to recreate the Latin words of the Angel's song. After some comically parodic attempts, they reconstruct the words accurately and benefit from them without translating them into English. The third shepherd remarks: '... hee sange "bonae voluntatis"; | that is a cropp that passeth all other' (VII: 426–7), and Trowle the boy adds 'Hee sange alsoe of a "Deo"; | me thought that heled my harte' (VII: 430–31). The mocking of Mercy's language and the parodic song of the shepherds both address objections in medieval society, and especially among the Lollards,[28] to the use of Latin as the language of the Church. Both plays propose that although the forms of language may be unfamiliar, they are none the less beneficial.

Mankind and *Wisdom* both address social and didactic topics which are also addressed in biblical plays. *Wisdom*, like the Passion plays of the biblical cycles, comments on corrupt lordship and corruption of the law. *Mankind* comments on the use of Latin, illustrating its benefits like the Chester *Shepherds'* play, but differing from the Towneley *Second Shepherds' Play*, which focuses on the marginalizing effect of Latin. Similarities also appear to exist between the forms and functions of transgressive language in the biblical plays and the Macro plays: similar forms of abuse occur in both genres, and in both transgressive language characterizes various degrees of sin, but in all cases similarities are outweighed by differences, and this applies equally to similarities between the moralities themselves.

While each Macro play uses transgressive language to represent the conflict between vice and virtue which is particular to the morality genre and not found in the biblical plays, each morality uses different forms of that language to emphasize different aspects of the conflict. *The Castle* uses easily identifiable forms of transgressive language to characterize the forces of evil; *Wisdom* uses less easily identifiable forms which nevertheless reveal a link between spiritual corruption and social evils; while *Mankind* uses highly entertaining and highly transgressive forms as it involves the audience in using transgressive language,

---

[28] Because of the late date of all the Chester manuscripts Lollard objections to Latin would have been superseded in society by Protestant objections, and Lawrence Clopper points out that at Chester 'in the 1560s and 1570s the struggle over whether to produce the plays was a struggle between two, perhaps more, Protestant factions'. Lawrence Clopper, 'Lay and Clerical Impact on Religious Drama and Ceremony', in Marianne Briscoe, ed., *Contexts of Early English Drama* (Bloomington: Indiana University Press, 1989), p. 103. Nevertheless, the Protestants themselves may have recognized that illiterate spectators at any time would have been reminded of the benefits to be derived even from imperfectly understood scriptural references; they may even have regarded the initial confusion of the Shepherds as justifying their demands for a vernacular Bible and liturgy.

in order to illustrate the ease with which any person may succumb to temptation. It also shows that the effect of such language is to encourage sin. Although *Mankind* shares its didactic topic with a biblical play, it uses very different transgressive language to show that words may be beneficial even when they are obscure.

The moralities all use transgressive language to characterize tempters and corrupted representatives of humanity who are personified abstractions, and in each Macro play transgressive language addresses a social problem and moral point which is particular to that play. However, the differences between the genres, and within the morality genre, illustrate the way such language was manipulated by dramatists who were not constrained by the biblical sources of the cycles. Morality dramatists use transgressive language which suits the allegory and audiences of their plays, in order to comment on social issues, some of which are also commented upon in biblical plays, but in the moralities there are marked differences in the ways transgressive language is used to present those issues.

The moralities extend transgressive language beyond insults, abuse, oaths and threats, to include language which expresses a willingness to commit sin and reject virtue, shameless boasting of sinfulness, and scatological language which is more than just a means of characterizing evil and expressing contempt. These extensions reflect the morality dramatists' relative freedom to address social and didactic topics, construct allegory, and create characters.

Transgressive language as it occurs in *The Castle* recalls its use in the biblical plays, perhaps because the play is intended for a large audience and outdoor performance. Insulting and scatological language define evil characters, but they also contribute to the martial allegory which dramatizes the battle between vice and virtue. In *Wisdom* the Mights' boasting of corrupt practices, after Anima's declarations of love for Wisdom, indicate a perversion of the ideal loving relationship between God and the soul. This is shown to be manifested in society as perversions of the law. The play also provides examples of the misuse of language which contribute to those perversions. Thus transgressive language in *Wisdom* defines corruption of the law in terms of its moral and social consequences.

Mankind, on the other hand, is a play about virtuous and sinful language. It uses highly entertaining scatological language to illustrate the ease with which people succumb to temptation. It shows how context changes the significance of language, and teaches that language is virtuous or sinful according to the effect it has. While the entertainment could be addressed to literate and illiterate spectators alike, the contextualization of scatological language, and the differentiation of language according to its effect, suggest that at least some members of the audience were highly educated.

The differences between the moralities in the use of transgressive language seem to indicate an increasing sophistication. In *The Castle* it characterizes evil, but in *Mankind*, written some fifty years later, it is used to consider language itself, and to demonstrate how moral significance is highlighted by context and defined by effect. This development of semiotic self-consciousness is not confined to the moralities. In the N-Town *Trial of Mary and Joseph* transgressive language is similarly used in a self-conscious representation of language as sin when the audience hear the slandering of Mary and then hear the Bishop condemn it as defamation (13: 108). The Chester *Shepherds'* play includes the contextualization of language, and further illustrates the way some dramatists developed the use of transgressive language from creating characterizations to the consideration of language itself.

Although growing complexity in the use of transgressive language is suggested, from its place in *The Castle* (1400–1420), to its use in *Mankind* (1465–70), this chronological development may be an illusion created by the scarcity of extant morality plays. In the case of the biblical plays, the N-Town *Trial of Mary and Joseph* is dated before 1468, since it is included in the Proclamation Play, while the earliest manuscript containing the Chester *Shepherds'* play is dated after 1591.[29] However, chronological development cannot be considered without a date for the composition of the Chester play. Nevertheless, it is clear that fifteenth-century dramatists working in both genres were interested in language itself, and the contemporary debates it provoked, as well as in its usefulness as a dramatic device.

While the functions of transgressive language which are recognizable in the Macro plays continue to be used in the sixteenth-century moralities, that concern with language, and the increasingly complex use of transgressive language in particular, are developed in the later plays. There, in response to altered auspices, different audiences, and playing spaces, transgressive language is adapted and extended in order to reflect the anxiety caused by cultural, political, and religious change.

---

[29] Mills, 'The Chester Cycle', p. 110.

Chapter 5
Magnyfycence: signs of change in the sixteenth century

John Skelton's play *Magnyfycence*, written in the second decade of the sixteenth century,[1] reveals major changes in the use of transgressive language as a dramatic device. However, the most influential difference between this play and the drama already examined in previous chapters is that *Magnyfycence* has a named author. Knowledge of Skelton's life and interests contribute substantially to the following interpretation of the relationship between the changes he makes to the use of transgressive language and the play's didactic purpose.

Thematic changes

Skelton's alterations to the use of transgressive language were governed by his choice of socio-political topics. In a development of the function of morality drama he addressed the topic of cultural change, rather than an aspect of Christian morality. He set this in the court of a prince,[2] a context appropriate, and familiar, to the learned and elite audience he wished to influence. The play's overt didactic purpose is the instruction of a prince, and Skelton gave this literary convention contemporary relevance by discussing the problem of choosing courtiers. The difficulty the prince, Magnificence, has in choosing suitable courtiers reflects upon Henry VIII's own misjudgements.[3] It also facilitates Skelton's discussion of the problems of judging any identity when the signs by which it is conventionally recognized are unstable and open to abuse.

Skelton's anxiety over cultural change is consistent with his opposition to the challenges which were confronting the use of medieval Latin and English in the early years of the sixteenth century. In 1501 Erasmus had written that the

---

[1] John Scattergood gives the date as 1515–16. John Scattergood, ed., *John Skelton: The Complete English Poems* (London: Penguin, 1983), p. 433. Greg Walker suggests 1519. Greg Walker, *Plays of Persuasion: Drama and Politics at the Court of Henry VIII* (Cambridge: Cambridge University Press, 1991), p. 66.

[2] Although *Magnyfycence* is set in the court of a prince this does not reflect the courtly setting of the fifteenth-century morality *Wisdom*. The court in *Magnyfycence* is temporal not spiritual.

[3] See Greg Walker on the problem of the 'minions' in *Plays of Persuasion*, p. 66.

'Latin scholarship ... is maimed and reduced by half without Greek'.[4] Humanist educators in England followed Erasmus's lead, rejecting medieval Latin, the language of learning and culture, in favour of classical styles such as that of Cicero, and promoting the introduction of Greek into the universities so that by 1519-20 'the academic community was split by what has become known as the Grammarians' War. The issue was the method of Latin instruction.'[5] Skelton took the side of the traditionalists, defending education in medieval Latin and English against the Erasmian humanists.[6]

The challenge to medieval Latin and English constituted an assault on the traditions and conventions by which literate and learned individuals expressed themselves, perceived their world, and situated themselves in it. Other culturally and socially significant signs were also under attack in the early decades of the sixteenth century. The Lollard heresy continued to challenge signs such as transubstantiation and the use of Latin as the language of religion, which were deeply significant in late medieval society.[7] The most obvious sign of personal status, clothing and personal adornment, continued to be the subject of official concern. Sumptuary laws indicate the significance of clothing to late medieval society, and were re-enacted during the reign of Henry VIII. As late as 1532-3 they were directed at

> the inordynate excesse ... used in the sumptuous and costly araye and apparell accustomablye worne in this Realme, wherof hath ensued ... sondrie ... inconveniences as be to the greate manifest and notorious detryment of the comon Weale, the subvercion of good and politike ordre

---

[4] *The Correspondence of Erasmus*, vol. 2, Letters 142-294, 1501-1514, trans. R.A.B. Mynours and D.F.S. Thomson (Toronto: University of Toronto Press, 1976), p. 25.

[5] Stanley Eugene Fish, *John Skelton's Poetry* (New Haven: Yale University Press, 1965), p. 128. See also Ian A. Gordon, *John Skelton: Poet Laureate* (Melbourne: Melbourne University Press, 1943), p. 95; and Alistair Fox and John Guy, *Reassessing the Henrician Age: Humanism, Politics and Reform 1500-1550* (Oxford: Basil Blackwell, 1986), p. 14.

[6] Skelton satirized the humanists' preference for Greek in his poem *Speke Parrott*, written in 1521, where he proposed that Greek was not well enough known to have any practical social use. Scattergood, ed., *John Skelton: The Complete English Poems, Speke Parrott*, ll. 141-7. The dates proposed for *Magnyfycence* suggest it was composed before the poem.

[7] A.G. Dickens suggests that as late as the second half of Henry VIII's reign, although 'everyone had heard of Luther, yet this did not make every heretic Lutheran'. A.G. Dickens, *The English Reformation*, 2nd edn (London: Batsford, 1989), p. 54. Eamon Duffy shows that at a date later than that proposed for *Magnyfycence* heresy still bore the marks of Lollardy. Eamon Duffy, *The Stripping of the Altars: Traditional Religion in England, c.1400-1580* (New Haven: Yale University Press, 1992), pp. 379-81. Christopher Haigh writes that after the Oldcastle rebellion 'Lollardy was not crushed, but it was an unpopular heresy' and that 'Protestant Reformation of individual conversions ... began in London, Cambridge, and Oxford from about 1520'. Christopher Haigh, *English Reformations* (Oxford: Clarendon Press, 1993), pp. 52, 14. The suggested date of *Magnyfycence* (1515-19) thus situates it during the transition between the old heresy and the Protestant Reformation.

in knowelege and distinccion of people according to their estates preemynences dignities and degrees.[8]

Continuing subversion of the visual signs of social rank, and the challenge posed, however ineffectively, to fundamental signs of the Christian faith, were compounded with the humanists' attack on language. It is hardly surprising, then, that Skelton, a poet of considerable, if controversial, fame in his own time, a devout Catholic, and former tutor to the king, should represent in *Magnyfycence* his concerns over the challenge to language: the fundamental sign upon which society is based.

In response to the humanists' challenge to the value of the traditional languages, Skelton contrasts the problem of judging the moral worth of individuals with judging the worth of language. He adapts the conventional functions of transgressive language in drama, which signify the spiritual and moral status of characters, to problematize the judgement of individuals within the courtly context. This creates innovations in morality genre characterizations which are developed further by John Heywood in his *Play of the Wether*, and John Bale in *King Johan*.

Since the overt didactic purpose of *Magnyfycence* is the instruction of a prince in the choice of counsellors, and the allegorical framework of *Magnyfycence* is the court of a prince, the representative of humanity is no longer a personified human attribute but a specifically princely one: Magnificence. Moreover, this character does not begin the play in a conventional state of virtue, but appears to be flawed from the start. Like the human representatives in the fifteenth-century moralities, Magnificence is tempted, but his tempters are not personifications of general evils, or devils, they are fools and personifications of evil which are pertinent to the courtly setting.

Magnificence's fall is both social and spiritual, unlike the entirely spiritual fall of human characters in the Macro plays. Skelton uses the conventional evil ruler's boast from biblical plays and promotes the significance of language as punishment as means of representing and commenting on this prince's corruption. After his fall Magnificence is confronted with a virtuous character who punishes him before he receives help towards repentance. In the earlier moralities, *Wisdom* and *Mankind*, the fallen human representatives are not punished before they repent.

These changes prompt alterations in the use of transgressive language as a means of characterization, and the definition of spiritual corruption through the use of transgressive language is frequently ambiguous. The changes Skelton introduces to the use of transgressive language within a morality structure must, however, be taken together with other semiotic devices of drama, such as

---

[8] Statutes of the Realm, vol. 3, 24 Henry VIII, c. 13 (abbreviations silently expanded).

costume, as Skelton plays them off against each other. Thus transgressive language functions as part of a dynamic of misinterpretation and ambiguity which would have been inappropriate to the characterization of good and evil characters in both the mysteries and the Macro plays.

Skelton adapts transgressive language in order to examine the misjudgement of identity from various perspectives, and the attention he draws to semiotic instability seems at odds with his defence of the traditional languages. He begins *Magnyfycence* by demonstrating that language offers conflicting signs which problematize judgements of identity. That conflict shades into malicious deception during exchanges between Magnificence, Felycyte, and Fansy. Fansy and the other conspirators, Counterfet Countenaunce, Clokyd Colusyon, Crafty Conveyaunce, Courtly Abusyon, and Foly, develop the theme of deception.

Having dramatized the causes of misjudgement, Skelton uses the comic interlude of Fansy and his bird to demonstrate that some signs of identity are stable and unalterable by virtue of their familiarity and usefulness. The introduction of cultural change as a topic at this point adds significance to Magnificence's corruption and fall. Although the prince's degradation serves to instruct a prince in the need for caution when choosing counsellors, it also comments on the danger to society of misjudging the worth of the traditional languages. Thus Skelton uses the temptation and fall of a prince as an allegory for the consequences of the cultural change promoted by the humanists. After Magnificence's fall, the morality structure is foregrounded, the linguistic signs of good and evil are no longer ambiguous, and cultural change is contextualized as spiritual and social degradation.

The complex relationship between the courtly allegory, didactic purpose, and theoretical concerns of *Magnyfycence* indicate that Skelton intended to address an audience composed, at least in part, of highly literate spectators.[9] It is important to understand the level of knowledge possessed by those spectators in order to interpret the significance of the play's various episodes. Skelton constructs areas of ambiguity, and manipulates dramatic conventions, in ways not found in the Macro plays, and which indicate an audience capable of understanding the significance of the changes he makes. The sophistication of sixteenth-century audiences is illustrated by Joel B. Altman's observation that Tudor plays 'functioned as media of intellectual and emotional exploration

---

[9] Greg Walker accepts Paula Neuss's suggestion that the play may have been performed before one of the London livery companies. Walker, *Plays of Persuasion*, p. 88. See also Paula Neuss, ed., *Magnyfycence* (Manchester: Manchester University Press, 1980), p. 43. However, the subtlety of Skelton's comments on linguistic change and semiotic instability suggest a learned and literate audience.

for minds that were accustomed to examine many sides of a given theme'.[10] Skelton's juxtaposition of various aspects of semiotic instability to stable signs of identity is consistent with this intellectual skill.

Because of the complexity of the play this chapter will concentrate on episodes in *Magnyfycence* which reveal Skelton's most significant changes to the use of transgressive language in the morality genre. The first section examines how Fansy's comic interlude illustrates Skelton's concern over the challenge posed by the humanists to the status of medieval Latin and English. The second section shows how he manipulates the conventions of transgressive language which create social and spiritual characterizations in the biblical plays and the Macro plays, in order to create ambiguous characterizations, and involve the audience in a metadramatic judgement of identity, mirroring the prince's own problematized judgement. The third section will examine the deception, downfall, and punishment of Magnificence as his increasingly obvious use of transgressive language dramatizes his spiritual corruption, and leads to his punishment through the legitimate use of abusive terms by a virtuous character.

Signs of stability and instability

In *Magnyfycence*, Skelton's most condensed, entertaining, and structurally significant dramatization of his concern with cultural change is the comic interlude which focuses on Fansy. We have seen in earlier chapters that medieval dramatists frequently use entertainment as a framework for their most important or contentious social and doctrinal ideas, and Skelton extends the significance of entertainment in *Magnyfycence* as he uses the conventions associated with it to comment on cultural change as well as providing instruction to a prince on choosing advisers.[11] Skelton uses the irrational language of Fansy's soliloquy and his comic exchanges with Courtly Abusyon and Foly as a means of commenting on the instability of signs, and the folly of change.[12] He demonstrates the need for conventions by assigning Fansy and Foly language consonant with their status as fools.

The interlude begins with Fansy's entrance during Courtly Abusyon's soliloquy. Fansy is carrying a bird which he addresses in the language of

---

[10] Joel B. Altman, *The Tudor Play of Mind* (Berkeley: University of California Press, 1978), p. 6.
[11] Peter Happé, '"Fansy and Foly": The Drama of Fools in *Magnyfycence*', *Comparative Drama*, 27:4 (Winter 1993–4), p. 43.
[12] Fansy's language is transgressive according to Richard Rolle's sermon condemning 'vayne speche, moche speche, fool speche ... idel wordes or wordes þat ben nat need'. Ogilvie-Thomson, ed., *Richard Rolle: Prose and Verse*, pp. 11–12.

hawking. Abusyon asks him: 'What the devyll hast thou on thy fyste? An owle?'[13] Fansy objects in scatological terms conventional to a corrupt character: 'Torde! Man, it is an hawke of the towre. | She is made for the malarde fat' (925–6). Abusyon does not agree, and tells Fansy: 'Methynke she is well becked to catche a rat' (927).

There are no stage directions to indicate what kind of bird Fansy should actually carry. Fansy calls it both 'hawke' and 'owle'. When Abusyon exits Fansy remarks 'It is best I fede my hawke now' (968), but a line later he says: '... all hayle, owle!' (970). Since he goes on to declare: 'Lo, this is | My fansy, iwys' (971–2), it may well be an owl that he chooses to pretend is a hawk, and this would be consistent with the mistake he apparently makes later when he says: 'Teuyt, teuyt!' (1004), only to curse himself in the next line for not keeping up the pretence. Fansy's praise of the bird does not help to identify it. He declares: 'There is many evyll faveryd, and thou be foule!' (969). This is a merry (rather than a harmfully deceptive) pun on 'foule' which not only refers to the difference between the fine appearance of a hawk and the tradition that the presence of an owl is ominous, but also draws specific attention to the bird as a stage prop, and not a real fowl at all.

If the bird is a hawk, or a representation of one, Fansy's references to it as an owl, taken in conjunction with his response to Abusyon, are jokes on Abusyon's misinterpretation of the identity of the bird, and are appropriate to the theme of judgement of identity in *Magnyfycence*. However, the thematic satirizing of upstarts in the play suggests the bird should be an owl. Fansy's pretence then fits more closely with the part played by deception, and the manipulation of conventional signs by the tempters in the play.

Fansy draws attention to the bird's hooked beak and sharp talons, but these are characteristic features of both owls and hawks. The differences between them in body, eye, and particularly head shape are ignored by Fansy, but would be obvious to an audience. There is, however, another difference between owls and hawks. The status of the birds is assigned by society according to the prey they hunt since this dictates their relationship to humanity.[14] Fansy declares his

---

[13] Scattergood, ed., *John Skelton: The Complete English Poems*; all quotations from *Magnyfycence* are from this edition.

[14] Skelton may have been drawing on literary tradition for the uncertainty over the bird's identity since 'the Owl and Falcon fable is one of the most familiar of its kind'. See J.W.H. Atkins, ed., *The Owl and the Nightingale* (Cambridge: Cambridge University Press, 1922), p. lxiii. The fable sets up the owl as the bird that fouls its own nest. In the late twelfth-century English poem *The Owl and the Nightingale*, the nightingale challenges the owl by retelling the fable in which the falcon's fledglings blame 'ure oȝe broþer | þe ȝond þat haveð þat grete heued', for fouling their nest. J.H.G. Grattan and G.F.H. Sykes, eds, *The Owl and the Nightingale*, EETS ES 119 (London: Oxford University Press, 1935), ll. 118–19. The interloper has been fostered like a cuckoo chick, and is only distinguished from the other fledglings by the size of its head (a distinction reminiscent of devils in medieval drama). The poem is a debate between the Owl and the Nightingale, cast in highly rhetorical terms, in part

bird is fit for catching game (926), while Abusyon says it is better suited to rat-catching (927).

Paula Neuss suggests that the bird 'symbolizes [Fansy's] own inconstant "fancy",[15] but I would argue that the bird symbolizes the stability of some forms of identity, in spite of attempts to change them. The audience would be able to see clearly the mismatch between the visual object and the references Fansy makes to it as he draws attention to aspects of the bird's appearance, and his pretence becomes an obvious and foolish act of deception. Fansy attempts to manipulate the conventional signs which differentiate the two birds, but the signs and conventions which establish the identity of each bird are so familiar that they subvert Fansy's attempts and confirm his status as a fool.

The manipulation of names, however, is associated with evil in didactic drama. Satan, in the N-Town *Satan's Prologue*, tells the audience:

> I haue browth 3ow newe namys, and wyl 3e se why?
> For synne is so plesaunt to ech mannys intent.
> 3e xal kalle pride 'onesté', and 'naterall kend' lechory,
> And covetyse 'wysdam' there tresure is present;
>
> Wreth, 'manhod', and envye callyd 'chastement'
> ....
> Glotenye, 'rest' (let abstynawnce beyn absent).
> (26: 109–15)

The fifteenth-century morality *Wisdom* dramatizes the corruption of the Mights, in part, through their changed names. The convention which associates name-changing with evil and corruption adds an evil dimension to Fansy's foolishness.

Throughout *Magnyfycence* name changes and the manipulation of linguistic signs of identity suggest the instability of signs. However, Fansy's inability to construct a convincing identity for his bird indicates that there are some identities which cannot be changed or manipulated without the attempt appearing to be an act of foolishness. The comic episode reveals that some signs remain stable because the conventions associated with them are easily recognized by society, and because the benefits they produce are valued in different ways by society. The naming of the bird illustrates the impossibility of changing some identities simply by calling them by another name. Although names can be changed, the identities they signify may be so well known that

---

about their usefulness to humankind. See James J. Murphy, *Medieval Eloquence* (Berkeley: University of California Press, 1978), pp. 198–230. The fable of the interloper who fouls the nest but is hard to distinguish and the linking of problematized identity, utility, and rhetoric would add emphasis to Skelton's comments on language in the comic interlude, as well as to the theme of upstarts, if the audience were familiar with it.

[15] Neuss, ed., *Magnyfycence*, p. 123, n. to l. 921.

society cannot be deceived into thinking that the identities are also altered. Those identities, and the signs that represent them, remain stable, and are not liable to change. Fansy can call his owl a hawk, but the visual and performative qualities associated with hawks are so firmly established in society that neither Courtly Abusyon, nor the audience, would be persuaded to accept Fansy's definition of his bird's identity.

In this episode Skelton is proposing that medieval Latin and English cannot have their identities altered simply by being called worthless, because society is already so familiar with their characteristic features that they cannot be manipulated without the manipulator looking like a fool. Similarly, a language which has not traditionally been useful cannot suddenly be called valuable in the expectation that society will simply accept it as such. Society's perception of something that it values cannot be changed simply by saying it is now of little value. Society will judge the worth of language in the same way that Abusyon judges the bird, and this is accomplished by familiarity with a combination of socially recognized factors. Even Fansy's name and declaration: '... this is | My fansy, iwys' (972) contribute to Skelton's comment on the changes being imposed on the status of language, and thus the character's name and foolish naming of his bird suggest that changes to the status of language are motivated by foolish whim, without consideration even for the possibility of making such changes.

The theme of Abusyon's soliloquy, delight in fashion, which immediately precedes Fansy's game with the bird, contributes to Skelton's examination of cultural change, and it is not surprising that Skelton uses the verse form of that soliloquy for Fansy's description of his bird. It functions as a structural allusion to the part played by fashion in cultural change. This is expanded as Fansy's soliloquy passes from the unsuccessful manipulation of his bird's identity to reveal a delight in change. That delight results first in the wild instability of Fansy's identity, as he declares:

> Nowe curteys, forthwith unkynde;
> Somtyme to sober, somtyme to sadde;
> Somtyme to mery, somtyme to madde;
> Somtyme I syt as I were solempe prowde;
> Somtyme I laughe over lowde.
> (1008–11)

The speech grows wilder, and more irrational, but also becomes more obviously critical of the change which is its theme. Fansy babbles on:

> ... it is I that other whyle
> Plucke down lede and theke with tyle;
> Nowe I wyll this, and nowe I wyll that –
> Make a wyndmyll of a mat –

....
And within an houre after,
Plucke down a house and set up a rafter,
....
Of a spyndell I wyll make a sparre.
(1025–35)

In the context of things which are useful, even vital, to society, the changing fashion in language may be understood by the audience as the topic under examination here, and this provides Skelton's most emphatic comment on attempts to change the status of language in English culture.

The impossibility of changing a mat into a windmill, and a spindle into a spar, emphazises the comedy of the speech, but also suggests the destabilizing of normality. The images of changing lead for tiles and putting up a rafter in place of a house suggests the destruction of what is solid and valuable for its protection; the worthlessness of what is put in its place; and the folly of making such changes. The destruction is also illogical, since the rafter that replaces the house could not stay up on its own. It is a useful part of a greater whole, but of no value on its own. The changes of which Fansy speaks have no permanence; neither have they any foundation: Fansy's delight in irrational change thus contextualizes the rejection of the traditional languages in favour of more fashionable ones as an act of wild, and evil, foolishness which will destroy something that is as valuable to society as a windmill, a house, or the propulsion unit of a ship.

Having commented on the folly of cultural change, Skelton shifts the emphasis of the comic interlude from problematic identity to the value of conventions in speech. Foly enters and greets Fansy. They discuss the bird he holds, and Fansy asks Foly about the 'pylde curre' he has with him (1054). Foly replies that he has sold the dog's skin. Fansy is surprised, and asks: 'What! Fleyest thou his skynne every yere?' (1058), to which Foly replies: 'Yes, in faythe, I thanke God I may here?' (1059). This begins Foly's entertaining pretence of deafness. Fansy asks to buy Foly's dog, to which Foly responds: 'Cockys harte! Thou lyest; I am no hogge' (1083). The exchange continues:

Fans: Here is no man that callyd the hogge nor swyne.
Foly: In faythe, man, my brayne is as good as thyne.
Fans: The devyls torde for thy brayne!
Foly: By my syers soule, I fele no rayne.
(1084–7)

Fansy does not challenge Foly over his misinterpretations of Fansy's words; he does not seem to remember that Foly has shown no signs of deafness before their comments about the dog, and has actually declared that he can hear. Foly makes communication break down between them by manipulating the conventions governing speech. His refusal to respond logically, his deception of Fansy by pretending deafness, and his intentional misinterpretation of the sounds of words subvert the conventional nature of verbal exchanges, making this one entertaining, but making intelligible communication impossible. Fansy's failure to call Foly's bluff by referring back to their earlier conversation suggests his own inability to discriminate between the rational use of conventions and their obvious manipulation.

The comic entertainment provided by Fansy and Foly's word games is conventional to evil fools such as the Worldlings in *Mankind*, and it signals the evil nature of the fools at other points in *Magnyfycence*, but in this episode it illustrates the need for the conventions which govern social exchanges, and without which meaningful communication becomes impossible. Word games demonstrate that words themselves are unstable because they can be interpreted in different ways, and the intention of the speaker may not accord with the interpretation of the hearer. Skelton uses this problem to suggest the need to observe the conventions of speech.

In this comic interlude Skelton shows that some signs are stable because they are recognized for their value to society. He suggests that change for the sake of fashion is foolish, and he illustrates that the consequence of disregarding the significance of familiar signs is the impossibility of meaningful communication. Skelton packs these important comments into an interlude which is dramatically significant as it challenges the inability to judge identity, which the play has represented until this point. It also contextualizes the action which follows, as Magnificence returns to the playing area and his fall is played out before the audience. The fall is caused by the prince's misjudgement of some signs of identity, and the tempters' cynical manipulation of others. The comic interlude does not help the prince to avoid temptation or degradation, since it takes place in his absence, but for the audience it contrasts with, and emphasizes, Magnificence's misjudgements of identity, by showing that signs which are socially significant and familiar remain stable.

Stable signs and characterization

Skelton uses the linguistic conventions associated with characterization in drama as a means of creating ambiguous moral identities in *Magnyfycence*. The only characters in the play who are unambiguously good are the four virtues, Good Hope, Redress, Cyrcumspeccyon, and Perseveraunce, who come to Magnificence's spiritual aid after his fall, and whose use of language is clearly beyond reproach. Two further characters, Adversyte and Poverte, who also belong in this group are, surprisingly, included by John Scattergood among the 'ten vices who cause [Magnificence's] fall and almost cause his death'.[16] However, while the characters Adversyte and Poverte may be regarded as representing personal or social evils, they are not evil tempters of the kind Scattergood is suggesting when he includes them with the vices.[17]

Although Adversyte uses the vocabulary of insults, he is God's messenger, and may be interpreted as a stern virtue whose language accurately reflects the prince's degraded condition. That language is also a means by which the prince should come to understand the extent of his error. Poverte is Adversyte's associate and is also an instructor. These interpretations of Adversyte and Poverte are consistent with the morality genre, and its illustration of the results of wilful folly for the benefit of the audience. It is likely that the original Tudor audience would have regarded the two characters as social horrors to be avoided and the punishments of God, by which corrupted individuals should understand that deprivation and degradation would be the result of their own foolish rejection of virtue.

Four characters are shown to be unambiguously evil according to their use of transgressive language, but this is revealed only to the audience before the corruption of Magnificence. The four conspirators, Counterfet Countenaunce, Clokyd Colusyon, Crafty Conveyaunce, and Courtly Abusyon, insult, abuse, and mock each other. Courtly Abusyon and Clokyd Colusyon, for example, meet and confront each other, and Colusyon demands: '... wenyst thow that I know not the, cankard Abusyon?', to which Abusyon responds: 'Cankard Jacke Hare, loke thou be not rusty' (757–8). Although they may be dressed as courtiers, the forms of transgressive language used by these characters, and its entertaining vitality, are consistent with the characterization of evil, and the audience would never be in doubt as to their corrupt natures or their function in the play. The same use of transgressive language situates the characters in the society to which the audience belongs so that their corruption is depicted as part of that society.

The unambiguous characterizations of these personifications of good and evil serve Skelton's didactic purpose. Their moral status, indicated by the use of transgressive language, conforms to the polarization of good and evil in the earlier moralities. It also provides examples of signs which are stable: good and evil remain unambiguous, and are identifiable by means of the language conventionally associated with them. The tempters in *Magnyfycence*, like those in the earlier morality *Mankind*, are characterized as evil by their 'vayne speche, moche speche, fool speche ... idel wordes, wordes þat ben nat nede',[18]

---

[16] Scattergood, ed., *John Skelton: The Complete English Poems*, p. 434.
[17] Pearl Hogrefe describes Adversyte and Poverte as 'agents of redemption'. Pearl Hogrefe, *The Sir Thomas More Circle* (Urbana: University of Illinois Press, 1959), p. 310.
[18] Ogilvie-Thomson, ed., *Richard Rolle: Prose and Verse*, pp. 11–12.

and their oaths and curses. The traditions of morality drama thus provide Skelton with stable signs which, in spite of the humanists' challenge to the status of traditional languages, including the vernacular, show that those languages continue to be capable of their most important signification – showing the difference between good and evil.

Unstable signs and characterization: the difficult judgement of identity

The moral status of all the characters in *Magnyfycence*, except the virtues and the four tempters, is made ambiguous by Skelton's manipulation of the conventions of transgressive language. Those characters include the prince himself, and the personifications of his three original princely qualities. The three characters Felycyte, Lyberte, and Measure are described by John Scattergood as 'the three virtues originally possessed by the hero',[19] but, in fact, this is by no means obvious when they first enter. As personifications of virtues or suitable qualities for a prince these characters are rendered ambiguous by Skelton's use of conflicting signs of identity, although Measure at least would undoubtedly have been understood as a virtue by the audience when he enters.

The first problematic characterization is that of Lyberte. Although this character would not have been considered a virtue in the late medieval period without some qualification, it is not until Magnificence has been corrupted that Lyberte uses insulting speech, and only after the prince's fall does Lyberte speak openly of the vicious tendencies with which he is associated. As the personification of one of the princely qualities, his identity is modified by the conduct of Magnificence, but his eventual viciousness cannot easily be deduced from his linguistic style at the beginning of the play.

Lyberte does not use the vocabulary conventional to a wicked character, and Skelton uses the audience's understanding of social conventions to maintain a degree of uncertainty about the character early in the play. The characterization demonstrates a mismatch between the conventions upon which the identity of a character is based in medieval drama, and linguistic signs which may influence the audience. Lyberte's name and its associations with all kinds of freedom are opposed to a constraint which has been placed upon him. This problematizes his identity, and might confirm a spectator's interpretation of Lyberte as a wicked character when he confesses to Felycyte that he has been 'lockyd up and kept in the mew' (35).

Lyberte's identity is further influenced, and complicated, by the way he is treated by other characters. He acknowledges this himself after Magnificence's

---

[19] Scattergood, ed., *John Skelton: The Complete English Poems*, p. 434.

fall when he declares: '... I am a vertue yf I be well used, | And I am a vyce where I am abused' (2101–2). However, the treatment he receives from Felycyte, Measure, and Magnificence suggests that either he is a victim of their oppression, if he is accepted according to his linguistic style, or that he is a vice *because* they insist on restraining him. Felycyte counsels Lyberte that:

> ... lyberte may somtyme be to large,
> But yf reason be regent and ruler of your barge.
> (37–8)

Lyberte agrees, saying: 'To that ye say I can well condyssende' (39). When Measure has lectured them both Felycyte declares: 'Measure is worthy to have domynyon' and Lyberte agrees again, adding modestly: 'So that lyberte be not lefte behynde' (127, 129). This request is for the quality of 'measure' (restraint or moderation)[20] to be used so that Lyberte is not ignored, and demonstrates Lyberte's own 'measure'.

Lyberte grows increasingly anxious at attempts to control him, but remains courteous and ready to obey, as he tells Measure: '... I my selfe hooly to you wyll inclyne' (182). In spite of his amenable and courteous attitude Lyberte is eventually given into Measure's charge by Magnificence. Lyberte indicates his belief that the prince's command will change his identity and he asks him: 'What, syr, wolde ye make me a poppynge fole?' (232). In his speeches he has shown that he is certainly not a chattering fool. However, it is not simply Measure's control to which he objects when he says: 'I wolde be rulyd and I myght for shame' (235). He is concerned that control will degrade his identity, and his concern highlights the effect of social interaction on an individual's identity.[21]

While Lyberte's characterization as a virtue or princely quality would be open to question and qualification in Tudor society, there should be no such problem with Felycyte, yet conventionally characters in morality drama who are entirely virtuous are not rude to other characters unless they have already been defined as vicious. Thus the morality tradition provides a convention against which Skelton may effect other changes. Felycyte treats Lyberte discourteously, offering him instruction in a speech full of aureate language which accords with his own status as a virtuous character. When he finishes Lyberte begins his reply, only to be interrupted by Felycyte's: 'Nay, suffer me yet ferther to say ...' (48). Felycyte denies Lyberte the opportunity to make his point on three more occasions. Lyberte asks Felycyte's permission to speak, matching his elevated diction:

---

[20] Scattergood, ed., *John Skelton: The Complete English Poems*, p. 434.

[21] An allusion to Skelton's own experiences may be present as he was both praised and attacked as an author, and was no longer in favour at court when he wrote *Magnyfycence*.

> But and you wolde me permyt
> To shewe parte of my wyt,
> Somwhat I coulde enferre
> Your consayte to debarre,
> Under supportacyon
> Of pacyent tolleracyon.
> (58–62)

Felycyte replies to this with equal courtesy: God forbyd ye sholde be let | Your reasons forth to fet' (63–4). Lyberte continues with the same use of the terms of formal disputation and Latinate vocabulary, saying:

> Brefly to touche of my purpose the effecte:
> Lyberte is laudable and pryvylegyd from lawe.
> Judycyall rygoure shall not me correcte –.
> (67–9)

Felycyte allows Lyberte only these lines before interrupting again, and his interruptions transgress conventions of courteous speech, both in drama and in life. If Lyberte had been shown to be thoroughly wicked, sinful, or corrupt, Felycyte's interruptions would seem less discourteous and could be interpreted as the privileged linguistic status of a virtuous character. While Lyberte's exact nature remains ambiguous it reflects unfavourably on the characterization of Felycyte, who is courteous in his speech but apparently discourteous in his interruptions. Simultaneously, Felycyte's discourtesy highlights Lyberte's courtesy, and suggests that the character in this instance does not represent a form of vice.

Felycyte appears discourteous, but he is not overtly insulting to Lyberte. Measure, however, who would be understood by a Tudor audience to be unequivocally virtuous, insults both Lyberte and Felycyte. Lyberte greets Measure courteously when he enters, beginning: 'Mayster Measure, you be come in good season' (84), to which Measure responds insultingly: '... it is wonder that your wylde insolence | Can be content with Measure presence' (85–6). Antagonism between personifications of the opposed qualities of liberty and measure, or restraint, may seem logical, but the audience has not witnessed any conduct which could be described as Lyberte's 'wylde insolence', thus the conventions governing the use of insulting language in drama would suggest that Measure is more corrupt than Lyberte.

Measure's reaction to Lyberte is followed by his response to Felycyte's and Lyberte's respectful request for instruction:

> Fel. Wolde it please you then –
> Lyb. Us to informe and ken –
> (87–8)

Measure replies:

> A, ye be wonders men!
> Your langage is lyke the penne
>
> Of hym that wryteth to fast.
> (89–91)

In view of the status of his supplicants – they are neither fools nor overtly evil – and considering the courtesy with which they address him, Measure's mocking response is also insulting since he implies that their speech is hardly intelligible.

Measure's use of insults challenges the conventional perception of this personification as being associated with wisdom and virtue. Virtuous characters in didactic drama use the vocabulary of insults as part of their condemnation of vicious and corrupt characters, and the words used will be an accurate signification of the condition of the character addressed. However, in the scene between Measure, Lyberte, and Felycyte the observable moral status of Lyberte and Felycyte is not so degraded as to make condemnation appropriate, and so Measure's use of insulting language casts doubt over his status as a virtue.

The characterization of Measure is open to question because of his insults to Lyberte and Felycte. His language and conduct viewed in terms already set up in the interaction between Lyberte and Felycyte does not match the quality he represents. In comparison to Lyberte's interrupted opportunities to speak, Measure speaks very freely, lecturing the other characters on the quality of 'measure':

> Where measure is mayster, plenty dothe none offence;
> Where measure lackyth, all thynge dysorderyd is;
> Where measure is absent, ryot kepeth resydence;
> Where measure is ruler, there is nothynge amysse.
> (121–4)

Learned exposition by virtuous characters is conventional in morality plays. However, while the rhetorical patterning and Latinate vocabulary of the whole speech are conventional, the anaphora builds up a sense of insistence which seems inappropriate to the quality of measure, or restraint, which the character should represent, although the form and content of the speech are consistent with a virtuous dramatic character.[22]

---

[22] Norma Phillips, 'Observations on the Derivative Method of Skelton's Realism', *Journal of English and Germanic Philology*, 65 (1966), p. 33.

Measure's use of insults not only affects his own characterization but that of Lyberte too. The audience would be aware of Lyberte's equivocal status as a virtue or suitable princely quality, but it would have seen nothing in the play so far to suggest that Lyberte should be interpreted in this instance as vicious or corrupt. However, his own confession that he has been 'lockyd up and kept in the mew' (35), if taken together with Measure's reference to Lyberte's 'wylde insolence' (85), give Lyberte a bad reputation, which, although it may accord with one interpretation of the quality of liberty known to the audience, nevertheless appears unjust in the context of the action they would have witnessed so far.

During the exchanges between Lyberte, Felycyte, and Measure the spectators themselves are involved in the difficulty of judging identities. They are confronted with verbal signs of the characters' identities which may conflict with their own prior understanding of the character, or do conflict with what they witness taking place before them. Skelton extends this problematizing of judgement using Measure. The character is set up as pompous and tendentious at the start of the play, but when he returns to the playing area he becomes a more sympathetic character as he is excluded from the court and duped by Clokyd Colusyon.

The episode takes place after Magnificence's corruption but before his fall. Colusyon enters with Measure, who is out of favour with Magnificence, and assures him that he will petition the prince on Measure's behalf. He leaves Measure by the door and approaches the prince, but the petition he makes out of earshot of other characters takes the form of advice to Magnificence that Measure is not suitable for his company. Colusyon is quite open about his deception of Measure, telling the prince:

> It were better he spake with you or he wente,
> That he knowe not but that I have supplyed
> All that I can his matter for to spede.
> (1662–4)

Skelton gives this episode a moral dimension when Colusyon goes to fetch Measure into Magnificence's presence. Colusyon assures Measure: 'By the masse, I have done that I can, | .... | I trowe ye herde yourselfe what I sayd' (1693, 1695). Measure replies:

> Nay, indede, but I sawe howe ye prayed,
> And made instance for me by lykelyhod.
>   ....
> Syr, God rewarde you as ye have deserved.
> (1696–7, 1701)

Measure has read the visible signs in conjunction with Colusyon's verbal assurances of help and concluded that Colusyon has spoken for him. His expression of gratitude in response to the act of deception is unwitting but appropriate. His words are a genuine and literal expression of gratitude and faith that God will reward Colusyon as he deserves. However, the spectators will understand the satisfying irony of Measure's words which predict a reward for Colusyon suited to his evil nature. It is an irony made possible by their prior knowledge of Colusyon's deception.

More significantly, the language in which Measure expresses his gratitude shows the process of his judgement which leads him to that expression. He has not foolishly jumped to a conclusion, but observed the visual and verbal signs given him by Colusyon and made his judgement according to these. Measure's erroneous judgements function as a metadramatic exploration of the process and limitations of judgement. The spectators are able to follow his interpretation of the signs they also observe, while Skelton's careful phrasing constrains their judgement. This process contextualizes Magnificence's own misjudgements of the signs of identity with which he is constantly confronted: they are shown to be, in part, the result of duplicity, and the limits of personal knowledge.

Measure's exclusion from the court through the evil influence of Colusyon draws attention to a political problem. Access to the king and the right to be heard appears to have caused contemporary concern. Greg Walker draws attention to the problem when he notes that in 1526 the Eltham Ordinances defined, controlled, and organized access:

> considering ... the great confusion, annoyance, infection trouble and dishonour, that enseweth by the numbers as well of sicklie, impotent, inable and unmeete persons, as of rascalls and vagabonds, now spred, remayning and being in all the court.[23]

The royal household was evidently not so organized at the time of the composition of *Magnyfycence* in the second decade of the sixteenth century. The socio-political consequences suggested by the play are that if 'unmeete' courtiers and advisers gained access to the king, they could then hinder the access of worthier people. The result of this in *Magnyfycence* is the financial and moral ruin of the prince.

Unstable signs and the deception of a prince

Magnyfycence challenges spectators to make metadramatic judgements of the moral identity of characters when the signs by which these judgements are

---

[23] Walker, *Plays of Persuasion*, p. 82.

conventionally made in drama are rendered ambiguous. The audience also witnesses the prince's misjudgements. The difficulty he faces throughout the play is his inability to distinguish between virtuous and vicious characters. He misreads, or ignores, the linguistic and visual signs by which their moral states may be judged. He is also deceived by the tempters' cynical manipulation of signs, to his ruin.

The characterization of Fansy marks a shift in the play from judgement of identity problematized only by conflicting signs, to judgement which is problematized by the cynical manipulation of conventions with the intention to deceive. Fansy's manipulation of the conventions associated with both courtiers and fools may seem playful at the start, but the signs made available to the audience increasingly point to its harmful intention.

The audience witnesses the condemnation of Lyberte, who does not transgress the conventions of polite speech. This is followed immediately by the action which leads to the acceptance of Fansy, the fool, into Magnificence's court. The difference in their treatment arises from the fact that while Fansy sets about constructing for himself an identity acceptable to the court, Lyberte's evident courtliness is subverted by other possible interpretations of his identity. Although Lyberte insults no one, attempts no trickery, it is Fansy whose display of courtly conventions wins him the right to be heard and accepted according to the identity he constructs, in spite of the verbal signs which suggest he is a fool and may be evil.

Fansy is the first character to introduce himself in conventionally transgressive terms and thus provide the audience with a recognizably sinful or evil characterization. However, to refer to this character as Fansy when he first enters is to misrepresent the knowledge available not only to Magnificence but also to the audience. They have no more information about the character than the prince himself has; but he enters, and without provocation insults Felycyte, telling him: 'Tusche, holde your pece! Your langage is vayne' (251). When Magnificence asks Fansy's name he replies: 'Largesse, that all lordes sholde love, syr, I hyght' (270). The name may be a joke since since Fansy is so small.[24] The character Counterfet Countenaunce draws attention to Fansy's size later when he jokes: 'So large a man, and so lytell of stature!' (523). In view of this, Magnificence, and Felycyte, show themselves unaware of the significance of the juxtaposition of size, speech, and name.

There are no stage directions to define Fansy's costume,[25] but Scattergood deduces that he 'appears to have been dressed in the costume of a professional

---

[24] Scattergood suggests Fansy 'was probably played by a boy'. Scattergood, ed., *John Skelton: The Complete English Poems*, p. 434.
[25] Costume in the Macro plays is a sign of a character's moral condition, and conventionally in medieval didactic drama fashionable clothes signify worldliness and moral corruption.

fool'.[26] Although there is textual evidence for this later in the play, when Foly observes: 'What, frantyke Fansy, in a foles case?' (1046), there is none at this point, and Peter Happé writes that three roles 'evil doer, accuser, and victim – have been seen as fundamental to stage fools'.[27] These roles are all aspects of Fansy's character, but Skelton introduces him as corrupt by his use of transgressive language, although this convention is modified by the additional convention which permits fools to use such language. If Fansy wears a fool's costume then his use of transgressive language contributes to his comic identity, and reveals his unsuitability as a courtier. However, after he has been accepted by Magnificence he tells Counterfet Countenaunce: '... Largesse I hyght; | And I am made a knyght' (520–21). If Fansy enters in a costume suited to the courtly status he is trying to achieve then the mismatch between his language, his size, and his costume is comic and similarly reveals his unsuitability. While both costumes should signal Fansy's unsuitability as an adviser, costuming him as a courtier would provide more opportunity for entertaining parody and satire.

Skelton provides further linguistic clues for understanding Fansy's character, when both Magnificence and Felycyte respond sharply to Fansy's opening insult and the little character interprets their remarks as a sign that they have mistaken his identity. He tells them:

> Nowe, *benedicite*, ye wene I were some hafter,
> Or ellys some jangelynge Jacke of the Vale.
> Ye wene that I am dronken, bycause I loke pale.
> (257–9)

Felycyte rebukes him again, so Fansy changes the nature of his speech to argue:

> ... upon trouth my reason I grounde:
> That without largesse noblenesse can not rayne.
> And that I sayd ones yet I say agayne:
> I say, without largesse worshyp hath no place,
> For largesse is a purchaser of pardon and of grace.
> (264–8)

The conventional vocabulary of formal disputation, which is packed into the first line, provides a frame of reference. Fansy also uses the rhetorical device *traductio* as he repeats his point about the link between largesse and nobility, with a slight variation and elaboration, but he pushes repetition to its limit by

---

[26] Scattergood, ed., *John Skelton: The Complete English Poems*, p. 434.
[27] Peter Happé, 'Fansy and Foly', p. 427.

repeating 'I say' rather too often, thus subverting his apparent competence in the art of disputation.

The audience would read the mismatches in Fansy's assumed identity. On the one hand, his name and costume may be appropriate to a courtier, on the other, his small size, transgressive language, and questionable rhetorical skill conflict with this assumed identity. Felycyte, however, is taken in by Fansy's rhetoric and commends him to Magnificence as a suitable courtier. Having come to this conclusion, Felycyte then interprets Fansy's later display of low-status language as simply a sign that he has 'a mery mynde' (292). Fansy is able to establish his identity as a courtier in Felycyte's mind, in spite of his earlier insult and Felycyte's disdain, by using linguistic conventions associated with the learned status of a wise courtier. That convention overrides all others in Felycyte's perception of Fansy, although his perception of Lyberte was not influenced to the same degree by Lyberte's use of similar courtly conventions. The arbitrariness of Felycyte's judgement is indicated by his different responses to Lyberte and Fansy, and suggests that judgements of identity made by means of similar conventions are subject to personal whim.

Magnificence is less easily persuaded than Felycyte by what he has heard from Fansy, and his caution links him to the representatives of humanity in the earlier moralities who are virtuous before they are tempted to evil. In his attempt to persuade Magnificence of his identity, Fansy almost gives himself away when his vocabulary slips into the common usage as he asks rhetorically: 'What avayleth lordshype, yourselfe for to kyll | With care and with thought howe Jacke shall have Gyl?' (286–7).

Proverbs such as this are not necessarily a form of transgressive language.[28] However, the use of proverbs in *Magnyfycence* seems, in practice, to be defined by Lyberte's declaration of his own identity: 'I am a vertue yf I be well used, | And I am a vyce where I am abused' (2101–2). Fansy's use of the proverb is interpreted correctly by Magnificence as a sign of low status. 'What! I have aspyed ye are a carles page' (288), the prince exclaims. Paula Neuss suggests 'carles' may be understood as 'carl's' meaning 'churl's'. This would characterize Fansy as the servant of a low-status man, diminishing his status to one entirely unsuitable for Magnificence's court. However, Fansy immediately interprets 'carles page' to mean 'careless boy' rather than the lowest kind of servant, and he tells the prince: 'By God, syr, ye se but fewe wyse men of myne age' (289). The interpretation of the prince's words deflects the challenge to Fansy's assumed status, and implies a degree of common sense, but, like other instances of puns and reinterpretations of words in the play,

---

[28] Paula Neuss, 'Proverbial Skelton', *Studia Neophilologus*, 54 (1982), p. 244. Robert S. Kinsman observes that 'the proverb or proverbial phrase helped [Skelton] to characterize the dialogue of the vice'. Robert S. Kinsman, 'Skelton's *Magnyfycence*: The Strategy of the "Olde Sayde Sawe"', *Studies in Philology*, 63 2 (April 1966), p. 102.

demonstrates how ambiguity of meaning allows language to be manipulated for the purposes of establishing an identity.

Fansy achieves recognition of his assumed identity in spite of the mismatch between his stature, the forms of speech he adopts, and his claims to status. However, his assertion of that identity prompts mockery from a character who already knows him. Counterfet Countenaunce addresses him as 'Fansy, my frende' (500). When Fansy tells him '... I am made a knyght' (521), Counterfet Countenaunce responds: 'A rebellyon agaynst nature – | So large a man, and so lytell of stature!' (522–3). The mocking remark is expressed in terms which should be obvious to Magnificence, Felycyte, and the audience. Counterfet Countenaunce is aware of the mismatch between the identity Fansy claims and his physical appearance. Because of the mismatch, Counterfet Countenaunce treats Fansy with scorn, rather than with the respect which knighthood would conventionally demand. Because the signs – Fansy's stature and his claim to the status of a knight – do not conform to the conventions associated with knights, he is mocked for his pretensions. This mockery is in direct contrast to the acceptance of Fansy by Felycyte and Magnificence, who have similarly been aware that Fansy does not measure up to the conventions of courtly conduct.

Magnificence accepts Fansy because he is unaware that the fool is manipulating the signs of his identity. This is the first instance of conventions being cynically manipulated by a character, but it is a process which contributes to the prince's downfall. Magnificence's misjudgement is contrasted with Counterfet Countenaunce's judgement of Fansy, and serves as instruction to princes by drawing attention to the reading of conflicting signs in order to judge identity.

Fansy's manipulation of conventions culminates with his production of a letter when the prince has finally grown tired of his insolence. Fansy announces that the letter is from Sad Cyrcumspeccyon, and this changes Magnificence's mood. He tells Fansy 'Thys wrytynge is welcome with harty affeccyon!' (313). While the prince reads the letter Counterfet Countenaunce enters 'singing'. This does not disturb Magnificence, but the sight of him disturbs Counterfet Countenaunce, who 'retreats softly' (s. d. 324). The incident might be interpreted by the audience as deference on unexpectedly encountering a prince, but Counterfet Countenaunce returns, calling 'What, Fansy, Fansy!' (325).

Until this moment the audience may suspect, but cannot be sure, that Fansy is an evil fool. His manipulation of his own identity is a deception of Magnificence and Felycyte, but not necessarily a harmful one. The audience is now given a new name by which to identify the character who calls himself, and is accepted by Magnificence, as Largesse. The slyness of this episode increases as Magnificence asks: 'Who is that that thus dyd cry? | Me thought he called Fansy' (326–7). Fansy lies, replying: 'It was a Flemynge hyght Hansy'

(328). Although the prince presses the point, Fansy directs his attention back to the letter and Magnificence seems too easily persuaded. The false name, and the slyness of Fansy's acquaintance, would, however, confirm the spectators' suspicion that Fansy is evil.

It is a dramatic moment when the spectators realize that Fansy is indeed a villain. The covert encounter between Fansy and another character who recognizes him by a name different from the one by which both the prince and the audience know him modifies the audience's perception of Magnificence. While his inability to judge Fansy from the conflicting conventions of language, conduct, and stature may characterize the prince as foolish, he is now clearly being deliberately deceived.

This episode marks a divergence between what Magnificence knows and what the audience knows: from now on the information given to the audience will conflict with that given to the prince. While he continues to be duped and to form his judgements according to the partial information he has, as the plot against him develops the audience's judgement of his foolishness has to be weighed against its increasing perception of the difficulty he faces in trying to make judgements when he is being constantly and cynically deceived. Some critics have suggested that through its representation of the tempters *Magnyfycence* satirizes Henry VIII's poor judgement in his choice of unsuitable young men as his companions and advisers.[29] However, Greg Walker interprets the play as a

> vehicle for praise of the king, rather than for criticism. The king who emerged from the play was strengthened by his experiences. His fall into folly was educational in its effects rather than corrupting.[30]

Satire against Henry would contribute to the play's instructional purpose, but after the revelation of Fansy's deception any satire directed at Henry's misjudgement of suitable courtiers is balanced by the implication that cynical deception was practised against him, as Skelton shows that Magnificence is corrupted not only through his own misjudgements, but by the malicious deception of Fansy and the other tempters. This deception alters the prince's identity.

Unstable signs and princely identity

Magnificence's identity is defined by the qualities associated with his name, 'princely authority and judgement, dignity, glory'.[31] The play demonstrates

---

[29] See Walker, *Plays of Persuasion*, p. 66.
[30] Ibid., p. 76.

Magnificence's deviation from these qualities, and from the conventions laid down in books of advice to princes such as the *Secretum Secretorum*, while he is preoccupied with living up to another set of conventions – those which he expresses in his soliloquy. Magnificence is punished for his deviation from the socially acceptable conventions of princely conduct and his punishment represents a further development in the dramatic functions of transgressive language at it uses the conventional vocabulary of insults to characterize Magnificence in his wholly corrupted condition.

The prince is morally flawed from the beginning of the play and this is a departure from the characterization of human representatives in the Macro plays. Magnificence's flawed condition is dramatized in the first instance by the ambiguous status of his qualities, represented by the characters Lyberte, Felycyte, and Measure. However, when he enters, the prince addresses these characters with proper courtesy, and this is conventionally a sign of virtue. This virtuousness is called into question by his responses to Fansy, but only as he succumbs to the tempters does Magnificence use explicit insults and abuse.

When Magnificence first speaks to Fansy it is in a way which would be insulting if used by a lower-status character. In response to Fansy's insult to Felycyte Magnificence remarks dismissively: 'Here is none forsyth whether you flete or synke' (254). This may be regarded as princely *hauteur*, but the tone of the remark is too colloquial and informal to be an adequate response from the prince to a character who has insulted one of his counsellors, and by that insult demonstrated his own low and probably corrupt nature. Magnificence's language also disregards the advice to princes which is found in the *Secretum Secretorum* and counsels that a prince should:

> with hys men, bothe in communicacion and in hys gesturis schew dyscrecion and wysdam ... And for þis he is feryd of hys men, qwan þei se hym eloquent in hys wysdam and is prudent in hys conceyte and hys dedys.[32]

Magnificence's language constantly tends towards transgressiveness when he is speaking to Fansy. This dramatizes the insidious corruption of a flawed, but not yet evil character, and may be compared with the dynamic corruption carried out by tempters in the earlier moralities. The effect Fansy appears to have on Magnificence's language suggests the corrupting power of the quality Fansy represents. Following an exchange of colloquial language Fansy lapses into insolent and ill-considered speech, telling Magnificence: 'In fayth, I wyll not say that ye shall prove a fole, | But ofte tymes have I sene wyse men do mad dedys' (301–2). The prince snaps back: 'Go shake the, dogge, hay, syth ye

---

[31] Scattergood, ed., *John Skelton: The Complete English Poems*, p. 434.
[32] M.A. Manzalaoui, ed., *Secretum Secretorum*, vol. 1, EETS 276 (Oxford: Oxford University Press, 1977), p.131.

wyll nedys!' (303), and orders Fansy to leave the court. Although the rebuke may be interpreted as the prince's expression of irritation, his participation in an exchange of low language, using the insult 'dogge', again subverts his status.[33] According to the morality conventions, Magnificence's language suggests a spiritual state which is already flawed, while in the context of the allegory, his identity as a character who represents temporal power and authority is modified, not merely by his use of low language, but specifically by his interaction with another character.

Magnificence's early characterization depends upon mismatches between dramatic and social conventions which would be expected to govern the conduct of a prince in a play or in society. His soliloquy is his act of self-representation after his corruption, and it provides an entertaining demonstration of dramatic conventions which subvert the intention of the user and show his judgement of princely identity itself to be flawed and inappropriate.

The prince's language during his soliloquy exhibits characteristics which are familiar from the boasting speeches of evil rulers such as Pilate and Herod in the biblical plays, and Mundus in *The Castle of Perseverance*. Magnificence declares himself '... lyke as a prynce sholde be; | I have welth at wyll, largesse and lyberte' (1457–8). As the speech continues it draws on both the poetic form and images conventional to the boasts of evil rulers. Magnificence announces: '... I am prynce perlesse, provyd of porte, | Bathyd with blysse, embracyd with comforte' (1471–2), and 'I reyne in my robys. I rule as me lyst, | I dryve downe these dastardys with a dynt of my fyste' (1485–6). In the York *Christ before Pilate (1)*, Pilate announces himself: 'Loo, Pilate I am, proued a prince of grete pride' (XXX: 19), while in the N-Town *Magi* Herod declares

> Now I regne ... kynge arayd ful rych,
> Rollyd in rynggys and robys of array.
> Dukys with dentys I dryve into þe dych.
> (18: 69–71)

The style and vocabulary of the speech contribute to the characterization of Magnificence. The speech is in rhyme royale,[34] consistent with his princely status, but alliteration is pronounced in the final lines of the stanzas in which Magnificence compares himself to ancient kings and heroes, and this recalls the heavy alliteration of the rants with which evil rulers begin biblical plays. The alliterative style associated with the boasts of these rulers in the biblical plays has been replaced by a courtly style which has the familiar linguistic signs of evil in drama imposed upon it. Although the use of rhyme royale

---

[33] Magnificence's ambiguous use of language here foreshadows the innovative characterization of the King in Bale's *King Johan*.

[34] Neuss, ed., *Magnyfycence*, p. 53.

accords with Magnificence's status, his corrupted condition conflicts with the high-style verse form and is represented by his boastful and bombastic tone. These turn the verse form associated with elevated subject matter and virtuous characters into a parody which reflects back on the speakers.

Conventionally the speeches of evil rulers exhibit the sin of pride and were intended by the biblical play dramatists to prompt mockery from an audience through their transgressive tone and content. The alliteration of such speeches is bombastic, the vocabulary often threatening, but in the ludic context the evil rulers who make such speeches are impotent and safe targets for an eclectic urban audience to vent its social grievances in the form of mockery. Magnificence, however, sees in himself the coincidence of those signs which he believes at this time demonstrate his princely status. For the audience, dramatic convention has already problematized all those signs so that the prince's use of conventions which already have pejorative significations make him an object of mockery, and perhaps pity, for the audience, since he confuses the significance of the conventions. His misjudgement may also touch on a social anxiety arising from an awareness of the difficulty of choosing between the many conventions associated with any social identity.

After being influenced by all the evil characters in the play Magnificence's use of transgressive language becomes unmistakable. To the wise counsel of Felycyte that: '... Lyberte without rule is not worth a strawe' (1378), the prince replies: 'Tushe! Holde your peas; ye speke lyke a dawe' (1379), and later, to Measure's plea to be heard:

> What! Woldest thou, lurden, with me brawle agayne?
> Have hym hens, I say, out of my syght!
> That day I se hym I shall be worse all nyght.
> (1722–4)

In this episode Skelton links language with vomit as Magnificence goes on to practise the kind of deception of which the tempters are guilty. He does so on the advice of Courtly Abusyon, who counsels him to feign nausea when he is displeased with someone. Having insulted Measure the prince exclaims: 'A bolle or a basyn, I say, for Goddes brede! | A, my hede! But is the horson gone?' (1728–9). His language is transgressive both because it is insulting, and because it deceives. His action indicates his rejection of his old, wise adviser through the influence of the vicious tempter. Morally, the feigning of sickness characterizes Magnificence's use of transgressive language as proceeding from his mouth like vomit. The image identifies his language as foul and unacceptable, and like vomit, a sign of inner sickness or disorder.

The increasing use and vehemence of Magnificence's transgressive language are signs of the corruption which is gradually taking place in his spiritual condition, unlike the rapid changes of spiritual condition which take place in earlier morality drama. In *Wisdom*, the Mights begin the play as entirely virtuous, but, having succumbed to the temptations of Lucyfer, reappear in a completely altered spiritual condition which is signalled by their expressions of delight in various forms of sinful conduct.[35] Although Magnificence shows signs of his flawed virtue before he leaves the playing area, he has not at that time encountered any character who would appear to the audience to be as unequivocally evil as the tempters in the early moralities, and although his corruption is apparent through his use of transgressive language when he reappears, the completion and full extent of his corruption remain to be played out in detail before the audience.

Skelton makes innovative use of the familiar and conventional vocabulary of insults in the punishment of Magnificence. Although punishment by means of language occurs in the cycles of biblical plays,[36] it has particular dramatic impact in *Magnyfycence*, as it challenges Magnificence's identity as a prince. The insulting terms 'losell' and 'lurden', which are found in all the biblical cycles and *The Castle of Perseverance*, are used in *Magnyfycence* to characterize the prince after his fall. Adversyte rebukes him saying: 'Vyle velyarde, thou must not nowe my dynt withstande', and 'Ly there, losell, for all thy pompe and pryde' (1878, 1880). Then, speaking to the audience, Adversyte continues: 'Thys losyll was a lorde and lyvyd at his lust; | And nowe lyke a lurden he lyeth in the dust' (1886–7). The familiar insulting terms here express the degraded condition of the prince and condemn him in low terms suitable to the degraded status to which his folly has brought him. When Adversyte calls Magnificence 'losyll' (scoundrel), and 'lurden' (vagabond), the words are insulting to Magnificence's former rank, but accurately name him in accordance with the conduct he has displayed and his beggar-like condition after his fall.

Following his degradation, Magnificence is subjected to mockery from the characters who have caused his downfall, which focuses on his changed identity. Counterfet Countenaunce enters while Crafty Conveyaunce and Clokyd Colusyon are arguing over who should take credit for ruining Magnificence, but Counterfet Countenaunce tells the others: '... had I not bene, ye bothe had bene hangyd, | When we with Magnyfycence goodys made chevysaunce' (2235–6). Magnificence hears this and responds: 'And therfore our Lorde sende you a very wengaunce!' (2237). Counterfet Countenaunce does not recognize the prince and responds haughtily: 'What begger art thou, that thus doth banne and wary?' (2238). Magnificence is not recognized until he announces his name, and even then the evil characters are not immediately convinced of his identity. When they are they mock his impoverished condition with their 'alms':

---

[35] Eccles, ed., *The Macro Plays, Wisdom*, ll. 551–620.
[36] See Chapter 2. Chapter 7 will show how John Bale in *King Johan* adapts this device, giving punishing language to the King and the widow Englande as well as to the virtue Veritas.

Crafty Con.	In faythe, I gyve the four quarters of a knave.
Cou. Cou.	In faythe, and I bequethe hym the tothe ake.
Clokyd Col.	And I bequethe hym the bone ake.
	(2252–4)

The alteration in Magnificence's observable identity brings about an alteration in the way he is treated. He has been beaten and stripped of his fine clothes by Adversyte, and wrapped in rags by Poverte. His former status is unrecognizable, and his name is no longer an adequate sign of his status because it conflicts with other signs which contradict its former significations of authority, judgement, dignity, and glory.

This is the climax of Skelton's exploration of the problems of judging identity. Princely identity is shown in *Magnyfycence* to be subject to many influences. The prince's misjudgements, although they are only partly his fault, lead to his corruption, social ruin, and spiritual downfall. He misreads the linguistic signs of evil in his first encounter with the evil fool Fansy, and accepts the wrong conventions of royal conduct. His fall leads to the onset of Adversyte and Poverte, and brings about the disregard of other characters. The regard of others is, in this way, characterized as a vital component of identity: a prince is only a prince as long as he is recognized and treated as one by other people. When he behaves foolishly he leaves himself vulnerable to those who, like the tempters in the play, will treat him as less than a prince. The process of his degradation is charted through his increasing use of transgressive forms of language which are familiar from earlier drama; in this way Skelton shows that although personal identity is open to many influences, the signs of spiritual degradation remain stable.

Magnificence's fall is also the climax of Skelton's comments on cultural change. He has shown how judgement of moral worth is problematized by conflicting signs, and by deception. He has also shown that some signs of identity are unalterable social conventions; and he has emphasized the role of society in constructing, defining, and altering identities. Magnificence's fall illustrates that misjudgement of other identities results in the loss of his own. This functions as a warning that misunderstanding the worth of the traditional languages which define cultural identity will result in the loss of that identity.

Cultural change is not foregrounded throughout *Magnyfycence*, but it is the underlying motivation for Skelton's adaptations of the dramatic conventions of transgressive language. His concern with this topic is consistent with his opposition to the linguistic changes taking place in early sixteenth-century education. He responds to the humanists' promotion of Greek and classical Latin by examining how identities may be judged for their moral worth or social value. He sets this examination in a context which is relevant, and entertaining, to his audience, and begins the play by involving them in a metadramatic judgement of characters whose moral worth is defined ambiguously by his manipulation of transgressive language.

In accordance with the literary convention of instruction to princes Skelton offers instruction in how to judge the worth of counsellors. Although his treatment of misjudgement may be read as satirizing Henry VIII's folly, and could also be justified as the charitable correction of that folly, Skelton is careful to show how judgement is problematized by mismatched signs of identity, and compounded by malicious deception.

Skelton manipulates the conventional uses of transgressive language in drama which characterize degrees of sin and moral corruption, to show that language is open to differing, sometimes contradictory, interpretations, and can be manipulated by unscrupulous characters. He takes language together with conventions of costume, to demonstrate that signs of identity can be unstable; but in Fansy's comic interlude he also shows that some signs are stable by virtue of their familiarity, and their usefulness to society. Throughout the play he emphasizes the role of society in constructing and maintaining identity.

Skelton does not use the comic interlude to reject the humanists' preferred languages, but to suggest that the relative worth of both new and traditional languages may be judged according to their usefulness to society. He links this to the need for speech conventions, without which communication breaks down. He also suggests that change for its own sake, or for the sake of fashion, is an act of folly leading to the rejection of what is valuable. By setting the comic interlude *before* the final corruption and fall of Magnificence, Skelton suggests that misjudgement of the worth of language, like misjudgement of the moral worth of individuals, leads to moral degradation, and thence to the social degradation of the language community.

Skelton's manipulation of the conventions associated with transgressive language which create ambiguous identities in *Magnyfycence* also draws attention to semiotic instability. His concern with the cultural change, which he proposes will result from the humanists' innovations in education, may thus represent part of a wider concern with language. However, in *Magnyfycence* it is the problem of cultural change which motivates the adaptations Skelton makes to the use of transgressive language. This secular concern foreshadows the motivation provided by political and religious upheaval for Heywood's use of bawdy and scatological language in *The Play of the Wether*, and the motivation provided by religious change for Bale's innovations in *King Johan*.

Chapter 6
The Play of the Wether: entertainment and religious anxiety

The changes Skelton made, in the second decade of the sixteenth century, to the use of transgressive language in drama were prompted by his concern with cultural change. The religious tensions of the 1530s were a far more dangerous topic for a playwright to address. This danger appears to govern the changes and innovations John Heywood made to transgressive language, and his use of fragmented allegory, in his *Play of the Wether*.

Richard Axton and Peter Happé suggest that *Wether* was first performed at Shrovetide 1533, but observe that their evidence is not 'conclusive and the play contains a great deal more worth considering as topical allusion'.[1] I will adopt this date since it situates the play at the time of Henry VIII's divorce from Katherine of Aragon, and the play appears to address this topic, and the religious changes it initiated. Heywood's innovations and changes enabled him to comment on these topical problems with varying degrees of circumspection.

Henry's divorce was inextricably linked to religious reformation. In order to obtain his divorce he had to persuade the Pope that the marriage should be annulled, or he had to assert sufficient authority over the Church in England for the bishops to annul the marriage in spite of papal authority. The solution to the impasse which developed was provided by Thomas Cranmer and Thomas Cromwell, who advocated royal supremacy. At the same time, loyal orthodox Catholics like Sir Thomas More, and Heywood himself, recognized the need for the reformation of long-standing abuses of ecclesiastical power and authority.[2] This recognition of the need for reform was different in degree from the Protestant desire for reformation, which was based on doctrinal differences, such as the rejection of transubstantiation. Both radical and moderate religious factions strove to influence the King over the divorce. The process and consequences of the factional struggle are allegorized in *Wether*.

Heywood significantly extends and adapts the dramatic conventions associated with transgressive language, and introduces innovations, in order to address with caution the concerns raised by the divorce and its religious tensions among a high-status and highly literate audience. This audience may have been a coterie of Catholic opponents of the divorce, but evidence from the

---

[1] Richard Axton and Peter Happé, eds, *The Plays of John Heywood* (Cambridge: D.S. Brewer, 1991), p. 50. All quotations from *The Play of the Wether* are from this edition.
[2] Walker, *Plays of Persuasion*, p. 155.

play itself suggests that it included the King. The Boy who comes to ask for snow says he and his companions have heard that

> ... god almyghty,
> Was come from heven by his owne accorde
> This nyght to suppe here wyth my lorde.
> (1025–7)

This reference to 'god almyghty' refers to the character Jupiter, who at times provides an allegorical representation of Henry in the play. Jupiter/Henry may, therefore, be differentiated from the lord of the hall in which the play takes place. However, if the performance took place in the royal court, the god was honouring the King with his presence. If the play was performed before the court the audience would probably have included representatives of both religious factions. Heywood does not appear to favour either in *Wether* although he does distinguish between virtue and corruption.

Innovations

While some of the examples and functions of transgressive language in *Wether* are familiar from earlier moralities, and retain much of their traditional and conventional significance, Heywood made important innovations. The most subtle and significant is in his use of transgressive language. He uses both conventional and innovative forms to introduce, signal, contextualize, and limit areas of important political and religious comment. The form he chooses may be a minor and conventional insult or a highly entertaining display of bawdy; nevertheless, where it occurs it serves Heywood's intention to comment on the political and religious situation in one or more of these ways.

Heywood made other important innovations in *Wether*. Unlike the main virtuous characters in the earlier moralities, Jupiter's moral and spiritual integrity is never seriously compromised (which suggests that *Wether* may have been performed before the King). Furthermore, Heywood uses fragmented allegory: Jupiter may be interpreted at times as an allegorical representation of Henry VIII; and at times Mery Report, the Vyce, may represent Thomas Cromwell or the reforming faction. He may also represent Heywood's, or public, opinion. This fragmented allegory is defined by the contexts in which it occurs, and allows Heywood to address dangerous topics by allusion where thematic allegory would allow no room for claiming misinterpretation.

Thirdly, Heywood draws on a classical source for the explicit theme of the play. Lucian's *Icaromenippus* is the source of the petitions for weather, providing Heywood with a framework which is far removed from the tensions of Tudor society but enabling him to satirize religious factionalism with a degree of wit which could deflect any animosity his satire provoked.

Fourthly, Heywood introduces into *Wether* an apparently new kind of character. He describes Mery Report as the Vyce in his list of characters.[3] Apart from Jupiter and the Boy, this is the only character not named according to his/her occupation or social position, and in a departure from morality convention, no other character is a personified abstraction. Although Mery Report's name suggests a departure from the allegorical personifications of human vices in the earlier moralities, his use of transgressive language and his clowning are conventional to such characters. He is by far the most frequent user of all forms of transgressive language, using insults, mockery, and scatological references, but specializing in bawdy language, something which occurs only briefly in the earlier drama. Wyll's comment in *Wisdom* 'Met and drynke and ease, I aske no mare, | Ande a praty wenche, to se here bare' (814–15), and New Guise's 'Alas, my jewellys! I xall be schent of my wyff!' in *Mankind* (381) can hardly be compared with Mery Report's imaginative displays.

Furthermore, unlike earlier moralities, *Wether* seems to have no evil tempter, no Titivillus or Crafty Conveyaunce. Although characterized by his language as evil or sinful, Mery Report deviates from conventional vicious characters in moralities as he does not declare his intention to tempt the chief virtuous character, who in this play is Jupiter, to accept a sinful way of life, nor do his actions initially suggest that this is his purpose, although he clearly tempts Jupiter later in the play. Mery Report is not like Fansy in *Magnyfycence*, nor the Worldlings in *Mankind*, even though he indulges in comic routines. While the language of the conventional vicious characters in earlier drama seems to have become simply entertaining as Mery Report uses it, transgressive language is, in fact, the clue which both disguises and reveals his activity as a genuinely vicious character.

In addition, Mery Report's abundant use of bawdy language is an innovation in the morality genre.[4] John Bale uses bawdy language in his morality *King Johan*, but in that play it has a vicious edge which is absent from the good-natured bawdy in *Wether*. Mery Report is, however, not the only character to use such language. Heywood introduces it into the speech of female characters together with scatological references. The Launder greets Mery Report with entertaining and reductive language of a kind conventional in earlier drama only to male characters. When Mery Report asks the

---

[3] I have adopted Heywood's spelling of Vyce to avoid confusion with vicious characters in the earlier moralities.

[4] Axton and Happé remark on Heywood's frequent use of sexual jokes in his debate plays. His use of bawdy language in a morality is an innovation. Axton and Happé, eds, *The Plays of John Heywood*, pp. 13 and 26.

Gentlewoman for a kiss, saying: 'I never desyred to kys you before' (867), the Launder asks him impertinently:

> Why, have ye alway kyst her behynde?
> In fayth good inough yf yt be your mynde.
> And yf your appetyte serve you so to do,
> Byr lady, I wolde ye had kyst myne ars to.
> (868–71)

No female character, not even Noah's wife in the biblical plays, uses scatological and bawdy language as freely as the Launder. The abrupt and startling speech appears to be an unequivocal assertion of the character's low status and comic function. If she is played by a large man in the manner of a pantomime dame she will, both in dramatic style and physical appearance, provide an entertaining comparison with the flirtatious Gentlewoman, making her even more attractive.

The Gentlewoman's social status suggests that she should not use transgressive language. However, her insult to the Launder when she speaks of '... such grose queynes as thou art' (900) calls into question her own status, and acts as an indication of her sinful vanity, characterizing her as attractive but morally flawed. Although the prince is characterized as morally flawed in *Magnyfycence*, this representation of a female character is an innovation in morality drama. While the prince's first response to Fansy the fool in *Magnyfycence* may be interpreted as princely *hauteur*, neither the Gentlewoman's status nor her virtue are great enough to justify her insult to the Launder. It does recall Procula's insults to the Beadle in the York *Christ before Pilate (1)* which subvert her apparent social status and challenge social ideals. Nevertheless, the use of transgressive language by female characters in *Wether* is a significant innovation as it uses the subversiveness of their language to comment on religious change.[5]

Heywood's extension of the conventions associated with transgressive language provides lively entertainment. The innovations serve the didactic purpose of the play, and emphasize the significance of the episodes in which they are used, but limit those episodes, and reassert the ludic context. The entertaining transgressiveness of Mery Report's scatological and bawdy language provides the ludic context within which Heywood was able to address the contentious political and religious topics which were important to the play's courtly audience during the spring of 1533. The bawdy and scatological language are dramatically more spectacular than Mery Report's simple insults, but Heywood uses each form to direct attention to his comments on the religious crisis.

---

[5] John Bale extends this innovation in *King Johan*.

The Vyce and entertainment

Heywood uses the tempter's conventional delight in word-play to introduce and characterize Mery Report, but more obvious transgressive language soon reveals an evil aspect to the entertaining characterization. However, that characterization seems initially more ambiguous than that of Fansy in *Magnyfycence*, who enters with an insult. When Mery Report first enters the hall he merely remarks to a servant near by: 'Brother holde up your torche a lytell hyer!' (98). When Jupiter takes Mery Report into his service and sends him away to start work, the Vyce leaves as he entered, addressing the bystanders as 'Frendes' (176). The forms of address suggest equality, differing from the characterization of vicious tempters in earlier moralities, but Jupiter refers to Mery Report's ' lyght ... araye' (110), and this costume is consistent with a tempter. When Mery Report returns his language has changed: it is full of the insulting vocabulary which conventionally marks evil. He tells the bystanders: 'Avaunte, carterly keytyfs, avaunt! | Why ye dronken horesons, wyll yt not be?' (187–8). The change in the Vyce's mode of address provides a context which becomes important later in the play.

Each episode in *Wether*, except Jupiter's opening and closing speeches, is to some extent marked by Mery Report's use of transgressive language. Sometimes it intrudes into the middle of an episode, as it does when he informs Jupiter that the Gentleman is a hunter who 'wolde hunte a sow or twayne out of this sorte' (249). This is supplemented by the stage directions that 'Here he poynteth to the women'. Sometimes it marks the beginning or the end, as it does when Mery Report leaves Jupiter, suggestively telling the crowd around the door: 'Thynke ye I may stand thrustynge amonge you there? | Nay by God, I muste thrust about other gere' (176–7). So he exits, leaving the audience laughing. These remarks set a comic tone and emphasize the ludic context for the rest of the play. The tone, context, and transgressive vocabulary of all Mery Report's speeches are significant for controlling the audience's reception of contentious material in *Wether*.

Mery Report's first encounter with Jupiter suggests the Vyce's corrupt nature. He replies to Jupiter's question: '... what arte thou that approchyst so ny?' (101), saying 'Forsothe, and please your lordshyppe it is I', to which Jupiter responds '... but what I?' (102–3). This provides the cue for Mery Report's entertaining and innovative parody of rhetorical and philosophical style. He declares:

> ... Some saye I am I perse I.
> But what maner I, so ever be I,
> I assure your good lordshyp I am I.
> (104–6)

This appears to be harmless fooling, but provides the audience with another clue to Mery Report's true nature. Word games indicate sinfulness in *Mankind*, and are characteristic of the evil fools in *Magnyfycence*, where Fansy also attempts a rhetorical style as he persuades the prince to accept him. Although Fansy's rhetoric is not so lively and entertaining as Mery Report's, both uses of rhetoric suggest an intention to deceive.

Greg Walker suggests that the characterization of Mery Report may satirize abuses of power committed by Court ushers.[6] The character's desire for influence at the god's court seems to prompt a degree of arrogance which is not present before Jupiter accepts him. It is, however, his effect on Jupiter which is the major innovation, since although he tempts the god, unlike earlier moralities, the temptation fails. Nevertheless, Mery Report's insult to Jupiter reveals the possibility that the Vyce's role provides an allegory which plays off allusions to the Usher. Mery Report tells Jupiter flatly that, for his own sake, he ought to take him into his service:

> For as I be saved, yf I shall not lye,
> I saw no man sew for the offyce but I.
> Wherfore yf ye take me not or I go
> Ye must anone whether ye wyll or no.
> (129–32)

Walker reads this as relentless logic,[7] but it is oddly insulting to speak to a god, or a king, in terms which imply compulsion. However, Jupiter does not take issue with Mery Report over his bluntness, even though he has already told him he is not suitable, but finally gives him the job.

A glance at the political situation suggests a context for interpreting the insult. By the 1530s Henry VIII was desperate to find a way to divorce Queen Katherine. Thomas More's resignation over the matter was eventually accepted in May 1532. Four months later Thomas Cranmer, who had been co-opted in 1529 to work on Henry's behalf in England and Europe,[8] was recalled from the imperial court to manage the business.[9] At the same time, Thomas Cromwell was trying to persuade the bishops to grant an annulment.[10] Mery Report's speech may allude to both men as Henry had no choice but to turn to them in order to achieve his aim. However, allusions to Cromwell appear to predominate in this episode.

---

[6] Walker, *Plays of Persuasion*, p. 142.
[7] Ibid., p. 138.
[8] Diarmaid MacCulloch, *Thomas Cranmer: A Life* (New Haven: Yale, 1996) pp. 45–54.
[9] Axton and Happé, eds, *Wether*, chronological table, p. xiv.
[10] Christopher Haigh, *English Reformations* p. 110.

Mery Report's subsequent bawdy account of his encounter with the widow is entertaining but may again point towards Cromwell, who married a widow when he returned to England after spending part of his youth abroad.[11] With this first use of bawdy language Mery Report explains to Jupiter the benefits of being able to express bad news in a pleasing manner, and this introduces two of the play's more accessible themes – marriage and sexuality. Mery Report says he pleases the widow not only by breaking the news of her husband's death in a cheerful way: 'Mynglynge the mater accordynge to my nature' (144), but also by providing sexual pleasure: '... in suche facyon I conjured and bounde her | That I left her meryer then I founde her' (149–50).

The bawdy story may also allude to Henry's early relationship with Queen Katherine. Heywood's personal closeness to Katherine and her daughter Mary may have prompted him to draw attention to that early relationship, couching the reminder in terms which complimented the King on his sexual prowess. Although such an allegorical reference appears to conflict with the interpretation of Mery Report as Cromwell, allegory in *Wether* is open to differing interpretations according to the dramatic context and the orientation of individual spectators towards the politics of the time. Such fragmented allegory is an essential feature of the play.

References which may point to the identification of Mery Report with Cromwell are fragmented and not obviously condemnatory. Any of the references which may be taken to allude to Cromwell can be interpreted as part of a harmless and conventional satire upon a familiar figure during the early part of the play. A low-status individual's rise to power may provoke envy, but is not essentially evil allusions to an individual's sexual prowess, in the form of Mery Report's comments about pleasing the widow, are not insulting. However, underlying all these references is the characterization of Mery Report. Heywood names him a Vyce, and characterizes him through forms of language and behaviour which were familiar from the conventional tempters and corrupters of earlier moralities. To staunch Catholics in the audience, and those opposing Henry's divorce, Cromwell, and the other supporters of both divorce and Protestant-led reform, may have represented the tempter who was leading the King towards the great sins of divorce and reformation. Moreover, not only Catholics saw the divorce as a plot. William Tyndale 'thought the divorce a nasty plot by Wolsey to lead the king astray'.[12]

Mery Report is the only male character who can be said with certainty to use bawdy language. The Water Miller's advice to Mery Report that his mill will not work 'Except ye be perfyt in settynge your stones' and 'Perchaunce your lydger doth lacke good peckyng' (741, 744), could be interpreted by an

---

[11] Guy, *Tudor England*, p. 154.
[12] Haigh, *English Reformations*, p. 101.

audience as bawdy in the context of Mery Report's preceding speech, but it is not in keeping with the rest of the Water Miller's characterization.

Bawdy language which entertains includes both references Mery Report makes to his own impotence. He complains to the Water Miller that his wife

> ... wolde have the myll peckt, peckt, peckt every day,
> But by god, myllers muste pecke when they may.
> So oft have we peckt that our stones wax ryght thyn
> And all our other gere not worth a pyn.
> (746–9)

The sexual innuendoes clearly suggest impotence here, as does Mery Report's exchange with the Launder when he complains:

> ... so farre at lest she hath made me to lyttell.
> ....
> Ye shall washe me no gere for feare of fretynge.
> I love no launders that shrynke my gere in wettynge.
> (974, 976–7)

Axton and Happé note that 'doubts about the King's virility ... were expressed in April 1533' by the imperial ambassador, and they observe that 'Heywood's play would feed such rumours'.[13] However, rather than being satiric comments upon the sexual competence of the King, these references to impotence add a topical point to the entertaining use of transgressive language, and make fun of all those who may have had doubts about Henry's virility. Anne Boleyn was known to be pregnant in December 1532. Although Axton and Happé's dating of the play puts its first performance *before* the ambassador's expression of doubt, it is possible that gossip about Henry's virility was already circulating, in which case the play's references to impotence would indeed raise a sensitive topic, but it would do so in order that it could be turned into a joke by the knowledge of Anne's pregnancy, challenging the gossip so the King (if he was present) and his supporters were able to laugh at his detractors.

Peter Happé has suggested that 'the overriding intention in *Wether* is reconciliation',[14] but while Anne's pregnancy would have subverted accusations of impotence against Henry, references to it could not have pleased Katherine's Catholic sympathizers. However, while Mery Report's remarks raise the topic of impotence, any interpretation of those remarks would be influenced not only by gossip about Henry, nor simply by Mery Report's role as the Vyce, but more importantly by his allusive association with reformers

---

[13] Axton and Happé, eds, *Wether*, n. to ll. 719–54.
[14] Peter Happé, 'Dramatic Images of Kingship in Heywood and Bale', *Studies in English Literature*, 39 (1999), p. 1.

and the reforming faction, thus his remarks about his impotence reflect back on that faction, as a joke against its power and influence.

Mery Report is characterized through his use of conventional, and innovative transgressive language. That language entertains, but frequently points to significant political and religious comments. However, Mery Report is always a Vyce and therefore both entertaining and transgressive. As a Vyce he has licence to transgress; if his transgressions recall the actions or character of identifiable people this may be interpreted as a comment on their conduct as vice-like. His role is to facilitate dramatic action but through his linguistic and behavioural association with earlier vices he also facilitates political and religious comment. While his bawdy language turns allegations of Henry's impotence into a joke, and challenges the power of the reformers, his scatological language focuses on the divorce.

Scatology and the divorce

While bawdy language is entirely fitting for comments on Henry's impotence, scatological language offers a comment on the divorce and the political measures needed to achieve it, contextualizing them in terms of low, offensive physicality. At the same time, Mery Report's use of transgressive language continues the entertainment. His response to the blowing of horns which signal the entrance of the Gentleman seems to be a gratuitous use of scatology with no other purpose than to provide entertainment through transgression. He remarks to the audience:

> Now by my trouth, this was a goodly hearyng.
> I went yt had ben the gentylwomens blowynge,
> But yt ys not so as I suppose,
> For womens hornes sounde more in a mannys nose.
> (216–19)

These observations may be understood as simply characteristic of the linguistic transgression of the Vyce representing verbally his inherent, conventional, and entertaining wickedness.

Keith Thomas offers an explanation for the inclusion of such a speech when he writes that 'the jokes made by Henry VIII's jester Will Somers, at which the king is said to have "laughed heartily" and been "exceeding merry", nearly all seem impossibly scatological today'.[15] Mery Report's remarks are clearly in keeping with a trend favoured at court, and may simply foreground the ludic

---

[15] Keith Thomas, 'The Place of Laughter in Tudor and Stuart England', *Times Literary Supplement*, 21.1.1977, p. 77.

context. However, the reference to horns would probably have been interpreted by a Tudor audience as a conventional reference to cuckoldry expressed in terms of offensive *flatus*. Such a topic might be considered at least indelicate, if not very dangerous, at a time when Henry had not yet secured his divorce from Katherine. However, the reference to 'women's horns' might imply that it was Anne who was likely to cuckold the King. Either interpretation would be likely to provoke royal anger, but this first scatological reference is quickly deflected as the Gentleman enters.

Mery Report's oath 'by Seynt Anne' (233), which introduces his mockery of the Gentleman brings the problem to the divorce more openly in play, and the Vyce's mocking inquiry: 'But who maketh al these hornes, your self or your wife?' (235) continues to imply cuckoldry. But the Gentleman responds with a light-hearted comment: 'Now by my trouth, thou art a mery one' (237). This cheerful disregard for Mery Report's imputation would, in earlier drama, indicate the Gentleman's own folly, but in *Wether* the remark contextualizes the Vyce's conduct and language as light-hearted and inoffensive, even when he is insulting someone by imputing marital infidelity. The Gentleman's comment acts as the dramatist's skilful directing of the audience's perception.

The scatological mockery continues when the Gentleman declares that he and his kind are 'the weale and heddes of all comen welth', and Mery Report asks him: '... I beseche your mashyp, whose hed be you?' The Gentleman replies: 'Whose hed am I? Thy hed' (296–8). Mery Report makes great play with this idea. He says it explains why he has so many foolish and variable states of mind; he always thought there were too many for one head, but now he understands he has two! The comic references to having two heads may well allude to the topical problem of royal supremacy. In 1531 the Convocation of Canterbury had been asked to recognize the King as 'supreme head of the English Church and clergy'.[16] This was a significant step which was intended to enable Henry to obtain his divorce from Katherine. For Catholics like Heywood the notion of having another head of the Church would have seemed an act of folly, and it may be this foolishness which Heywood was satirizing through Mery Report's comic routine of the two heads.

At the level of social satire, the humorous imputation of folly to the Gentleman is followed by scatological remarks from Mery Report. Axton and Happé note that this episode calls for some physical contortions from the actor playing Mery Report as he tells the Gentleman: 'One feate can I now that I never coude before | .... | I can set my hedde and my tayle to gyther' (308, 310). His bending over would indeed set his 'tayle' closer to his new 'hedde' – the Gentleman. The action and the speech continue the traditional use of

---

[16] Haigh, *English Reformations*, p. 107.

scatological insults and mockery to imply the intention to degrade. In this instance it is comic, and mocks the pretensions of gentlemen.

Mery Report again uses scatological references as he prepares to lead the Gentleman into Jupiter's presence. He observes:

> ... when ye dyd blow yt
> Harde I never horeson make horne so goo.
> As lefe ye kyste myne ars as blow my hole soo.
> (253–5)

In the context of 'hornes' as a reference to cuckoldry this might be read as Mery Report's humorous anxiety over being cuckolded, but the vocabulary and sentiments are so typical of vice characters that cuckoldry may be obscured. On the other hand, the political significance of Mery Report's scatological language frequently differentiates it from similar language used in earlier drama.

Insults and religious tension

In his examination of *Wether* Greg Walker refers to the 'curious lack of any clerical figures normally so well represented in social satires'.[17] However, four kinds of clerics may be identified in the play, and their presence and didactic significance are signalled by Mery Report's use of insults. Heywood's familiarity with Chaucer contributes to anticlerical satire in *Wether*, and together with contemporary opinions, enables him to comment on dangerous contemporary topics.

The first instance of an insult which opens up anticlerical satire in the play is Mery Report's greeting to the Merchant: 'Mayster Person, now welcome by my lyfe! | I pray you, how doth my mastres your wyfe?' (329–30). The Merchant takes this as an insult and rebukes Mery Report with an insult in return, saying: 'Syr, for the presthod and wyfe that ye alledge, | I se ye speke more of dotage then knowledge' (331–2). The humour in this exchange depends on anticlerical sentiments, and Mery Report's mistake refers to a confusion which should not have been possible.

Satire aimed at clerical abuses is not in conflict with Heywood's loyalty to Catholicism. Complaints had been made since at least the time of Chaucer about the wealth of the clergy and their unchastity. Christopher Haigh observes that in 1510 'John Colet, dean of St. Paul's ... argued that worldliness among the clergy was a greater danger than heresy among the laity'.[18] Thomas More

---

[17] Walker, *Plays of Persuasion*, p. 163.
[18] Haigh, *English Reformations*, p. 77.

recognized the need to reform the abuses which were rife in the Church, while the reformation Parliament of 1529 declared that 'clerics were forbidden to indulge in trading'.[19] When Mery Report apparently mistakes a merchant for a parson he also comments on the venality of orthodox priests, and the complaint that many kept concubines. However, the mistake may also draw attention to those Protestant reformers who had taken wives as part of their rejection of Catholicism.[20]

The Ranger, like the Merchant, is greeted by Mery Report with an insult. The Ranger gives the courteous greeting 'God be here! Now Cryst kepe thys company!' (400). Mery Report tells him rudely: 'In fayth ye be welcome evyn very skantely' (401). The Ranger appears to represent peripatetic clerics or minor clerical officials such as the friars and pardoners to whom Simon Fish referred in *A Supplication for the Beggars* printed in 1528.[21] Although Fish was a Protestant polemicist, peripatetic clerics were traditionally the subject of criticism. Chaucer constructed pejorative portraits of such characters in *The Canterbury Tales*, and Heywood's play *The Pardoner and the Frere*, performed just two months after *Wether*, indicates the playwright's interest in the contribution pardoners and friars made to endangering the Church through their self-serving disputes.[22]

The area for which the Ranger and his kind are responsible, 'forestes, parkes, purlews and chasys' (413), suggests the need to travel around, as friars, pardoners, and specially appointed monks were accustomed to do.[23] The Ranger's complaint reinforces this interpretation when he bemoans his poverty in view of the price of meals when he is travelling:

Alas for our wages, what be we the nere?
What is forty shyllynges or five marke a yere?
Many tymes and oft where we be flyttynge
We spende forty pens a pece at a syttynge.
(416–19)

He goes on to say that 'wyndefale' is the main supplement for his low wages. This may refer to actual wood; it may also refer to the charitable donations of the faithful to friars, monks, and pardoners. Moreover, the Ranger is not a man to be denied his livelihood, he tells Mery Report:

---

[19] A.G. Dickens, *The English Reformation*, p. 124.
[20] This interpretation would have been particularly pertinent at this time as Cranmer had married his second wife in 1532. See MacCulloch, *Thomas Cranmer*, p. 21.
[21] Axton and Happé note that the Ranger's greeting is the English version of the friars' *Deus hic* greeting, *Wether*, n. to l. 400. See also Haigh, *English Reformations*, p. 65.
[22] Axton and Happé, eds, *The Plays of John Heywood, The Pardoner and the Frere*, p. 17.
[23] Larry D. Benson, ed., *The Riverside Chaucer, The Canterbury Tales: General Prologue*, l. 166, and *The Shipman's Tale*, ll. 62–6.

> ... yf I can not get god to do some good
> I wolde hyer the devyll to runne thorow the wood
> The rootes to turne up, the toppys to brynge under.
> (426–8)

His hasty and violent alternative echoes the viciousness of the Summoner and the Friar about whom Chaucer's pilgrims tell tales. The Summoner attempts to extort money from a poor widow: '"Pay me" quod he, "or by sweete seinte Anne, | I wol bere awey thy newe panne"',[24] and the insulted Friar flies into a rage and vows vengeance: 'But I on oother wyse may be wreke, | I shal disclaundre hym over al ther I speke.'[25] The Ranger's words also echo those of the Chester Antichrist who declares: 'Nowe wyl I turne, all through my might, | trees downe, the rootes upright.'[26] Thomas More uses an image of the devil tearing off branches in his *Confutation of Tyndale's Answer*, writing:

> yet shall [God] neuer neither suffer [the Church] to be distroyed / nor the flocke that remaineth how many braunches so euer the deuyll blow off, to be brought vnto scarcite either of faithe or vertue.[27]

The Ranger's threat does not simply indicate his belligerent nature, but characterizes him as ready to destroy the established Church for his own benefit.

Mery Report's response to the Ranger's blasphemous declaration is ironically insulting; he tells the Ranger: 'Very well sayd. I set by your charyte | As mych in a maner as by your honeste' (430–31). Heywood's rhyming and ironic use of 'charyte' and 'honeste' as non-attributes of a character who is only responsible for land and 'all maner game', together with Mery Report's remark 'I see ye care not who wyn or lese | So ye may fynde meanys to wyn your fees' (434–5), points to the more significant interpretation of the Ranger as representing those peripatetic clerics and minor clerical officials who were notorious for preying on the faithful poor.

Mery Report's insults seem to draw attention to anticlerical satire, and his insults during the Millers' episode may continue this trend. This episode is significantly different from those which precede it. It is the first in which pairs of characters present conflicting suits for weather, and the only one with a binary structure comprising two soliloquies followed by a debate. Interpretation of the episode depends on the observation of linguistic style,

---

[24] Ibid., *The Friar's Tale*, ll. 1613–14.
[25] Ibid., *The Summoner's Tale*, ll. 2211–12.
[26] Lumiansky and Mills, eds, *The Chester Mystery Cycle*, play XXIII, *Antichrist*, ll. 81–2.
[27] *The Complete Works of St. Thomas More*, vol. 8, *The Confutation of Tyndale's Answer*, p. 617.

vocabulary, social status, and the treatment the Millers receive from Mery Report.

When the Millers enter they command deference. Each speaks to the audience for twenty-seven lines. Mery Report does not interrupt these opening speeches, and this is in marked contrast to his insulting interruptions of earlier petitioners. The Gentleman enters with a greeting to the audience: 'Stande ye mery, my frendes everychone!' (220), to which Mery Report responds arrogantly 'Say that to me and let the reste alone' (221). The Gentleman's social status, and perhaps even the Merchant's, would make deference from Mery Report appropriate (although his insults to them represent conventional disrespect from a tempter or vice). Mery Report's deference towards the Millers, who certainly have a lower social status than the Gentleman, therefore suggests that they are particularly significant.

Mery Report's insults and interventions mark off transitions in the Millers' episode and contribute to its significance, but in order to identify the significance of the episode in the context of Mery Report's insults, we need to look briefly at the language of the Millers themselves, although it is not consistently transgressive. The Millers' language during their soliloquies suggests a Christian significance. Both use images and references which may be drawn from Scripture, and the Tudor audience's familiarity with biblical texts is likely to have made these references more accessible than they may be to present-day readers. The Millers also speak of their occupations in terms consistent with good and bad aspects of the priesthood. The deference Mery Report shows them, and their long, uninterrupted speeches, accord with such clerical status.

Both Millers refer to the grinding of corn, which is their occupation, but they do so in different ways. The Water Miller asks:

> ... what avayleth to eche man hys corne
> Tyll it be grounde by suche men as we be.
> There is the losse yf we be forborne.
> (451–3)

The corn he refers to may be interpreted as a conventional metaphor deriving its significance from biblical sources such as the parable of the sower. Christ tells his disciples *Est autem haec parabola: Semen verbum dei* ('Now the parable is this: the seed is the word of God').[28] The Book of Isaiah also provides a quotation which seems remarkably apt in the context of the play, when God says:

> *quomodo descendit imber et nix de caelo et illuc ultra non revertitur, sed*

---

[28] Weber, ed., *Biblia sacra*, Luke 8: 11. My translations.

inebriat terram, et infundit eam et germinare eam facit et dat semen serenti et panem comedenti sic erit verbum meum quod egredietur de ore meo. ('as the rain and snow comes down from heaven, and does not return there, but saturates the earth, and makes it germinate, that it may give seed to the sower, and bread to the eater: so shall my word be that goes forth out of my mouth').[29]

Corn may be understood as the word of God, but according to orthodox Catholic belief this required the intervention, instruction, and exegesis of the Church before it could be assimilated by the faithful. So the image of grinding may be interpreted as referring to the ministry, to preaching and exegesis by which the word of God becomes spiritual nourishment, in the same way that corn must be ground into flour before it can provide nourishment for the physical body. The conjunction of images is familiar from Christ's statement: *scriptum est non in pane solo vivet homo sed in omni verbo quod procedit de ore Dei* ('it is written man shall not live by bread alone but by every word that proceeds from the mouth of God').[30] Margaret Aston, moreover, draws attention to images of the 'mill of the host' such as that in a now missing twelfth-century window in Canterbury Cathedral. Manuscripts note its accompanying Latin text: 'What the old law and the new grind as a pair of millstones, this food is your passion, cross, and word, O Christ.'[31] The association of grain, milling, and faith was clearly well established.

The Water Miller speaks of the circumstances under which he and his fellow 'water millers' make their living, telling the audience:

> For touchynge our selfes, we are but drudgys
> And very beggers, save onely our tole,
> Whyche is ryght smale and yet many grudges.
>   ....
> Yet, were not reparacyons, we myght do wele.
> (454–8)

In theological terms these are not rich priests and prelates living in luxury, a reference which might have struck a topical chord with the audience who would still remember the greatly resented splendour of the late Cardinal Wolsey. These are poor priests, living on the tithes which were traditionally a cause of resentment among many ordinary parishioners. The 'reparacyons', which the Miller speaks of in terms appropriate to milling, may be interpreted as repairs to the physical fabric of churches which depleted the financial resources of poor priests, but it also means spiritual restoration or salvation, again indicating that the Miller should be understood as representing a good

---

[29] Ibid., Isa. 55: 10–11.
[30] Ibid., Matt. 4: 4.
[31] Margaret Aston, 'Corpus Christi and Corpus Regni', p. 30.

priest, one who cares for the spiritual welfare of his parishioners although it is a heavy responsibility. As he says:

> In thys and mych more so great is our charge
> That we wolde not recke though no water ware,
> Save onely it toucheth eche man so large,
> And ech for our neyghbour Cryste byddeth us care.
> (462–5)

The Water Miller seems to represent the good priests who work hard, not for personal gain but to enable the word of God to become spiritual nourishment. The Wynd Miller's speech does not suggest that he works for anyone else's benefit. Moreover, it expresses concern that pride has caused the problems now suffered by 'wind millers'. He reminisces:

> ... in time past when gryndynge was plente
> Who were so lyke goddys felows as we?
> As faste as god made corne we myllers made meale.
> Whyche myght be best forborne for comyn weale?
> But let that gere passe! For I feare our pryde
> Is cause of the care whyche god doth us provyde.
> (524–9)

When the Miller asks 'Whyche myght be best forborne for the comyn weale', the audience's attention might have been drawn to complaints that exegesis (the making of 'meale') had become more important to the Church than the word of God (corne). The Wynd Miller's comments may be seen as referring to bad priests who were lacking in discrimination between the benefits of human teaching and the word of God.

This had been a Lollard complaint in the fourteenth and fifteenth centuries, but humanists of the early sixteenth century held similar opinions. John Guy observes that for Erasmus

> The Bible of the medieval church, the Latin Vulgate translation, symbolized the corruption of ecclesiastical tradition and [in 1516] Erasmus added notes in which the Vulgate's errors were exposed. Scholars and laymen were delighted; at last they drank the pure waters of the fountainhead.[32]

However, by the time *Wether* was performed Thomas More regarded as heretics a group of 'English reformers ... because they believed the Bible to be a superior authority to the church'.[33] The difference between More's and

---

[32] Guy, *Tudor England*, p. 118.
[33] Ibid., p. 119.

Erasmus's outlooks may have contributed to Heywood's concern over the fragmentation of the Christian brotherhood, and his allegorical representation of a common anticlerical complaint thus gains special significance in the context of the political and religious tensions of the 1530s, as does Mery Report's reminder to the Millers that they are brothers.

Mery Report's first intervention in the episode ends the Water Miller's soliloquy as he prevents the Miller approaching Jupiter to make his petition. Mery Report tells him rudely: 'What, ye come in revelynge and reheytynge | Even as a knave myght go to a beare beytynge!' (474–5). The Miller objects to the insult, calling on the audience to bear witness: 'Herke how famylyerly he calleth me knave' (477), but he rebukes Mery Report with restraint and in terms appropriate to Christian teaching, advising him:

> ... syr, you shulde never call
> Your felow knave or your brother horeson,
> For nought can ye get by it when ye have done.
> (479–81)

Mery Report takes this as an insult in his turn, and this sensitivity is an echo of similar incidents in the biblical plays where evil or sinful characters are quick to interpret a remark as insulting or mocking. Mery Report responds haughtily: 'Thou arte nother brother nor felowe to me, | For I am goddes servaunt' (482–3), an erroneous assertion, since all Christians would be considered servants of God and brothers in Christ. However, if Mery Report represents an Usher, and even more significantly, if he represents Cromwell, at this point his arrogance suggests that those who now control access to the King have rejected the Christian model of relationships.

Mery Report's insulting intervention at this point is structurally significant as it reasserts the ludic context, limits the soliloquy, facilitates the expression of a reference with Christian significance, moves the play forward rapidly to the point at which the Wynd Miller enters, and looks back to the Vyce's insolence after he was appointed Jupiter's Usher.

Later Mery Report intervenes in the Wynd Miller's soliloquy and tries to mediate, telling the Millers: 'Come on and assay how you twayne can agre – | A brother of yours, a Miller as ye be' (546–7). This time, Mery Report's language is not transgressive, but the Water Miller replies arrogantly:

> By meane of our craft we may be brothers,
> But whyles we lyve shall we never be lovers.
> We be of one crafte but not of one kynde.
> (548–50)

His denial of Christian brotherhood echoes that of Mery Report and subverts his identity as a good priest. It is significant that Mery Report's intervention and the Water Miller's denial of brotherhood within the shared 'crafte' raise the issue of Christian brotherhood even as they mark the transition into the Millers' debate. In the context of the religious debate which was troubling Tudor society in the 1530s, these references suggest that the Millers are not simply priests, but represent the theologians of both factions who were engaged in the religious debate.[34]

An insulting intervention by Mery Report ends the Millers' debate. He tells them: 'Stop folysh knaves, for your reasonynge is suche | That ye have reasoned even ynough and to much' (710–11). It seems like an interruption in conventional insulting terms from a vice-like character by which he intends to degrade the debate, but which, given the Millers' low status, simply limits their parody of a debate. However, if the Millers' episode is read in terms of a dramatized complaint against the debate between the religious factions, Mery Report's insult can be interpreted as a complaint that the religious debate is as irritatingly unproductive as the Millers' debate, and that the participants are behaving as foolishly.

Heywood appears to juggle condemnation with reconciliation as Mery Report continues to insult the Millers. He declares in an aside:

So help me God, the knaves be more then madde!
Nother of them both that hath wyt or grace
To perceyve that both myllys may serve in place.
(713–15)

Mery Report seems to recognize the presence of the pro-divorce and reformation faction with his use of the term 'grace', since the doctrine of grace was a cornerstone of early Protestantism. This would encourage an interpretation of his speech as a plea that both forms of religious belief should exist together, an apparently radical proposition, but consistent (as an orthodox Catholic interpretation) with Mery Report's characterization as transgressive and potentially dangerous, and also consistent with the theme of reconciliation in *Wether*.

Mery Report's final insult to the Millers again addresses them as 'knaves'. They exit and he remarks to the audience: 'Now be we ryd of two knaves at one chaunce – | By saynt Thomas, yt is a knavyshe ryddaunce' (764–5). Use of the conventional insulting term suggests Mery Report's self-importance, and continues to emphasize the similarity between the Millers. However, Mery Report's oath is more significant than his insult. It permits several interpretations. One is to Doubting Thomas the disciple, implying lack of faith,

---

[34] For a discussion of the topicality of the Millers' debate in the context of religious controversy see Lynn Forest-Hill, 'Lucian's Satire of Philosophers in Heywood's *Play of the Wether*', *Medieval English Theatre*, 18 (1996), pp. 142–60.

but other allusions to Thomas Becket, Thomas Wolsey, Thomas More, Thomas Cromwell, and Thomas Cranmer, as well as the great theologian Thomas Aquinas, are possible, and all could be regarded as controversial figures in the context of the religious climate of 1533, depending on the religious orientation of individual spectators. Becket put his loyalty to the Pope before his loyalty to Henry II. Wolsey had failed Henry VIII, while More had refused to assist the King to his divorce. Cromwell and Cranmer, on the other hand, had devised the means by which it might be achieved, but this meant a challenge to papal authority. Mery Report's simple and unspecific oath emphasizes the factionalism represented by these men, while his insult denies any difference between them.

Although Mery Report treats the Millers with equal deference, and disrespect, Heywood distinguishes between them. The Water Miller speaks first in 'the higher quatrain form'.[35] The Wynd Miller speaks in the less markedly high form of rhyming couplets. This distinction is significant for the interpretation of the Millers' episode, since it suggests the relatively higher status of the Water Miller. Moreover, while the Water Miller grinds corn for the benefit of the people, the Wynd Miller says he wants wind because with '... wynde contynuall, | Then shold we wyndemyllers be lordes over all' (544–5). However, both Millers are shown to be spiritually flawed by their use of oaths when they enter, and the Water Miller's willingness to participate in the debate shows him to be no better than the Wynd Miller. During the debate he speaks in the couplets which have characterized both his dialogue with Mery Report and the Wynd Miller's speech. This recalls the degrading effect of Fansy's speech on the prince in *Magnyfycence*.[36]

In order to understand the allegorical significance of the Millers we should note that neither Miller is characterized by references which indicate allegiance to heresy or to the reforming faction. Only Mery Report's later reference to 'grace' might suggest this. Heywood appears not to be taking sides. Moreover, the debate he dramatizes was not between the polarized factions supporting either orthodox belief or heresy; he is acknowledging, as many devout Catholics did, that in the Catholic Church there were bad priests, and bad practices. He demonstrates the degree to which the sin of pride had infested the bad clergy when the Wynd Miller asks: 'Who were so lyke goddys felows as we?' (527). As a result of the abuses of the bad priests, the good priests, personified by the Water Miller, are now ignored, as he complains: 'We water myllers be nothynge in regarde' (445). At the same time, the good priests are as willing as the bad to enter into the fruitless theological debate, and because of this the Church is threatened not merely with reform of its vices, but with a serious challenge to its authority and practices.

---

[35] Axton and Happé, eds, *The Plays of John Heywood*, p. 25.
[36] See Chapter 5 above.

It seems strange at first that Heywood includes both a parson and a priest in his anticlerical satire; but each serves his examination of clerical abuses. The Merchant/parson represents the financial abuses for which the clergy were condemned, including the practice of pluralism, and the great wealth of some prelates, while the Wynd Miller/priest represents lower clerical status, and self-seeking pride.

It is not by coincidence that the Merchant mistaken for a parson, the Ranger, and the Wynd Miller all sue to Jupiter for the same kind of weather. A biblical quotation provides a link between wind and doctrine in St Paul's epistle to the Ephesians, where he wrote: *circumferamur omni vento doctrinae in nequitia hominum* ('we are carried about by every wind of doctrine among the worthlessness of men').[37] The Merchant, Ranger, and Miller, as parson, minor peripatetic cleric, and priest, rely on wind, or doctrine, as their means of making a good living. Grouped together by their desire for wind they represent the vices traditionally alleged against clerics: greed, unchastity, pride, and self-seeking. Mery Report's insults are the clues to their identities as each is addressed in terms of conventional anticlerical satire. Both Millers, however, are insulted in terms consistent with a pejorative opinion of the religious debate.

Heywood uses Mery Report's simple insults to signal anticlerical satire; the insults are appropriate to the forms of corruption he intends to illustrate. However, Heywood signals the significance of the Millers' episode by its paired characters and binary structure, and by varying the use of Mery Report's transgressive language. Insults referring to brotherhood introduce a Christian significance which becomes a context for the debate. Mery Report's insulting intervention halts that inconclusive debate, and expresses his irritation at its tediousness. By naming both Millers 'knaves' he makes no distinction between them, although Heywood indicates that differences exist. The same insult provides unspoken criticism of the great theological debate. Heywood's economical use of insults is a subtle device by which he could address an audience, which may have included hostile spectators, and comment on the religious tensions they were provoking. This subtlety might have escaped some spectators, but while it indicates caution, it may also indicate Heywood's delight in his own skill and erudition.

Bawdy, scatology and schism

Bawdy and scatological language take on a complex significance after the Millers' episode as the religious debate is extended by the immediate entry of

---

[37] Weber, ed., *Biblia sacra*, Eph. 4: 14.

the Gentlewoman. This introduces the second pairing of characters in an episode with a binary structure (although this accommodates only the women's individual comments on weather, and each other). These similarities with the Millers' episode suggest a link between them, and at a didactic level the second episode has a causal link with the first as it dramatizes the effects of the theological debate.

The interpretation of Mery Report as Cromwell, or at least as an allegorical personification of the pro-divorce and reformation faction, becomes clearer and more satirical as the Gentlewoman enters to plead her case for mild weather before Jupiter. Her entrance gives rise to entertaining *double entendres* from Mery Report which mock her. She complains:

> What sholde I do where so mych people is?
> I know not how to passe in to the god now.
> (768–9)

Mery Report replies: 'No, but ye know how he may passe into you'. She continues: 'I pray you, let me in at the backe syde', to which Mery Report responds: 'Ye, shall I so, and your foresyde so wyde?' (770–71). The bawdy exchanges are entertaining, and play on the expectation of the Gentlewoman's embar-rassment, which does not happen, but as the episode proceeds they form part of the incremental representation of her sexual sophistication, until she thanks Mery Report for singing with her, telling him:

> Ye have done me pleasure, I make god a vowe.
> Ones in a nyght I longe for suche a fyt,
> For longe tyme have I ben brought up in yt.
> (855–7)

Axton and Happé note that 'fyt' has a sexual connotation, which means that in these lines the Gentlewoman is admitting to being sexually experienced ('brought up in yt'), and 'longing for it'.

Mery Report refuses to let the Gentlewoman go to Jupiter, but approaches him on her behalf. He does not ask the god to grant her an audience, nor does he present her suit for her; he tells Jupiter:

> Here is a derlynge come, by saynt Antony!
> And yf yt be your pleasure to mary
> Speke quyckly, for she may not tary.
> In fayth I thynke ye may wynne her anone.
> (781–4)

Mery Report is presenting the Gentlewoman herself, thus acting as her pimp.[38]

---

[38] Walker, *Plays of Persuasion*, p. 140.

Mery Report's oaths by 'Seynt Anne', spoken to the Gentleman and the Merchant (233; 396), may suggest Anne Boleyn.[39] Mery Report's oath 'by Saynt Antony' is not obviously a reference to her although from a Catholic perspective it may have seemed appropriate. The story of the sexual temptations which troubled St Anthony at night was well known, and may have provided an underlying satirical comment in Anne's relationship with the King, implying that she was the succubus tempting him to sin. Mery Report uses another oath during the episode with the Gentlewoman, swearing by 'saynte Quinteyne' (834), and Richard Axton proposes that this 'may be dictated by wordplay (ME queynte: pudendum; quintain: a mark to be tilted at – often used in a bawdy figurative sense)'.[40] If this is the case then the two oaths taken together would add a condemnatory emphasis to the otherwise playful sexual references in the episode.

At this point in the play it is more accurate to interpret the Gentlewoman as the allegorical personification of the reformed religion rather than as Anne Boleyn because Mery Report has remarked to the Gentlewoman that Jupiter is 'makynge of a new moone' (795). The succeeding episode with the Launder confirms the relevance of a new interpretation. In terms of topical references, if Anne was already known to be pregnant by the time *Wether* was first performed then it would be anachronistic for the Gentlewoman to represent her while Jupiter (Henry) was engaged in sexual intercourse with another woman (making a new moon). Pregnancy clearly refers to Anne at this time, which leaves the Gentlewoman as a personification of something else which is new and potentially attractive to the King, but which he, for the moment, dismisses, as Jupiter tells Mery Report: 'Sonne, that is not the thynge at this tyme ment' (786). It is the reformed religion which is being offered to the King for his delectation, but which he has so far refused.

At this point the pro-divorce and Protestant reforming faction, and perhaps specifically Cromwell, are being contextualized, through Mery Report's activities, as pimps, prepared to exploit Anne Boleyn's sexual attraction as the means by which they present the King with a new and attractive but morally corrupt bride in the form of a reformed Church.[41] The Church had long ago been allegorized as the Bride of Christ by patristic writers.[42] The offering of the reformed Church as a bride for the King is thus a blasphemous parody which may have been intended by Heywood to reflect what Catholics regarded as the

---

[39] Axton and Happé, eds, *Wether*, n. to l. 396.
[40] Ibid., n. l. 834.
[41] More addressed Luther insultingly as *leno* ('pimp') in his *Responsio ad Lutherum* (1523). John M. Headley, ed., *The Complete works of St. Thomas More* (New Haven: Yale University Press, 1969), vol. 5, *Responsio ad Lutherum*, p. 322, and Commentary, p. 819.
[42] The image had been reiterated in Dean Colet's Convocation Sermon of 1512, when he referred to 'the spouse of Christe, the churche'. Ernest William Hunt, ed., *Dean Colet and his Theology* (London: SPCK, 1956), p. 84.

improper relationship between the King and the Church which the reformers were proposing. Such an interpretation would, of course, amount to serious defamation of the reformers by the dramatist if his opponents could assert with conviction that this was what he meant. The degree of bawdy entertainment provided by this episode, the compliment to the King which is embedded in the reference to Jupiter making a new moon, thereby refuting the gossip concerning the King's possible impotence, and Mery Report's characterization as a Vyce, all serve to distance the episode from the more controversial interpretation.

Mery Report's encounter with the Gentlewoman heralds the second phase of the debate on religion which began with the arrival of the Millers. The full impact of the episode is revealed by the comparison which the Launder provides.[43] If the Gentlewoman is the new, attractive, but morally corrupt reformed religion, then the Launder is the old, hard-working, and virtuous established religion, less attractive, as the character says, because she was not prepared to prostitute herself simply to avoid hard work and retain her looks. She tells the Gentlewoman:

> When I was as yonge as thou art now
> I was wythin lyttel as fayre as thou
> And so myght have kept me yf I hadde wolde
> And as derely my youth I myght have solde
> ....
> But I feared parels that after myght fall,
> Wherfore some besynes I dyd me provyde.
> (904–10)

This speech reiterates conventional teaching on the dangers to the soul of idleness, and condemns the Gentlewoman for her morally degenerate life of pleasure. But the work the Launder has chosen provides a biblical allusion. She cleanses physical dirt, and she goes on to tell the Gentlewoman:

> ... I thynke yt farre better
> Thy face were sone-burned and thy clothis the swetter,
> Then that the sonne from shynynge sholde be smytten
> To kepe thy face fayre and thy smocke beshytten.
> (932–5)

---

[43] While the Launder is an innovative character in morality drama she belongs to a tradition of religious instruction which would have added significance to her appearance in *Wether*. G.R. Owst notes that 'the laundress and her task are old and favourite topics of the medieval preacher'. G.R. Owst, *Literature and the Pulpit* (Cambridge: Cambridge University Press, 1933), p. 36, n. 1.

The scatological bluntness of her comments is in keeping with her lower social status, which is defined by her manual occupation and her use of other forms of transgressive language. Although it is a rebuke to the Gentlewoman it is not punishing condemnation of the kind spoken by Adversyte to the corrupted Magnificence, and by Veritas to the three Estates in Bale's *King Johan*. They use abusive terms as a means of defining the corrupted characters' fallen condition. The Launder does not abuse the Gentlewoman, and this is a sign of her morally higher status, in comparison to the Gentlewoman, who refers to 'suche grose queynes as thou art' (900).

The image of external beauty concealing filth refers the audience to Christ's accusation in St Matthew's Gospel:

> *vae vobis scribae et Pharisaei hypocritae quia similes estis sepulchris dealbatis quae a foris parent hominibus speciosa intus vero plena sunt ossibus mortuorum et omni spurcitia* ('woe to you scribes and Pharisees, hypocrites, who are like whited sepulchres, which from outside appear beautiful to men, but inside are full of dead mens' bones, and all filth').[44]

This extends the significance of the Launder's words to the cleansing of the soul which was a function of the Church. It also provides a context for the Water Miller's remarks during his 'debate' with the Wynd Miller. He argues the need for water, saying:

> Yf ye take water for no commodyte,
> Yet muste ye take it for thynge of necessyte
> For washynge, for skowrynge, all fylth clensynge
> Where water lacketh, what bestely beyng!
> ....
> Wythout water coulde lyve neyther man nor best,
> For water preservyth both moste and lest.
> (658–11, 664–5)

The last line provides the clue for interpreting the images: 'moste and lest' applies to the ranks of society. The apparently commonplace remark, which previously appeared to be a low-status example appropriate to an unlearned man, may now be interpreted in the context of cleansing souls of their sins, and as a reference to the necessity for baptism – the use of water which preserves the souls of all ranks of society.

As the Millers have represented the factions within the established Church, and their debate the impotent wrangling within it, the episode with the two women represents the next stage in the political and religious upheavals taking place in the 1530s. The desire for a new, reforming movement comes after the

---

[44] Weber, ed., *Biblia sacra*, Matt. 23: 27.

unresolved wrangling. The play is thus mimetic of the process Heywood perceives going on in society.

It is in keeping with the balance Heywood appears to maintain throughout the play that no decision should be made in favour of either faction. Mery Report responds to the Launder with insults which limit the impression of her moralizing and emphasize the ludic context. He may address the audience as much as the Launder when he declares: 'Such a raylynge hore, by the holy mas, | I never herde in all my lyfe tyll now!' (937–8), but he continues:

> In dede I love ryght well the ton of you,
> But or I wolde kepe you both, by Goddes mother,
> The devyll shall have the tone to fet the tother!
> (939–41)

At first glance it seems that Mery Report obviously refers to the Gentlewoman in the first line, but finds both women so much trouble he would gladly be rid of them both. Earlier in the episode, however, he has wittily declared his feelings for the Gentlewoman. After their song he tells the audience ironically:

> I fere my selfe, excepte I may entreat her,
> I am so farre in love I shall forget her.
> (862–3)

He does not love her; she has aroused his interest but only so long as he gets what he wants. If he does not he will simply forget her. This may be another powerful comment on the relationship of the King to the Protestant reform movement, this time in the context of the divorce. In this instance Mery Report expresses a fickle attitude which may be interpreted as that of the King. Mery Report is suggesting that as long as the Protestant faction can achieve the divorce Henry desires he will favour it. Another interpretation, and one more closely tied to Heywood's personal loyalties, may also be evident here. Thomas More, his wife's uncle, opposed the divorce and had resigned as Chancellor, he was therefore no longer favoured by the King.

These interpretations of Mery Report's speech are complicated by its Catholic references. Since Mery Report does not love the Gentlewoman the one he loves 'ryght well' must be the Launder, the old established Church. His oaths 'by the holy mas' and 'by Goddes mother' emphasize this interpretation. However, both factions are causing so much irritation that the only option seems to be to dismiss them both. This maintains the tone of impartiality Heywood appears to have adopted for the play, while Mery Report's 'bargain', 'The devyll shal have the tone to fet the tother', returns the play to the level of entertaining transgression, and since he is the Vyce it is fitting that he should commit both women to the devil.

Both women wish Mery Report to make their petitions for weather but their demands are too much for him. They are expressed in bawdy terms as the Gentlewoman asks, 'Syr, yf ye medyll, remember me fyrste' (950) and the Launder objects: 'Then in this medlynge my parte shalbe the wurst' (951), to which Mery Report responds in exasperation:

> Now I beseche Our Lorde, the devyll the burst!
> Who medlyth wyth many I hold hym accurst.
> Thou hore, can I medyl wyth you both at ones?
> (952–4)

Mery Report is used to express the exasperation of the individual, as he was at the end of the Millers' episode, as Heywood sets out his anxiety that the good, virtuous aspect of Catholicism has been devalued first by its association with the bad aspect, and second by the manner in which it pursues the dispute with the corrupt Protestant faction.[45]

The patter speeches of Mery Report and the Launder appear to be elaborate insults which continue the entertainment set up by their bawdy exchange centred on the sexual connotations of 'medlynge' (951–6). The insulting exchange is terminated by Mery Report's allusions to impotence when he refers to the shrinking of his 'gere' (974–7). In this instance, entertainment brackets religious comment which is itself given the form of entertaining nonsense. The nonsense, in fact, acts as a satiric comment on the wrangling between the religious factions, as the Millers' debate functioned earlier in the play. Mery Report tells the Launder:

> The more ye byb the more ye babyll,
> The more ye babyll the more ye fabyll,
> The more ye fabyll the more unstabyll,
> The more unstabyll the more unabyll
> In any maner thynge to do any good.
> (960–64)

The most accessible image here is of drunken speech. To 'byb' or drink leads to babbling speech, and the fabrication of fictions which cannot be sustained. Mery Report, representing the reforming faction, is likening the arguments of the orthodox faction to drunken fables, having no truth in them, which renders them ineffective. His reference to drinking may also allude to the reformers' dismissal of the orthodox doctrine of transubstantiation as a fiction, or 'fabyll'.

---

[45] Heywood may have been reflecting current popular opinion, or his own anxiety, but he may also have been influenced by More's example of the 'poore symple woman' who, More suggests, if confronted by himself and Tyndale locked in theological debate, 'wold not lette to byleue and saye so to, that we were two madde folys and false heretykes bothe'. Thomas More, *The Confutation of Tyndale's Answer*, p. 391.

The reformers' attitude towards miracles performed by images of saints may also be included in the 'fabyll' reference, while 'babyll' may refer to their definition of the Latin liturgy.

The Launder counters Mery Report's insults, telling him:

> The les your sylence the lesse your credence,
> The les your credens the les your honeste,
> The les your honeste the les your assystens
> The les your assystens the les abylyte
> In you to do ought!
> (966–70)

The underlying religious interpretation is that the more the reformers speak out the less they are believed, the less worthy they seem, and the less likely they are to succeed in their purpose.

The Launder's parting lines complete the religious significance of the episode. She leaves Mery Report with an insult:

> Now wolde I take my leve yf I wyste how.
> The lenger I lyve the more knave you!
> (980–81)

Axton and Happé suggest that the first line indicates the Launder's 'social discomfort in the hall and also her recovery of sufficient dignity to deliver the proverbial sentence'.[46] This interpretation ignores the preceding characterization. The Launder's 'discomfort' suggests a sudden sensitivity in the character which was not apparent during her brief flytings with Mery Report when she exchanged bawdy and insulting remarks with him with considerable confidence, in front of the audience. And the 'proverbial sentence' is, in fact, a deviation from the usual form 'the longer *thou* livest the more knave thou'. However, if the Launder's final lines are considered in the religious context then they refer to the inability of the established Church to separate from society, and the longer it continues the more it proves its detractors, like the abusive and light-minded Mery Report, to be knaves – or scoundrels.

Heywood's use of transgressive language in *Wether* constantly signals, contextualizes, and provides clues to the contemporary significance of the petitions for weather. His innovations in transgressive language, characterization, and fragmented allegory, provide the means by which he can comment on the political and religious tensions, and their causes, obliquely and cautiously, while his most radical sentiments are submerged beneath the entertaining transgressive language of his innovative Vyce, Mery Report, which also introduces or limits all the episodes in the play.

---

[46] Axton and Happé, eds, *Wether*, n. to ll. 980–81.

Mery Report's scatological remarks contextualize Henry VIII's divorce, while his bawdy innuendo contextualizes the King's relationship with Anne Boleyn. Where both forms occur together in any episode they contextualize the process and effects of those events. Mery Report's insults direct attention to conventional anticlerical abuses which provide contexts for interpreting the Merchant, the Ranger, and the Wynd Miller as self-seeking clerics. His least emphatic insults are addressed to the Millers, but when taken in the contexts provided by Christian and anticlerical references in the Millers' episode, and the religious conflict in Tudor society, they represent pointed, and dangerous, condemnation of contemporary theologians and the religious debate prompted by the King's divorce. Mery Report's lively bawdy and scatological exchanges with the women direct attention to the effects of the factionalism and debate, and suggest the exasperation it was causing in society.

Mery Report's insults to both Millers and both women seem at first to suggest Heywood's impartiality towards the religious factions, a view apparently emphasized by the end of the play in which no petitioner achieves preferential treatment.[47] However, closer examination of the religious concerns of the play reveals that Heywood is not impartial: his own judgement is always in favour of virtue. He uses conventional anticlerical satire to acknowledge that abuses existed in the Church in Tudor England, but Mery Report's bawdy language suggests the spurious attractions of the reformers' alternative. Heywood makes his support for the good, virtuous aspect of Catholicism clear in the Water Miller's soliloquy, which he presents in quatrain form, giving the Miller a vocabulary suggesting biblical allusions, and a virtuous Christian attitude. It is only when the Water Miller engages in debate with the Wynd Miller that his verse form and linguistic style degenerate. The bad infects the good and when Mery Report calls both Millers 'knaves' there really is nothing to choose between them. Mery Report's dialogues with the women also distinguish between virtue and vice. The women's use of bawdy and scatological language, which is itself an innovation, creates unexpectedly subtle characterizations which represent the orthodox religion as virtuous but unattractive, and the reformed faith as attractive but morally corrupt. The end of *Wether* defines Heywood's resolution of his anxiety over the factional wrangling. Change does take place as the petitioners abandon their self-interested claims and willingly acknowledge that they are all under the authority of the same God, Jupiter. In contemporary terms this represents the acknowledgement of that brotherhood in Christ which the Millers/priests have previously rejected, and this is Heywood's proposal for reconciliation.

In *Wether* Heywood made innovations in transgressive language which enabled him to make radical comments on the political and religious situation

---

[47] Walker, *Plays of Persuasion*, p. 166, and Altman, *The Tudor Play of Mind*, p. 123, both suggest that *Wether* ends without anything being changed.

in ways which may have been especially apt, but are disguised as entertainment. He created innovative characterizations in the play, but the political and religious significance of all the characters are open to interpretation according to the political and religious orientation of individual spectators. Heywood's innovations thus represent the caution with which he attempts political intervention.[48] On the other side of the religious controversy, however, caution appears to have been ignored.

---

[48] See Arthur B. Ferguson, *The Articulate Citizen and the English Renaissance* (Durham, N.C.: Duke University Press, 1965), pp. 157–8, on the duty of the educated citizen to give counsel.

Chapter 7
King Johan: the language of virtue and reformation

John Heywood's innovations in *The Play of the Wether*, which enabled him to make dangerous comments on the unstable situation of the 1530s, illustrate the caution with which he addressed political and religious change. At first glance, caution does not seem relevant as a description of the ways in which John Bale used transgressive language in his morality play *King Johan*, but as we shall see, he did, in some instances, exercise a degree of caution, to powerful dramatic effect.

Bale made radical changes to the forms, functions, and use of transgressive language in *King Johan*.[1] These changes may be seen as, in part, the response of a Protestant dramatist who perceived the value of drama as a medium of instruction and persuasion, but rejected those traditions which were associated with the earlier use of instructional drama in the service of Catholicism.[2] The changes are the result of Bale's polemical intention, and play to the Protestant sympathies of his audience, who may have included Cromwell and Cranmer.[3]

The first known performance of the play in 1538 came at a time when the religious reforms which had been made were threatened by Henry VIII's acceptance of the Act of Six Articles.[4] The Articles upheld auricular confession, transubstantiation, communion in one kind, votive masses, clerical celibacy, and vows of chastity. *King Johan* offers a protest against this anti-reformation legislation, as it dramatizes what it defines as an historical

---

[1] The complex history of revisions to the text altered the amount of transgressive language in the play, which was modified according to the changing political and religious climate of the times. This study of *King Johan* uses Peter Happé's edition of the play which gives priority to the 1560–63 final version of the text, but will refer to the political events which would have influenced the reception of the play in its earlier (1538) version. The later version does not seriously misrepresent the earlier one, and Happé's edition enables significant additions to the amount of transgressive language to be traced from one version to the other. See Peter Happé, ed., *The Complete Plays of John Bale*, 2 vols, vol. 1 (Cambridge: D.S. Brewer, 1985). For a detailed discussion of the relationship between the 1538 and 1560–63 versions see Peter Happé, *John Bale* (New York: Twayne, 1996), pp. 89–91. Happé notes that 'Bale incorporated virtually everything from the A text into the B text', p. 104.

[2] Rainer Pineas, *Tudor and Early Stuart Anti-Catholic Drama* (Nieuwkoop: B. de Graaf, 1972), p. 6.

[3] Walker, *Plays of Persuasion*, p. 173. See also Robert Duncan, 'The Play as Tudor Propaganda: Bale's *King Johan* and the Authority of Kings', *University of Dayton Review*, 16: 3 (1983–4), p. 67; and Happé, *John Bale*, p. 90.

[4] Haigh, *English Reformations*, p. 152.

conspiracy by the Catholic Church against royal authority, and links this to auricular confession.

Bale addresses the Six Articles and makes his political and religious points with varying degrees of vehemence in the play, but the reputation as 'bilious Bale',[5] which he acquired after his death because of the violently abusive language in his prose works, falls short of an accurate representation of his use of transgressive language in *King Johan*. Ritchie Kendall has remarked that 'to overcome a millenium of rote response to Christian worship, each word of nonconformity had to jolt and disturb ... as well as guide and educate'.[6] While Bale can be seen to follow such a reformist trend in his use of a violent polemical style, he was not alone in using such language, nor was such a linguistic style the preserve of Protestant reformers. Moreover, in *King Johan*, Bale's use of transgressive language does not always take the form of strident polemic even though it dramatizes and satirizes the abuses of the Catholic Church, its attitudes to its congregation; and to the secular power.

Bale's language in *King Johan* deserves to be seen not only in the context of a Protestant polemical style but also in relation to a debating vocabulary and style which were linked to traditional attitudes towards language in drama and society, and to newer literary fashion. By the time Bale wrote *King Johan* both sides of the Reformation debate had already used vehement abuse as a weapon in defence of their particular Christian beliefs. In the 1520s Luther had abused Henry VIII in scatological terms for his book *Assertio septem sacramentorum*, which was the king's response to Luther's *Babylonian Captivity*. Luther wrote:

> *ius mihi erit pro meo rege, maiestatem anglicam luto et stercore conspergere; et coronam istam blasphemam in Christum pedibus conculcare* ('It will be my right, on behalf of my king [Christ], to spatter his English majesty with mud and shit and to trample underfoot that crown which blasphemes against Christ').[7]

Thomas More defended Henry in the same terms, replying:

> *licebit alijs pro maiestate anglica, lutum et stercus omne, quod uestra putredo damnabilis egessit, in uestrae paternitatis os stercoreum, et stercorum omnium, uere sterquilinium regerere: et in coronam uestram ... omnes cloacas et latrinas effundere.* ('others will be allowed, on behalf of his English majesty, to throw back all the mud and shit which your damnable rottenness has poured out into your paternity's filthy mouth,

---

[5] This epithet was given to Bale by Thomas Fuller in his book *Worthies of England*, published 1662; see Happé, *John Bale*, p. 137, and Happé, ed., *The Complete Plays*, p. 16.

[6] Ritchie Kendall, *The Drama of Discontent* (Chapel Hill: University of North Carolina Press, 1986), p. 100.

[7] *The Complete Works of St. Thomas More*, vol. 5, *Responsio ad Lutherum*, p. 311.

truly the cesspit of all filth, and to empty out all the sewers and privies onto your crown').[8]

Bale's polemic in *King Johan* is never so shockingly scatological as the exchange between More and Luther.[9] Although his characters frequently use ferociously insulting language, Bale nevertheless demonstrates his ability to modulate his use of linguistic transgression in order to achieve more interesting drama. While reformers in the audience no doubt enjoyed a sense of satisfaction as they watched and heard the abuses of the Church played out before them in highly offensive terms, Bale's innovations and use of comedy and subtlety to vary the pace and tone of the play enabled him to address issues of doctrinal, political, and liturgical reformation upon which Henry VIII, and even some fellow reformers, remained ambivalent at the time of the play's first performance.[10]

By situating Bale's linguistic style in *King Johan* in the context of the language of the reformation debates and earlier tradition we see more clearly Bale's restraint as well as the scale and significance of his innovations. In accordance with earlier convention, evil characters in *King Johan* are defined by their use of transgressive language, but in this play the virtuous characters also use abusive, insulting, and contemptuous language. The early sixteenth century had witnessed a fashion for 'flytings' which were not the simple verbal quarrels of the kind implied by references to 'flyting' in the biblical drama, but debates or arguments, carried on in writing by learned men, characteristically

---

[8] Ibid. William Tyndale used violent language in his *Practice of Prelates* (1530), calling the Pope 'the father of all hypocrites' and 'the devil's vicar' as well as referring to 'these vile begging friars out of hell'. William Tyndale, *The Practice of Prelates*, ed. Henry Walter, Parker Society (Cambridge: Cambridge University Press, 1849), pp. 273, 274, 277. More responded to Tyndale's writings in insulting terms, calling him, among other things, 'a dedly deuelyshe heretyke'; see *The Confutation*, p. 119.

[9] Stephen Greenblatt locates this exchange in specific cultural contexts when he observes that 'for More scatology normally expresses a communal disapproval.... For Luther, the Devil dwells in excrement, and his dominion over the world is made possible by the world's excremental character.' Stephen J. Greenblatt, *Learning to Curse* (New York: Routledge, 1990), p. 72.

[10] John D. Cox and David Scott Kastan draw attention to the problem of Bale's audiences, suggesting that he was 'writing for the socially diverse audience that he and his players would have been expected to address on tour'. John D. Cox and David Scott Kastan, eds, *A New History of Early English Drama* (New York: Columbia University Press, 1997), p.137. Nothing is known with certainty about the audience for *King Johan*, and Bale's vituperation in it may have been intended to address Catholic spectators, perhaps in the tradition of punishing language. However, Bale modulates his linguistic style when addressing the most sensitive aspects of Catholic doctrine, a feature which reinforces the notion of a diverse audience, but problematizes the extent to which he intended to be openly controversial.

employing an abusive and obscene vocabulary.[11] Rainer Pineas suggests that 'the Reformation had changed the meaning of the terms "virtue" and "vice",[12] and while Bale's innovations do just this, they may also reflect the literary fashion which used language as a weapon. This fashion, like Bale's use of vituperation, is related to use of transgressive language by virtuous characters in biblical and earlier morality drama who punish sinful characters by using the vocabulary of abuse to name the sinners, and their misdeeds, accurately without compromising their own virtue.

The use of abusive language by virtuous characters in *King Johan* consequently inverts its use as a signifier of spiritual status and change. As characters reject Catholicism their language becomes violently abusive of it, simultaneously asserting their new-found virtue. But transgressive language is not always used in the service of Bale's polemic; occasionally it takes the form of entirely naturalistic language – an insult or an oath may be spoken in irritation, having none of the special moral significance which such language had in earlier drama.

Since transgressive language alone is no longer a reliable indicator of moral status, other conventions contribute to defining the difference between good and evil characters. Names continue to carry moral significance as they had traditionally done, but in *King Johan* they define a character's vicious or virtuous condition according to the play's Protestant morality. Bale introduces historical characters in the play alongside conventional allegorical personifications, and his transformation of allegorical characters into named historical figures is an innovation. The name of the historical figure contributes to Bale's condemnation of Catholicism, while the use of historical figures distances his play from earlier Catholic moralities in which all the characters were allegorical personifications.

New forms of transgressive language are introduced by Bale as a result of his inversion of the moral significance of conventional transgressive forms. The language of evil in *King Johan* is that which expresses support for the Pope and the Catholic Church against the King. It is the language of treason. Evil is also characterized by the self-revelatory language of the characters who support Catholicism, and who thus demonstrate their pride, contempt, and complacency. This language is itself a parody of the Catholic confession, since it does not connote the speaker's wish for forgiveness but his ignorance or acceptance of his own viciousness. Bale includes more overt parodies of Catholic rituals, ceremonies, and sacraments which reduce the language of Roman Catholicism itself to a form of transgressive language.

---

[11] The best known are Skelton's flytings *Agenst Garnesche* (*c.* 1513) and *Against Dundas* (*c.* 1515), and the Scottish *Flyting of Dunbar and Kennedy*, published in 1508. See Scattergood, *John Skelton: The Complete English Poems*, pp. 424–5.

[12] Pineas, *Tudor and Early Stuart Anti-Catholic Drama*, p. 15.

Bale accommodates Protestant disquiet over religious drama and further extends the forms of transgressive language in *King Johan* by using words associated with dramatic performances as insults, and as part of his satire of Catholic rituals. This enables him to differentiate between Protestant and Catholic forms of drama, and to degrade Catholic rituals to the level of theatrical performances. The extensions to, and adaptations of, transgressive language in *King Johan* testify to Bale's interest in language itself, and the problem he faced when using language which was already ideologically loaded with significance he wishes to condemn.

Transgressive language and virtuous characters

The use of familiar forms of transgressive language – insults, abuse, and mockery – by virtuous characters is greatly extended in *King Johan*. In *Magnyfycence* the stern virtue Adversyte reviles the fallen prince with names taken from the vocabulary of common insults,[13] but these insulting names are, in fact, apt descriptions of the prince in his degraded state. They confirm his degradation and punish him as they signify the antithesis of his name and former rank. Bale's virtuous characters, King Johan, Englande, Veritas, and Imperyall Majestye, use transgressive language which at times is startling in its abusive vehemence. Since the use of transgressive language in medieval drama is traditionally a means of characterizing sin and evil, it is, at first, difficult to understand how Bale constructs these characters as virtuous *through* their use of such language. However, the political and religious orientation of the audience, together with the names of the characters, would ensure that these characters would be understood as virtuous, and this prior understanding controls the audience's reception of the characters' use of transgressive language. That language appears in the play as a response provoked by the abuses and evils perpetrated by the Church, and accurately representing them. The abusive language of the virtuous characters condemns and characterizes as low, corrupt, and evil all aspects of the Catholic clergy and papal authority, and it takes on the form of punishment after the death of King Johan.

In his prose writing, Bale justifies the use of abusive and insulting language to characterize and condemn people who are regarded as enemies of the faith. He cites Scripture as his model when he declares: 'Yea, Christ owr most gentyll and pacyent redemer, spared not to call them ... theues ... murtherers ... swyne ... adders ... deuyls ... and many other names of great

---

[13] Scattergood, ed., *John Skelton: The Complete English Poems*, *Magnyfycence*, ll. 1878–87.

indignacion.'[14] The vehemence of the language used by virtuous characters in *King Johan* against the characters who defend or represent Catholicism is part of Bale's polemic, for which he offers this justification.

Englande is the first of the virtuous characters to condemn the clergy in violently abusive terms. She appears dressed as a poor widow, and complains to King Johan, saying: 'Alas, yowre clargy   hath done very sore amys | In mysusyng me ageynst   all ryght and justyce'.[15] The King gently rebukes her, telling her 'They are thy chylderne;   thow owghtest to say them good' (68). Englande retorts:

> Nay, bastardes they are,   unnaturall by the rood!
> Sens ther begynnyng   they ware never good to me.
> The wyld bore of Rome –   God let hym never to thee –
> Lyke pyggys they folow,   in fantysyes, dreames and lyes,
> And ever are fed   with his vyle cerymonyes.
> (69–73)

Only if individual spectators are already sympathetic to the Protestant cause can this speech be recognized as that of a virtuous character, condemning in vivid terms the relationship between the Catholic clergy and the state of England represented by the character. The naming of the Pope as the 'wyld bore of Rome' and the clergy as 'pyggys' is unquestionably insulting. The description of the Roman rite as 'vyle cerymonyes' is equally offensive. However, the language may also be seen from the reformers' point of view as accurately representing the conduct and relationship between England, the Pope, and the clergy. The characterization of the relationship between the clergy and England in terms of the relationship between mother and child suggests ties of duty and affection, but the relationship to which Englande refers is unnatural because the duty and affection which the clergy owe to England, as to a mother, is diverted to the Pope. Englande's characterization of the relationship of the clergy to the Pope degrades it in terms of the behaviour of animals, contrasting it with the ideal human relationship between mother and children.

Although Englande uses highly insulting terms, she at no time takes on the aspect of a flawed or vicious character. Her use of transgressive language is an

---

[14] Thora Balslev Blatt, *The Plays of John Bale: A Study of Ideas, Technique and Style* (Copenhagen: G.E.C. Gad, 1968), p. 220. In William Tyndale's English translation of the *New Testament* Christ tells the Pharisees, among other things, 'Ye are serpents and generation of vipers' (Matt. 23); John the Baptist uses the same condemnatory language (Luke 3). David Daniell, ed., *Tyndale's New Testament* (New Haven: Yale University Press, 1989).

[15] Happé, ed., *King Johan*, l. 27. All quotations are from this edition. It is a feature of Bale's writing that each line of the play except those in Latin includes a medial caesura; I reproduce this form in all quotations from the play.

inversion of its traditional function since it calls attention to the evil nature of the influence and power exercised by the Catholic clergy. It does not characterize Englande as evil because she directs attention to the destructive power and dangerous influence of the Church signified in the image of the wild boar. Thus Englande's abuse is actually a sign of her virtue, since by the vehemence of that abuse she emphasizes the dangers which beset the nation.

King Johan himself uses insults to condemn the evils caused by the Catholic Church, and they represent truth-speaking in terms of the play's Protestant interests. The King's use of transgressive language also takes on the form of a weapon with which he tries to defend his authority and his realm.[16] A further significant function of his use of such language is as a means of defining the evil characters.

King Johan's simple insults occasionally have the impact of metaphors. He names the clergy 'thes cormerantes' (483) and Bale's choice of image reinforces the complaints already made by Englande and the King concerning the greed of the clergy by naming it as the bird which was a proverbial image of greed in the sixteenth century. The King also calls Clergye 'thu wycked Pharyse' (1465), recalling Christ's condemnation of Pharisees, but especially recalling their conspiracy which led to His death; this then provides a context for interpreting the betrayal of the King in the play.

Some of the King's insulting metaphors have more specific cultural significance; for example, he rejects the idea of the Catholic Church, declaring it '... no Holy Chyrch, nor feythfull congregacyon, | But an hepe of adders of Antecristes generacyon' (492–3). This is an apocalyptic image echoed later in Bale's paraphrase of the Book of Revelation: 'These are the prelates of antichrist's church ... These are the ... adders'.[17] The paraphrase was published in 1545, but the association of the papacy with the Antichrist is much older than *King Johan* or the Reformation. At his trial for heresy in 1413 Sir John Oldcastle named the Pope Antichrist, repeating the insult used earlier in the Lollard tract *The Lanterne of Li3t*.[18] Other insults take on the lurid vitality which led to Bale's reputation as 'bilious'. The King rebukes Nobylyte saying:

> I rew yt in hart that yow, Nobelyte,
> Shuld thus bynd yowre selfe to the grett captyvyte
> Of blody Babulon the grownd and mother of whordom –

---

[16] John R. Knott, *Discourses of Martyrdom in English Literature 1563–1694* (Cambridge: Cambridge University Press, 1993), p. 49.

[17] John Bale, *The Image of Both Churches*, ed., Henry Christmas, *Selected Works of John Bale*, Parker Society (Cambridge: Cambridge University Press, 1849), pp. 438–9.

[18] Alan J. Fletcher, *Preaching, Politics, and Poetry in Late Medieval England* (Dublin: Four Courts Press, 1998), pp. 284–5. *The Lanterne of Li3t* is dated c. 1409–10; see Lilian M. Swinburn, ed., *The Lanterne of Li3t*, EETS OS 151 (London: Kegan Paul, Trench, Trübner, 1917), p. xiii.

> The Romych Churche I meane, more vyle than ever was Sodom.
> (367–70)

Bale's reference here to the Whore of Babylon contributes a sense of apocalyptic danger and carnal corruption to King Johan's condemnation of the Catholic Church, as well as likening its hold over England to Babylon's enslavement of Israel.[19] Bale uses the rhetorical force of his polemical style in place of dramatic action to impress upon the audience the consequences of subjection to papal authority. This technique would be most fully appreciated by learned spectators who could be expected to understand the significance of the abusive allusions, especially those from biblical sources, but also those which recalled that England had fostered a long tradition of resistance to papal authority, which then gained political urgency from Henry VIII's break with Rome and theological momentum from Luther's gravitational pull.

When King Johan is openly faced with the threat to his power and authority he responds with language which condemns his opponents in mocking and insulting terms. Privat Welth/Cardynall brings the Pope's instruction to the King that he must restore the privileges of the Church, regardless of whatever the King can find in the Gospels to support his own authority. The King responds with scornful anger:

> Yowre father is sharpe   and very quycke in sentence
> Yf he wayeth the word   of God nomor than so.
> (1323–4)

As the Cardynall persists, King Johan insults him in unmistakable terms, telling him: 'Avant, pevysh prist!   What, dost thow thretten me?' (1340), and goes on to condemn the priesthood, declaring: 'I can not perseyve   but ye are becum Belles prystes, | Lyvyng by ydolles;   yea, the very antychrystes' (1354–5). Until King Johan concedes his authority, the forms of transgressive language he uses mark his resistance to the demands of the Pope. His transgressive language may be regarded as rebukes against the presumptuousness of the Church, and as correct, and therefore not insulting, representations of the forces ranged against him.

Other virtuous characters in *King Johan* use abusive language to rebuke and punish characters who are corrupted by Sedicyon the Vyce. Bale transforms the temptation plot, which is conventional to morality plays, into political coercion. It is more complex than temptation in earlier moralities, such as

---

[19] Knott, *Discourses of Martyrdom*, p. 103. The use of Babylon as a pejorative metaphor for the Church can be traced back to Martin Luther's *De captivitate Babylonica ecclesiae praeludium* (1520), in which he declared: 'I now know for certain that the papacy is the kingdom of Babylon.' Timothy F. Lull, ed., *Martin Luther's Basic Theological Writings* (Minneapolis: Fortress Press, 1989), p. 268.

Wisdom, where representatives of humanity are tempted away from the virtuous life, endangering their souls. Corruption in *King Johan* does not focus on the King, the main virtuous representative of humanity, but on the three Estates, represented by the allegorical personifications Clergye, Cyvyle Order, and Nobylyte, who are coerced by Sedicyon into betraying their allegiance to the King. These characters are simpler personifications than the social estates in *The Play of the Wether*, which represent religious factionalism.

After King Johan's death the character Veritas enters and begins to rebuke the Estates for the part they have played in the King's destruction. He does this in general terms at the start, declaring that:

> Saynt Hierome sayth also that he is of no renowne
> But a vyle traytour that rebelleth agaynst the crowne.
> (2231–2)

The name 'vyle traytour' is not an insult in this instance but an accurate representation of the rebellious subject. However, Veritas's rebukes become more specific and more directly insulting. He tells Clergye that he thinks the philological root of the word *clergy* derives not from *Cleros*, but from *Clerus*, 'A very noyfull worme, as Aristotle sheweth us, | By whome are destroyed the honeycombes of bees' (2252–3). By means of the pastoral image Bale likens the Catholic clergy to destructive parasites, while England takes on the aspects of sweetness and industriousness associated with the production of a honeycomb. Veritas next rebukes Cyvyle Order, and perhaps Nobylyte, saying:

> ... yow, lyke wretches, cast over both contreye and kynge.
> All manhode shameth to see your unnaturell doynge.
> Ye wycked rulers, God doth abhorre ye all.
> (2265–7)

He ends by asserting: 'The Turkes I dare saye are a thousande tymes better than yow' (2305).

Nobylyte, Clergye, and Cyvyle Order make little effort to defend themselves against Veritas's rebukes, and eventually his condemnation is more than they can bear. The power of his accusations and the terms in which they are expressed overwhelm them. Nobylyte begs: 'For Gods love, nomore! Alas, ye have sayde ynough' (2306). Clergye acknowledges that 'All the worlde doth knowe that we have done sore amys' (2307), and Cyvyle Order pleads, 'Forgyve it us so that we never heare more of thys' (2308). Their pleas indicate the power of words to persuade, enlighten, and turn hearts and minds away from treachery. This persuasive power, in its turn, represents a defence of the use of drama by reformers for political purposes. Bale's representation of the power of language may be compared with Mercy's complaint in *Mankind*:

'wythout rude behauer I kan not expresse þis inconvenyens' (737), which draws attention to the power of transgressive language even as it rejects it.

In a dramatically and politically significant confrontation, the virtuous character Imperyall Majestye rebukes Clergye in insulting terms when Clergye attempts to show his change of heart by telling Imperyall Majestye:

> If it be your pleasure ....
> ....
> ... your grace shall be the supreme head of the Churche.
> To brynge thys to passe   ye shall see how we wyll wurche.
> (2387, 2389–90).

This brings a rebuke from Imperyall Majestye:

> The crowe wyll not chaunge her hewe |
> ....
> I wyll the auctoryte   of Gods holy wurde to do it
> And it not to aryse   of your vayne slypper wytt.
> (2395, 2397–8).

Imperyall Majestye's rejection of Clergye's offer is an important statement of the Protestant view of royal supremacy as authorized by Scripture, as the reference to the proverbial crow suggests the impossibility of making the clergy understand that they have no right to make, or break, kings. The crow image also contributes a sense of malevolence from the bird's blackness. The reference to Clergye's 'vayne slypper wytt' defines the means by which the clergy have sought to control the monarchy. The significance of Imperyall Majestye's rebuke is extended by interpretations of the character, such as that suggested by Greg Walker, who sees him as 'the figuration of Henry VIII as Godly Prince'.[20] Thus it is Henry who perceives the duplicity of the clergy in his own time, and condemns it with just rebukes.

Naturalistic use of insults

King Johan's use of transgressive language contributes significantly to the characterization of the evils represented by the papacy and the clergy. It also represents an innovation in drama, since it includes colloquial insults which suggest the King's human rather than allegorical condition.

King Johan's transgressive language, which expresses his displeasure, irritation, and anger, does not characterize him as evil, nor even flawed, as such language characterizes the prince in *Magnyfycence*. The King's use of

---

[20] Walker, *Plays of Persuasion*, p. 210.

transgressive language helps to characterize his awareness of his own authority, and the challenge to it. It also contributes to his characterization as human rather than simply as a personification of kingly virtue. King Johan responds like a human ruler; he is involved in the troubles which beset his realm, not a distant image of god-like wisdom as Jupiter is in *Wether*, nor an exemplar of princely folly like Magnificence.

King Johan's rebukes to Sedicyon, like Magnificence's early rebukes to Fansy, are made in language which would be unquestionably insulting if spoken by a lower-status character, and they grow increasingly emphatic. The King commands Sedicyon: 'I saye holde yowre peace and stond asyde lyke a knave!' (112). He goes on to tell Sedicyon bluntly:

> Thow semyste by thy wordes to have no more wytt than a coote.
> I mervell thow arte to Englonde so un naturall:
> Beyng her owne chyld thow art worse than a best brutall.
> (176–8)

Sedicyon does not respond as might be expected to this condemnation. He does not challenge the insult to his intelligence or object to being described as a wild beast, but objects strongly to being mistaken for Englande's child, and replies with his own insults:

> I am not her chyld: I defye hyr, by the messe!
> I her sonne, quoth he! I had rather she wer hedlesse.
> (179–80)

In this instance Bale uses King Johan's speech as a means of characterizing Sedicyon, and the political and religious evils he represents by his response, rather than the King.

Although King Johan's later insults again characterize Sedicyon accurately, they also represent the King's increasing irritation. He tells Sedicyon: 'Gett the hence, thow knave, and most presumptuows wreche' (221). The King's language is unmistakably a colloquial insult and may be spoken as much to himself as to the audience when he again curses Sedicyon saying: 'The devyll go with hym! The unthryftye knave is gon' (313). The King's exasperation does not mark his own descent into folly or degradation, but it is justified by Sedicyon's insolence; the curse is therefore much closer to the realistic representation of speech associated with human anger than the curses of characters in earlier didactic drama. The King's curse on friars, as he deplores the poverty of Englande and Commynalte, has similar significance as he tells Englande: 'I beshrew ther hartes, they have made yow two full nedy' (1597).

In the biblical plays, figures of evil authority demonstrate a sensitivity to insults and mockery which leads them to challenge innocent remarks. In the N-Town *Trial before Herod*, for example, Herod defines Christ's silence in this way when he demands: 'Hast þu skorne to speke to þi kyng?' (30: 222). King Johan's interpretation of the Church's conduct as scorn does not, however, connote his vicious sensitivity, but his anxiety. The King tells Clergye:

> Nowther thow nor the Pope shall do pore Englond wronge,
> I beyng governor and kyng her peple amonge
> Whyle yow for lucre sett forth yowr popysh lawys
> Yowr selvys to advaunce ye wold make us pycke strawes.
> Nay, ipocrytes, nay! We wyll not be scornyd soo
> Of a sort of knavys.
> (470–5)

The difference between the vehemence with which King Johan speaks to his adversaries and his naturalistic oaths is an effective modulation in Bale's use of transgressive language which produces tonal variety in the characterization of the King, and further demonstrates his ability to modulate his polemic in the interests of drama.

Virtuous language and spiritual change reversed

As anti-Catholic abuse becomes the language of virtue in *King Johan*, the language of spiritual change reflects this innovation. After the rebukes of Veritas, the Estates' change of heart is confirmed, in traditional fashion, by the change in their language, or rather by the change in the political and religious orientation of their language as they express anti-Catholic sentiments. Bale inverts the traditional use of changed vocabulary and tone in order to demonstrate the change of heart which Nobylyte, Clergye, and Cyvyle Order undergo as a result of the rebukes. Having earlier submitted to the Pope's authority (1180–83), Nobylyte joins in general condemnation of him, declaring in vividly abusive language:

> Thys bloudy bocher with hys pernycyouse bayte
> Oppresse Christen princes by frawde, crafte and dissayte,
> Tyll he compell them to kysse hys pestylent fete
> Lyke a levyathan syttynge in Moyses sete.
> (2407–10)

Nobylyte ends by naming the Pope '... that beaste and slauterman of the devyll, | That Babylon boore whych hath done so muche evyll' (2413–14).The terms of abuse he uses echo those used earlier by King Johan and Englande to characterize and condemn the Pope, but Nobylyte goes further by referring to him as a 'levyathan' or devil. These echoes indicate Nobylyte's understanding of the 'true' nature of the papacy, the one defined by the reformers.

Cyvyle Order follows with equally lively abuse of the Pope, saying:

> I thynke he hath spronge out of the bottomlesse pytt
> And in mennys conscyence in the stede of God doth sytt,
> Blowynge fourth a swarme of grassopers and flyes
> Monkes, fryers and priestes, that all truthe putrifyes.
> ....
> Exyle thys monster and ravenouse devourar
> Wyth hys venym wormes, hys adders, whelpes and snakes,
> Hys cuculled vermyne that unto all myschiefe wakes.
> (2423–6, 2428–30)

It is a spectacular innovation to use so much abuse in order to characterize what, in terms of the play's Protestant polemic, is a change from vice to virtue, in this case specifically a change from the vice of supporting papal authority to the virtue of supporting royal supremacy. The violence of the language indicates the thoroughness of the speaker's rejection of his former allegiance to papal authority. At the same time, the violently abusive language characterizes the papacy and its influence not only by images, but by that violence of tone and style. It again describes the papacy in apocalyptic terms which Bale would later use in his paraphrases of the Book of Revelation, including references to 'this greedy leviathan ... with his devouring locusts'.[21] The use of biblical imagery as insults in *King Johan* is particular to characters who condemn Catholicism, and reflects Protestant insistence on scriptural authority.[22]

Transgressive language and evil characters

While Bale introduces transgressive language into the speeches of virtuous characters, he does not reject its conventional use for characterizing evil. The character Sedicyon enters with all the entertaining transgressiveness of tempters in earlier moralities, but he does not tempt either King Johan or Englande. Sedicyon is presented as a Vyce, but he is more obviously evil than Mery Report in *Wether*. He resembles the conspirators in *Magnyfycence*, but unlike them declares his evil intentions directly to the King. Bale's innovation is to present his Vyce as a political rather than a moral evil, as the character's language expresses his opposition to royal authority. Bale emphasizes the transgressiveness of such language by placing it in the mouth of a character who bears all the visual and dramatic characteristics of traditional tempters.

---

[21] Bale, *The Image of Both Churches*, p. 425.
[22] Rainer Pineas, 'The Polemical Drama of John Bale', in W.R. Elton and W. Long, eds, *Shakespeare and the Dramatic Tradition* (Newark: University of Delaware Press, 1989), p. 197.

Sedicyon's transgressive vocabulary includes sexual references, but there is no hint of Mery Report's bawdy wit in Sedicyon's sexual jokes and insults. His sexual insults to Englande recall similar insults in the biblical plays and earlier moralities, but Bale extends Sedicyon's abuse of Englande, as two revised sections of the play end with the Vyce using similar sexual slurs. Bale may have extended the Vyce's transgressiveness in response to the growing popularity of such characters, but Sedicyon's protest: 'Thys queane doth not els but mocke our blessed storyes' (1907), recalls the sensitivity to mockery displayed by villains in the cycles of biblical plays, so that his protest emphasizes the rightness of Englande's condemnation.

As a Vyce, Sedicyon would be expected to use all forms of transgressive language including scatological references, but his scatological remarks are unlike Mery Report's in *Wether* both in tone and effect. Sedicyon uses scatological terms in his attacks on Englande, and on his fellow conspirators, where they emphasize his evil nature, but also reflect on his political role. The first instance is an insult to Englande, representing his defiance, and suggesting his desire to impose upon her a form of allegiance to his authority which is characterized as obscene by his scatological assertion.

Englande asks King Johan 'Commaund this felow to avoyd' (92), but Sedicyon tells the King: 'I wyll not awaye for that same wedred wytche; | She shall rather kysse wher as it doth not ytche' (95–6). In terms of political allegory Englande cannot get rid of the evil represented by Sedicyon. He intends to force the nation into his allegiance. However, in place of the kiss of fealty Sedicyon proposes one which is obscene and degrading. This characterizes those people who oppose royal supremacy, and what Bale represents here as the wishes of the nation, as being potentially in an obscene and degrading relationship with the political evil represented by Sedicyon.

Sedicyon's scatological insults represent a conventional attempt to degrade the significance of Englande's protests against the papacy. She complains: 'So noble a realme to stand tributarye, alas, | To the Devyls vycar!' (1755–6). Sedicyon responds: 'Out with thys harlot! Cockes sowle, she hath lete a farte!' (1757). However, this attempt to degrade Englande's complaint emphasizes Sedicyon's anger and disquiet, and illuminates the virtue of the complaint by comparison with the Vyce's response.

The hierarchy of evil authority in *King Johan* might be expected to have Usurpid Powre/the Pope at its head, since it is by his authority that the conspirators confront the King. Bale makes an important political statement, however, when he sets up Sedicyon iconographically and linguistically as the highest form of evil. Sedicyon's language is far more transgressive than Usurpid Powre's, and he has the ability to command all the other conspirators to carry him in order to demonstrate how the evils which the conspirators represent contribute to the entry of sedition into a kingdom. While Dissymulacyon has led in Privat Welth, and he has brought in Usurpid Powre,

Sedicyon demands that they should all carry him. They do so, and demonstrate iconographically how the evils represented by Dissymulacyon, Privat Welth, and Usurpid Powre support the political evil of sedition. The iconography is supplemented by Sedicyon's scatological threat to his porters: 'I wyll beshyte yow all yf ye sett me not downe softe' (804).

The Protestant audience would no doubt enjoy the threat, and the image it conjures up of their political and religious opponents being defiled and degraded. It is also a statement of the power that Sedicyon has achieved. The struggle in Protestant terms is no longer merely against papal authority, but against the treason and rebellion which is supported by the Church and threatens the peace of the realm. A Bakhtinian reading of Sedicyon's threat would imply the fertility and regeneration of ecclesiastical evils and abuses through the agency of sedition.

Bale links all the conspirators to Sedicyon through their use of transgressive language, and their changes of name. These shared characteristics provide stylistic links with the Vyce which reinforce the connections between the political evil which Sedicyon represents and the evils represented by the other conspirators. It is conventional for vices in morality plays to change from names representing preliminary abstract qualities to names representing altered abstract qualities; for example, Counterfet Countenaunce takes the name Good Demeynaunce in *Magnyfycence* in order to be accepted at court. In *King Johan*, however, the characters personifying evil change their names from abstractions such as Sedicyon and Usurpid Powre to the names of historical figures who were associated with the degradation and death of the historical King John. These name changes represent an innovation in morality drama.

Sedicyon takes four different names during the play, but the name Stevyn Langton identifies him with the historical figure who was appointed Archbishop of Canterbury against the wishes of King John; Usurpid Powre names himself Pope Innocent the Third, while Privat Welth is created Cardynall Pandulphus. The name changes in the play are remarkable not only because they refer to historical figures but because the original names of the characters signify the evil quality or purpose which Bale ascribes to the historical figure.

Historical details recorded in the chronicles indicate the nature of the involvement of the real Stephen Langton in the political and religious events in England during the reign of King John. As Peter Happé points out, the characterization of the historical figure is subject to Bale's 'polemical objectives';[23] nevertheless, the use of an historical character and aspects of his life for propaganda purposes in drama provided Bale with a concrete, rather than purely allegorical, means of illustrating the cost to king and country if

---

[23] Happé, ed., *The Complete Plays of John Bale*, p. 119, n. to l. 934.

support for royal supremacy should waver. This argument would have been persuasion in 1538, but if the 1560 version of the play was performed, then the representation of Langton's activity against John, and the reflection of that situation in the troubled times of Henry VIII, would have been received by the Elizabethan audience as confirmation, rather than persuasion, of the wisdom of maintaining supremacy.

Names become a form of transgressive language in *King Johan* as they signify political transgression in the form of resistance to royal supremacy.[24] The names and status of the historical figures make their conspiracy relevant to the audience since the Pope, cardinals, archbishops and monks were all involved in the struggle for power between Henry and the Church. Bale thus uses names in the play in accordance with his concern to support and promote Protestant reform, while the historical framework of the play ensures that all forms of language which express support for papal authority rather than royal authority would be interpreted as treason, and are therefore transgressive in both political and religious contexts.

New forms of transgressive language

Treason

Bale extends the range of transgressive language to include treasonous language, defined in the play as the rejection of the religious and political reforms made during the reign of Henry VIII, especially the denial of royal authority in favour of papal authority. Bale uses traditional forms of transgressive language to complement this innovation.[25]

In order to contextualize treasonous language, Bale begins the play with a declaration of divine right as King Johan introduces himself and defines the source of his authority, telling the audience:

> To shew what I am   I thynke yt convenyent:
> Johan, Kyng of Ynglond,   the cronyclys doth me call.
>   ....
> By the wyll of God   and his hygh ordynaunce,

---

[24] Pineas, 'The Polemical Drama of John Bale', p. 205.

[25] Treasonous language had particular contemporary significance at the time of the earlier (1538) version of the play: in 1534 the Act 26 Henry VIII, c. 13 had made it high treason to 'slanderously and maliciously publish and pronounce, by express writing or words, that the King ... should be heretic, schismatic'. G.R. Elton, *The Tudor Constitution* (Cambridge: Cambridge University Press, 1962), pp. 61–2. However, Bale appears rather to treat the much older offence of praemunire – support for papal authority against the crown – as treason. Ibid., pp. 330–32.

In Yerland and Walys, in Angoye and Normandye,
In Ynglond also, I have had the governaunce.
(8–9, 15–17)

The assertion that the King derives his authority directly from God implies the degree to which treason against the King is also an act of disobedience to God.[26]

Polarization of loyalty between royal and papal authority provides the dramatic movement in *King Johan*, and the vehemence with which that polarization is presented suggests the homogeneous nature of the audience. Sedicyon is unequivocally opposed to Johan's kingship, and he makes this plain in language which, while it does not use the vocabulary of insults, nonetheless insults the King. Sedicyon makes his attitude absolutely clear in a short arrogant speech in which he tells King Johan:

As I sayd afore, I am Sedycyon playne:
In every relygyon and munskysh secte I rayne,
Havyng yow prynces in scorne, hate and dysdayne.
(186–8)

His arrogance continues when he declares:

I hold upp the Pope as in other places many,
....
For his holy cawse I mayntayne traytors and rebelles,
That no prince can have his peples obedyence,
Except yt doth stand with the Popes prehemynence.
(212, 218–20)

Language which transgresses by openly scorning the legitimate power of a temporal king is an innovation.[27] In *Magnyfycence* the prince is only ridiculed *after* he has been ruined and degraded. His right to rule is not challenged before his fall.

The Estates adopt the language of treason after they have been corrupted, but Clergye makes a slip of the tongue *before* Sedicyon openly corrupts him. Early in the play, Cyvyle Order and Clergye seem to accept the authority of King Johan. He pardons their misdeeds and tells Clergye: ' aryse, and ever be obedyent, | And as God commandeth yow take us for yowre governere' (510), to which Clergye responds: 'By the grace of God, the Pope shall be my rulare' (512). The King questions this declaration, but Clergye corrects himself, saying: 'Ha, ded I stomble? I sayd my prynce ys my ruler' (514).

---

[26] Pineas, *Tudor and Stuart Anti-Catholic Drama*, p. 37.
[27] Although, significantly, it occurs in the cycles of biblical plays, though in a different form, when evil characters speak scornfully of Christ's kingship.

Clergye's excuse and correction are hardly convincing, and allow various interpretations: his allegiance to the Pope is so profound that he cannot make the change; the slip is an unwitting revelation of his true allegiance; or perhaps his oath is not a mistake but a mocking assertion of his continued allegiance to the Pope which he cynically supposes he can pass off as a slip of the tongue. This last alternative represents an insult to the King, but all the possible interpretations condemn the attitude of the clergy towards the secular power. *King Johan* dramatizes the corruption of the three Estates of society through their acceptance of papal authority, and their rejection of their allegiance to the King. They become responsible not for their own downfall, but for that of the King, through their acts of treason. This is a development of the process Skelton presents in *Magnyfycence* where the treatment of one character by others affects his identity. Bale dramatizes the part the Estates play in the subjugation of their King, but also draws attention to their importance by casting them in the significant moral role of the tempted.

Although Nobylyte eventually turns his back on his excommunicated King, he does not succumb to Sedicyon's corruption without protest. He asserts: 'Yt is clene agenst the nature of Nobelyte | To subdew his king with owt Godes autoryte' (1176–7). Nevertheless, when King Johan objects: '… this is no tokyn of trew nobelyte | To flee from yowre kyng in his extremyte' (1452–3), Nobylyte replies:

> I shall dyssyer yow as now to pardone me;
> I had moche rather do agaynst God, veryly,
> Than to Holy Chyrche to do any injurye.
> (1454–6)

Nobylyte's speech illustrates the consequences of the pressure exerted by the Church. Bale implies that the support which the English nobility have given the Church in its challenge to the King's authority is a form of sedition, or treason, but he does not condemn them. Although Nobylyte eventually betrays his King out of duty to the Church, he also acknowledges that his duty to his King is intimately connected with his duty to God. Bale thus characterizes allegiance to the Catholic Church as a challenge against God as well as against the King, and illustrates Nobylyte's reluctance to accept the choice which is forced upon him.

The distinction between the reluctant treason of Nobylyte and that of Cyvyle Order is Bale's politic apportioning of blame among the Estates. He does not criticize the Tudor nobility as savagely as the clergy and lawyers, but he uses the treasonous speeches of these latter characters to dramatize the way in which the Estates support and defend each other although their conduct is to the detriment of their King and the realm. Clergye's support for the Church is a willing act of treason; indeed, Sedicyon calls Clergye 'my frynd' (1238), suggesting a close link between the English clergy and betrayal of the state.[28] The forms this betrayal takes are expressed in Clergye's declaration of the means by which he will follow Sedicyon's injunction that he 'must mennys conscyence grope | .... | Every wher sture them   to make an insurreccyon' (1239, 1242). Clergye says he will:

>   saye throwgh his occacyon
> All we are under   the danger of dampnacyon;
> And this wyll move peple   to helpe to put hym downe,
> Or elles compel hym   to geve up septur and crowne.
> (1245–8)

As Clergye agrees to betray the King for the sake of the Pope and the Church, so Cyvyle Order, who frequently supports Clergye during the play, agrees to the same treason 'For the clargyes sake' (1258). Bale satirizes the sophistry of the legal profession as he condemns its part in the betrayal of the King when Cyvyle Order declares:

>   I wyll in every border
> Provoke the gret men   to take the commonys parte.
> With cautyllys of the lawe   I wyll so tyckle ther hart
> They shall thynke all good   that they shall passe upon,
> And so shall we cum   to ower full intent anon;
> For yf the Church thryve   than do we lawers thryve.
> (1258–63)

The part played by lawyers in the corruption of the magnates, and possibly of parliament, is defined as being founded in self-interest, and having no foundation in religious beliefs.

The corruption of the Estates illuminates the way the Catholic Church promotes and facilitates treason to maintain its power. The language of treason illustrates the process of, and the political and religious background to, the downfall of King Johan, while the parts played by the Estates in this downfall are carefully revealed by Bale through the characters' use of treasonous language so that the Tudor nobility are warned of their culpability, but not condemned absolutely.

Language expressing treasonous sentiments is a new form of linguistic transgression serving Bale's political purpose in *King Johan*, but as a Protestant dramatist he varies the forms of language through which he attacks the Church to extend the range and dramatic effectiveness of that attack.

---

[28] Bale's linking of the clergy with treason had contemporary relevance, given the clergy's opposition to royal supremacy which resulted in the 1534 Act for the submission of the clergy (25 Henry VIII, c. 19). See Haigh, *English Reformations*, pp. 108–15, and Elton, *Tudor Constitution*, p. 339.

Innovative use of new and existing forms signal the difference between his reforming play and earlier Catholic drama to an audience which shares his Protestant views, but might be critical of his use of traditional dramatic devices. Bale's use of ludic references extends the forms of transgressive language, associates Catholicism closely with its own use of drama, and simultaneously condemns it as fictive spectacle.

Ludic references as transgressive language

Bale uses terms associated with drama to condemn both the deceit and the superficial ceremony which he and other Protestants attributed to the Catholic Church. Virtuous characters use ludic references to mock and insult the Catholic clergy and Catholic rites.[29]

'Disguising', in the sense of acting in plays, is used in *King Johan* as a term which criticizes the Catholic clergy and defines their preaching as specious role-playing. Englande describes the clergy as: 'Such lubbers as hath dysgysed heades in their hoodes' (36). 'Disguising' in the sense of acting condemns the priesthood for superficiality, but Englande's reference also recalls the representation of evil characters in earlier moralities, like Clokyd Colusyon in *Magnyfycence*, who tells the audience 'Two faces in a hode covertly I bere' (710). This image always connotes deception, and in *King Johan* it emphasizes the insult to the Catholic clergy.

The Catholic characters in *King Johan* also use ludic references, but not as insults. As they use them, the references are one form of the self-revelatory language which expresses their seditious, proud, complacent, and contemptuous sentiments.

Self-revelatory language and confession

Self-revelatory language is Bale's extension of the conventional self-revealing language of tempters in earlier moralities, which he uses to satirize the cynicism and vices of the Catholic Church and clergy and illuminate the folly of their congregations. The significance of this language lies in its use by characters who represent the evils of Catholicism.

The significance of drama as a manifestation of Catholicism is highlighted when Privat Welth tells his fellow conspirators Dissymulacyon and Sedicyon: 'Of me, Privat Welth, cam fyrst Usurpyd Powre: | Ye may perseyve yt in pagent here this howre' (785–6). The relationship between Privat Welth and the Pope is important in terms of Bale's representation of a structure or

---

[29] Walker, *Plays of Persuasion*, p. 191.

hierarchy of political evil in *King Johan*, and when Privat Welth identifies the dramatization of that relationship as a 'pagent' he adds significance to the dramatization.

The word 'pagent' refers only to the episode in the play which dramatizes the connection between Privat Welth and the power of the Pope; it does not refer to the whole play, but is used by Bale in contradistinction to it. 'Pagent' is significant for its association with the Catholic cycles of biblical plays, and its Latin root *pagina* recalls the privileged place of Latin in Catholicism. For Bale and other Protestants the biblical plays represented part of the Catholic neglect of Scripture in favour of mediated spectacle.[30] The 'pagent' not only dramatizes the relationship of various forms of clerical evil and abuse, but does so in terms of Catholic didactic drama. The superficial spectacle implied, in Protestant terms, by a 'pagent' becomes a revelation of evil, and by identifying the episode which illustrates the relationship between Privat Welth and the Pope as a 'pagent', Bale suggests the theatrical nature of Catholicism itself.

Privat Welth's reference to the 'pagent' problematizes the association of a dramatic style and genre with Catholicism. The character's use of the term reveals his complacent acceptance, in contrast to the Protestant audience's rejection, of a religion depending heavily on spectacle and theatricality. Other characters use this revelatory mode of speech, and it constitutes another new form of transgressive language which characterizes the evil of the Catholic characters.

Self-revelatory language transgresses as it expresses sentiments which uphold the power and corrupt practices of the Catholic Church and clergy, or defies the authority of King Johan.[31] Sedicyon's expressions of treasonous sentiments are the most explicit and frequent form of self-revelatory language in the play, but there are others. Sedicyon hears Dissymulacyon approaching and makes the insulting observation: 'Lyst, for Godes passyon! I trow her cummeth sum hoggherd | Callyng for his pyggys: such a noyse I never herd!' (637). His language recalls and continues logically the pig imagery used by Englande at the beginning of the play. While such insulting language is consistent with Sedicyon's characterization as a Vyce, his use of the same terminology as Englande suggests his contempt for the Church and justifies the Protestant condemnation of Catholicism.[32] Sedicyon's contempt demonstrates that those who support the authority of the Church over the King do not, in fact, do so out of religious conviction, but make use of it for their own treacherous purposes. It is significant to the dramatic impact of the play that

---

[30] Ibid., p. 193.
[31] Edwin Shepard Miller, 'The Roman Rite in Bale's *King Johan*', *PMLA*, 64 (1949), 804–22, p. 804.
[32] Pineas, 'The Polemical Drama of John Bale', p. 205.

Sedicyon's contempt precedes the episode in which he is carried by the other conspirators.

King Johan uses the image of priests as mummers as an insult, but one of the conspirators also speaks of 'mummyng'. Dissymulacyon tells Sedicyon how he controls the activities of the clergy in order to make money. He says:

> I appoynt yche man his place:
> Sum to syng Latyn, and sum to ducke at grace;
> Sum to go mummyng, and sum to beare the crosse.
> (698–700)

Dissymulacyon's use of 'mummyng' is an echo by which he unintentionally confirms the King's opinion of priests as actors merely performing a role without any real devotion to the religion they serve and preach.

The priest Treason reveals the cynicism of the priesthood and extends the satire on external show when he speaks of holy water, altars, ashes, and other signs pertaining to Catholic rituals as 'suche lyke trashes' (1830), thus acknowledging the priesthood's awareness of the falseness of the ceremonial and symbols of the Church. Bale does not, however, include in the list any of the signs or symbols of Christianity, only the accoutrements of the Church and priesthood.

Dissymulacyon boasts of the power of Latin, not for its liturgical significance, but as a means of making money, when he declares:

> I can make Latten to brynge this gere to the boxe.
> Tushe, Latten ys alone to brynge soche mater to passe;
> Ther ys no Englyche that can soche profyghtes compasse.
> And therfor we wyll no servyce to be songe,
> Gospell nor pystell but all in Latten tonge.
> (715–19)

Dissymulacyon's support for Latin derives its force ultimately from the reformers' long-standing objections to the use of Latin, which denied the individual the facility for understanding either the liturgy or the Bible without the mediation of priests, but the speech mocks popular devotion to the traditional use of Latin in the liturgy by showing that the Church's insistence on the retention of Latin is not based on religious or doctrinal grounds, but on the money that could be made from its use. At the same time, this satirizes the continuing devotion of many people to a language they could not understand.[33]

Bale frequently attacks the Church in *King Johan* for what he depicts as its preoccupation with making money out of its congregation, but when he addresses the issue of the clergy's reluctance to submit to taxation it is in comic

---

[33] Kendall, *The Drama of Discontent*, p. 97.

terms which nevertheless reveal the political orientation of the Church as it disadvantages the kingdom and the people. Nobylyte and Clergye discuss the problem, and at this point in the play Nobylyte is still loyal to his King, and defends him against Clergye, who complains: 'He demaundeth of us the tenth parte of owre lyvyng | .... | ... to recover that he hath lost in Fraunce' (593–5). Nobylyte asks: 'And thynke ye not that a mater nessesary?' to which Clergye replies: 'No, sur, by my trowth, he takyng yt of the clergy'. This prompts an objection from Nobylyte: 'Ye cowde be content that he shuld take yt of us?' and Clergye responds with comic honesty: 'Yea, so that he wold spare the clargy, by swet Jesus! | This takyng of us myght sone growe to a custom' (597–601). To an audience composed of men accustomed to paying taxes, Clergye's response would be a comic and derisive reflection on the freedom from taxation permitted to the Church.

Other forms of self-revelatory language are less obvious than Clergye's. Bale uses the concept of lying, but this differs markedly from Skelton's use of lies in *Magnyfycence* where the lies of his characters are a means of excusing princely misjudgement. In *King Johan* the lie covertly addresses the most sensitive and dangerous topic in English religion during the Reformation. A fundamental difference in belief between Catholics and reformers was, as it had been since the time of Wyclif, their attitudes to transubstantiation, but only some reformers at this time denied the real presence of Christ in the Eucharist. Henry VIII continued to believe in the doctrine of transubstantiation,[34] as did Cranmer.[35] By 1539, and with Henry's support, one of the Six Articles laid down the penalty of death by burning 'without opportunity for recantation' for denial of transubstantiation,[36] so Bale's criticism of this belief, which he included in the 1538 version of the play, is understandably subtle and cautious.

Dissymulacyon tells Sedicyon of his plan to murder King Johan by poisoning him, and he wants Sedicyon's help in justifying the crime. Dissymulacyon tells Sedicyon: '... thys must thu saye to colour the thynge | That a penye lofe he wolde have brought to a shyllynge' (2022–3). Sedicyon objects: 'Naye, that is suche a lye as easely wyll be felte' (2024), but Dissymulacyon explains:

> Tush, man, amonge fooles it never wyll be out smelte,
> Though it be a great lye. Set upon it a good face,
> And that wyll cause men beleve it in every place.
> (2026–8)

---

[34] Walker, *Plays of Persuasion*, p. 203.
[35] Cranmer did not change his view until 1546. See MacCulloch, *Thomas Cranmer*, p. 102.
[36] Haigh, *English Reformations*, p. 153.

As Sedicyon suggests that some lies are just too obvious to fool anyone, Bale draws attention to clerical contempt for the people who Dissymulacyon depicts as easily deceived as long as the deception is carried off boldly; and Bale satirizes those who are duped by such obvious lies. The inflated price of the penny loaf, however, together with Dissymulacyon's mockery of the ease with which a gross deception may be practised, suggests an allusion to the most radical reformers' view of transubstantiation. People would believe the lie that the value of the penny loaf had been increased by the King to what appears to be an unbelievable degree simply because it is told boldly. To radical reformers the changing of bread into the real body of Christ was just such an unbelievable lie, and people were convinced of its truth simply because the Church maintained the fiction boldly. However, like the lie which Dissymulacyon proposes Sedicyon should tell about the King, the real presence was also a fiction concocted by the clergy for their own devious purposes.

The full impact of Bale's comment on belief in transubstantiation is felt in Sedicyon's objection that Dissymulacyon's lie is unbelievable, since this suggests the Church's own understanding of the degree to which it was maintaining a fiction. Transubstantiation is linked by Bale in this brief exchange to the cynical duplicity of the Church which in turn is revealed in its connection to the evil represented by Sedicyon, and the deadly deceit by which Dissymulacyon is about to cause the death of King Johan. Transubstantiation, as Bale represents it, is not merely a doctrinal problem, but is related to political evils which will bring about the destruction of secular power.

Bale uses the revelatory language of the Catholic characters in the play to focus attention on the cynical attitude of the Church towards its most devoted supporters as the conspirators discuss the support given to the Church by the Irish. This episode not only exposes the Church's attitude but mocks the rebellious Irish, as Usurpid Powre remarks:

> They gett no money, but they shall have clene remyssion,
> For those Yrysh men are ever good to the Church;
> When kynges dysobeye yt then they begynne to worch.
> (967–9)

Privat Welth adds: 'And all that they do ys for indulgence and pardon' (970), and Sedicyon adds, with Vyce-like cynicism: 'By the messe, and that is not worth a rottyn wardon' (971). His cynical observation concerning the worth of indulgences mocks the Irish, and confirms the Protestant view of these Catholic practices, adding to the entertainment. The mockery of the unsophisticated Irish continues in Usurpid Powre's final remark: 'What care we for that? To them yt is venyson' (972).

Mockery of the Irish would have been entertaining to a Protestant audience in 1538, and in 1560. The Irish rebellion of 1534 would have been fresh in the memories of the play's influential spectators at the former date.[37] The unrevised A text in which the reference to the Irish occurs pre-dates Bale's own unsuccessful appointment as Bishop of Ossory and so it would originally have been relevant to the political events rather than to Bale's own prejudice, although Ireland continued to be a problem throughout the Tudor era and mockery of the Irish would have been acceptable entertainment for the later audience. The mocking of a rebellious faction by those it is rebelling against is amusing propaganda, but mockery of a rebellious faction by those who are supposed to be its friends not only makes fun of the innocence of the faction, but illustrates the hypocrisy of the friends, and provides particular entertainment for those who are at odds with both.

A conventional form of transgressive language, self-revelatory language, and the sacrament of confession all coincide as Dissymulacyon asks for absolution from Usurpid Powre. He kneels, saying: '*A pena et culpa* that I may this day stand clere' (848). Usurpid Powre asks: '... dost thow not preche the Gospell?' (855), and Dissymulacyon replies: 'No, I promyse yow, I defye yt to the devyll of hell!' (856). This reply is almost farcical in its transgressiveness, while Usurpid Powre's response: 'Yf I knewe thow dedyst thow shuldest have non absolucyon' (857) continues the comedy as it suggests that absolution is given for the wrong reasons. The Protestant audience would enjoy the transgressiveness as Usurpid Powre's interest in Dissymulacyon's preaching confirms the Protestant allegation that the Catholic clergy rejected the word of God.

Throughout the play self-revelatory language represents a parodic and perverted form of confession in which the speaker declares his, or the Church's, deeds and opinions, unaware, or unconcerned that he is actually confessing to treason or deception. A character who 'confesses' in this way unknowingly, as Clergye protests against taxation, makes himself look foolish, but a character such as Sedicyon who boldly 'confesses' his treacherous allegiance to Rome indicates his pride, and complacency. Neither kind of character understands his fault, and so neither asks forgiveness – the primary purpose of confession in the Catholic Church. This unawareness and complacency form part of Bale's careful attack on the sacrament of confession in *King Johan*.

The language of Catholicism problematized

The language of the Catholic sacraments, liturgy, and doctrine are all problematized by Bale in *King Johan*. Auricular confession did not have

---

[37] Guy, *Tudor England*, p. 357.

Henry's unequivocal support in 1538,[38] and parody of confession recurs in the play. Bale, nevertheless, treads a fine line between offending Henry and persuading him that the practice of confession was corrupt and open to abuse. The attack on confession throughout the play focuses on the dissemination of treason facilitated by the secrecy attending the sacrament. By focusing on the misuse of the sacrament as a means of subverting royal authority, Bale could criticize confession through an appeal to patriotism.

When Sedicyon, in the human, historical form of Stevyn Langton, takes on the role of confessor, his identity as the Vyce confers an extra dimension of evil on the character of the Archbishop, and mocks the sacrament as he administers it. Sedicyon hears the confession of Nobylyte but will not absolve him until he has preached the Pope's message against King Johan to Nobylyte. Bale dramatizes the use of the confessional as a means of suborning the population and as he parodies the blessing he draws attention to the source of authority which confession disguises. Sedicyon tells Nobylyte:

> I assoyle the here from the kynges obedyence
> By the auctoryte of the Popys magnifycence:
> *Auctoritate romani pontyficis ego absolvo te*
> From all possessyons gevyn to the spiritualte,
> *In nomine domini pape, amen.*
> (1184–8)

The speech makes a series of significant points as it parodies the confessor's blessing. Nobylyte is absolved not from his sins, but from his duty to his King; it is done on the authority of the Pope, rather than on God's authority, but more than this, it is the 'magnificent' Pope who provides the authority. The image of temporal magnificence would remind the audience of the greed of Rome and conflicts with the spiritual significance of confession and absolution. This is done in English; but in his parody of the Latin words of absolution Sedicyon comically absolves Nobylyte of all the possessions he has donated to the Church. This is the playfulness of the Vyce which Bale uses to subvert the spirituality associated with the sacrament.

Confession is linked to the fate of the King in the structure of the play, as well as in its plot. The Estates – Nobylyte, Cyvyle Order, and Clergye – are all given absolution in exchange for their disloyalty to King Johan. The King himself, having submitted to the Pope's authority, undergoes confession, but even this is a parody, as the King says: '*Confiteor Domino Pape et omnibus cardinalibus eius et vobis, quia peccavi nimis exigendo ab ecclesia tributum, mea culpa*' (1789–90). The sin to which he confesses is that of exacting taxes

---

[38] Walker, *Plays of Persuasion*, p. 213. See also Haigh, *English Reformations*, p. 153.

from the Church. He confesses to the Pope and is absolved in the name of the Pope, Langton, and the Apostles Peter and Paul, not in the name of God.

This parody of confession dramatizes the Protestant view of the sacrament. The absolution King Johan receives does not represent the mercy and forgiveness of God, since it is spoken in the name of the Pope, nor does it represent the forgiveness of the Pope or the Church. It does represent the worthlessness of a ceremony which is detached from God's authority, and the duplicity which lies behind it, and far from signalling the mercy of the Church, King Johan's confession signals only the assertion of its power. The full significance of this power is revealed in the parodic confessions which follow the King's.

Auricular confession is satirized for its association with the treachery of priests as the priest Treason is brought before the King, who remarks in surprise: 'A pryste and a traytour? How maye that wele agree?' (1811), to which Treason replies: 'Yes, yes, wele ynough, underneth *Benedicite*' (1812). He goes on to explain how, under the secrecy conferred by the confessional, he has made 'Twenty thousande traytour' (1817) and 'made Nobylyte to be obedyent | To the Churche of Rome' (1819–20). Treason's admission is part of a long revision in which King Johan's authority to judge the criminal priest is contested vigorously by Sedicyon, the Cardynall, and Treason himself, who defends his right to benefit of clergy in spite of his crimes. In both the earlier and later versions of the play the King's attempt to assert his authority fails. The revision links the treachery of the priesthood to confession with an explicitness which would have been impolitic in 1538.

Confession in *King Johan* represents a channel of power which directly conflicts with that of the King, and it is dramatized in such a way as to illustrate the process by which auricular confession facilitates the dissemination of plans and ideas posing a direct and personal threat to the sovereign and his authority. Once that authority has been undermined by the corruption of the Estates through the medium of confession, there is nothing, and no one, to stand between the realm and its destruction by its enemies. Bale makes the point that royal resistance to the Church is not enough to secure the safety of the realm, that the Church's power to alienate the Estates must be curbed, and that power is wielded through confession. He also makes the telling observation that the sovereign's acceptance of confession does not lessen the danger, but rather increases it. The Latin associated with confession: '*Benedicite*', '*A pena et culpa*', and '*ego absolvo te*', itself becomes transgressive as it is shown to be the language which brackets acts of treason in the play. Other forms of language specifically associated with Catholicism become transgressive as Bale illustrates the deception and treachery which they signify.

The use of oaths, which characterizes sinfulness in earlier drama, takes on a particular Catholic significance in *King Johan*. Bale's delight in reduplication serves to emphasize Catholic devaluation of their own language of devotion, by turning it into common oaths. Sedicyon's most frequent oath is 'by the masse', which he uses eighteen times. Bale uses one oath as a subtle means of drawing attention to Catholicism as superficial spectacle. Clergye protests at King Johan's criticism of the ceremonies and external signs of the Catholic faith: 'Yow wold have no churche, I wene, by thes sacred bones' (428). By his oath Clergye restates his allegiance to external signs, rather than faith itself, since 'sacred bones' refers to the relics treasured by the Catholic Church.

Catholic devotion to the Virgin Mary is cast as a challenge to the ties of affection between state and people in the exchange between Englande, Commynalte her son, and Cardynall Pandulphus. Commynalte has been overawed by the Cardynall and tells King Johan 'I must nedes obbay whan Holy Chirch commandyth me' (1609). Englande tells Commynalte: 'Yf thow leve thy kyng take me never for thy mother' (1610). Her passionate statement is mocked by the Cardynall, who calls after Commynalte as he leaves 'Tush, care not thow for that, I shall provyd the another' (1611).[39] The subversion of filial affection which the Cardynall's words imply are a comment on the Church's willingness to destroy the firmest ties of loyalty and affection, not only between mother and son, but more significantly between the King and his subjects. Through this exchange Bale also mocks the devotion of the people to the Virgin Mary, which leads them away from the love of king and country, personified here as the natural loving relationship between mother and son. This represents the ideal relationship between the people and the state, and through his satire Bale questions whether the people believe there can be another relationship which provides the unique exchange of love, loyalty, and support which is personified in the image of Englande as mother.

Bale extends his condemnation of the Catholic Church and its ceremonies, and significantly extends the forms of transgressive language, by parodying the language of the Catholic liturgy. The Litany is parodied as Dissymulacyon enters singing:

Sancte Dominice, ora pro nobis.
...
Sa[n]cte Francisse, ora pro nobis.
(639, 641)

---

[39] In his *Confutation of Tyndale's Answer*, More wrote of 'the mother of all chyrches the chyrche of Rome', and in his *Responsio ad Lutherum* that 'every church of the faithful recognises and venerates the holy see of Rome as mother'. Bale may have had Catholic opinions such as these in mind when he constructed the Cardynall's speech. More, *The Confutation of Tyndale's Answer*, p. 917, and *Responsio ad Lutherum*, p. 345. Janette Dillon observes that 'the strategy of the Tudor state ... was to present an image of the monarch as caring parent'. Dillon, *Language and Stage*, p. 99.

He continues with a parodic *Pater noster* in which he prays for the death of King Johan, 'Or elles Holy Chyrche shall never thryve' (645).

Sedicyon asks Dissymulacyon: 'Tell me, good felowe, makyste thow this prayer for me?' (646). Dissymulacyon replies:

> Ye are as ferce as thowgh ye had broke yowre nose at the buttre.
> I medyll not with the, but here to good sayntes I praye,
> Agenst soch enmyes as wyll Holy Chyrche decaye.
> (647–9)

He prays again for help against King Johan although he is confronted with a character who bears the visual characteristics of a devil, in the shape of Sedicyon's swollen nose.[40] Dissymulacyon makes a choice which satirizes the function of the Church by avoiding confrontation with the enemy of humanity. Even if the audience do not make the visual connection with the devils of earlier drama, the circumstances to which Dissymulacyon attributes the swollen nose suggest that the Church avoids confronting sin as it appears in the world, preferring to persecute virtuous reformers, like King Johan, who will bring about the downfall of the Church, rather than confronting the devil, who will bring about the downfall of human souls.

The parody of the Vespers for the Dead sung by Usurpid Powre and Privat Welth signifies their unity, and is an early allusion to their murderous purpose. It is also a subtle addition to Bale's polemic which suggests the alien nature of the Catholic Church as it rejects the word of God. Usurpid Powre begins the song: '*Super flumina Babilonis suspendimus organa nostra*' and Privat Welth continues: '*Quomodo cantabimus canticum bonum in terra aliena*' (764–5). In the Psalm from which these lines derive it is *canticum Domini* which cannot be sung,[41] but Privat Welth sings 'How shall we sing a *good* song in a strange land'. The simple change Bale makes from *domini* to *bonum* is all that is required to construct his satire.

The altered biblical reference serves Bale's thematic criticisms of the Church by suggesting that the papacy, represented by Usurpid Powre, and the clergy, represented by Privat Welth, regard England as an alien land,[42] and by illustrating the Catholic Church's manipulation of biblical texts. The substitution of the word 'good' for the biblical 'lord's' song also suggests that the Church rejects the 'lord's' song, or the word of God, in favour of something else it mistakenly regards as 'good'.

This parody, turning on the substitution of one word, demonstrates Bale's skill, and challenges his reputation as 'bilious Bale'. While he is notorious for

---

[40] Happé, *The Complete Plays of John Bale*, n. to l. 647.
[41] Weber, ed., *Biblia sacra*, Ps. 136: 4.
[42] Pineas, 'The Polemical Drama of John Bale', p. 207.

attacking his religious opponents with robust insults, the criticisms of Catholicism he constructs around that one altered word illustrate his ability to work at a more subtle, and perhaps more effective level, because it shows a degree of wit which would have appealed to his educated, élite audience, and provides modulation in the tone of his polemic which makes for more effective drama.

Language against language

King Johan reveals Bale's deep concern with the use and abuse of language. The excommunication of the King and interdiction of Englande represent the exercising of supreme papal authority through the medium of language, but Englande is not impressed by the curse of excommunication, and in her resolution to continue her association with the King she defies ecclesiastical law, telling Cardynall Pandulphus: 'I beshrow yowre hartes so have ye me onpursed. | Yf he be acurssed than are we a mete cuppell' (1617–18). Not only does she transgress by defying the law governing association with excommunicants,[43] but she does so with a curse of her own: 'I beshrow yowre hartes', which is a form of linguistic transgression more familiarly associated with sinful and evil characters.

Englande's curse has both dramatic and moral value, although it may not seem to be indicative of virtue. It can be interpreted as a naturalistic oath; it may, however, be interpreted as robust, and virtuous, defiance of the Catholic Church as the vernacular English curse is set against the traditional language of ecclesiastical authority. King Johan has already challenged that authority in more formal terms after he has been informed of his excommunication. Cyvyle Order tells him: '... ye are a man defylyd' (1423). The King asks: 'How am I defylyd?' (1424), and Cyvyle Order replies: 'By the Pope's hye powre ye are excommynycate' (1425). King Johan makes a statement which puts forward the reformist belief when he declares: 'That sentence or curse that scriptur doth not dyrect | In my opynyon shall be of non effecte' (1432–3). Englande's curse may refer back to this statement, so that by her defiance of the Great Curse, against which she utters the most colloquial and common curse, she defines papal excommunication as no more effective than her own transgressive language.

Englande's curse denies the power of the traditional language of authority, and defines the Church's use of language as an abuse of its power and authority.[44] Throughout *King Johan*, Bale contrasts Catholic abuse of language

---

[43] See Chapter 1 above.
[44] Duncan, 'The Play as Tudor Propaganda', p. 70.

to the virtuous characters' language of abuse. He demonstrates the persuasive power of language in the correction of the Estates, but he also problematizes its signifying power as he shows how the language of confession conceals treason, and how lies may be accepted if told with sufficient conviction. As he parodies the language of the liturgy he demonstrates that even the most traditionally authoritative language is open to perversion and manipulation, and its signifying power is therefore unstable unless grounded, like royal authority, in Scripture.

Bale himself comes close to transgressing the limits of politic language for a Protestant simply by writing *King Johan*. However, a play which does not represent the mysteries of religion avoids the primary source of Protestant disquiet. Bale's use of historical characters as part of his allegory, and the changes he makes in his use of traditional forms and functions of transgressive language, also distance and differentiate *King Johan* from Catholic drama.

The degree to which virtuous characters use transgressive language is an innovation in this play. It does not characterize them in any pejorative sense, but, because they speak in support of royal supremacy, the abusive terms they use function as vivid and accurate metaphors for the conduct and corruption of the papacy and clergy. Conversely, language which supports the Catholic Church or is associated with its rites and ceremonies is contextualized as transgressive.

Corruption in *King Johan* is focused on the Estates, and is a political rather than a personal, moral danger, since the King's virtue is never compromised. The corruption and recuperation of the Estates is signalled through a further innovation, as Bale inverts the traditional device of linguistic change signifying spiritual change. In *King Johan* the change is from language which supports the Church to language which reviles it in the most violent terms, but represents virtue in accordance with reformist views.

Bale's ample use of transgressive language, together with the variety of techniques he uses (comedy, parody, word-slips, and mockery), drive the play towards its climax in which the King abdicates. However, by his continued use of the same techniques after this reversal, Bale shows that nothing has actually changed, nor does it change until after the King's death. This represents a powerful political comment on the necessity for the contemporary monarch to withstand the Catholic Church.

The abusive terms Bale uses to characterize the evils he associates with Catholicism are often memorable in their violent transgressiveness, and they would have entertained an audience of influential reformers. However, Bale's polemic is structured to take into account the continuing attachment of Henry VIII, and less radical reformers, to some aspects of Catholic doctrine, and is cautious and subtle in its approach to these topics. *King Johan*, therefore, provides evidence that Bale's reputation as 'bilious', and Thora Balslev Blatt's comment that his use of invective tends 'to accumulated tediousness'[45] are both ill-deserved in this instance. Moreover, *King Johan* demonstrates Bale's skill and subtlety in his use of transgressive language, as he varies its forms to create effective and entertaining drama, which is thus more effective propaganda.

The frequent metalinguistic references in the play foreground language as the site of cultural conflict. The King, for example, tells Sedicyon: 'Thow semyste by thy wordes to have no more wytt than a coote' (176). This denial of value and meaning to Sedicyon's language is echoed in his own insult to Englande: 'Holde your tunge, ye whore, or by the messe ye shall repent!' (1714), representing a Catholic attempt to prevent Protestant speech. The power struggle dramatized in Bale's use of transgressive language reflects, in part, real conflicts fought through the medium of language in the first half of the sixteenth century, such as that between More and Luther and that which John Guy has called the 'battle of the books', between More and Christopher St German.[46] Such conflicts would no doubt have destabilized the old moral polarities associated with language, and since language was the battleground of the Reformation, we should understand Bale's use of vituperation in *King Johan* in its wider cultural context.

In his use of transgressive language Bale broke down the traditional moral significance associated with specific forms of language. Dramatists before Bale had not challenged or altered that moral significance even when, like the *Mankind* playwright, and John Skelton, they had perceived the semiotic instability of language. For these Catholic writers that instability was a cause of anxiety, for Bale it enabled him to make his most important innovations in *King Johan*. His naturalistic use of insults and the use of transgressive language by virtuous characters in the play show that words signify virtue or vice according to the contexts in which they are used, including the purpose of the speaker, rather than in accordance with an authorized tradition of signification. His use of transgressive language in support of Protestantism denied language a moral privilege derived from tradition by showing clearly that it has no inherent moral significance but derives this from the purposes for which people use it.

---

[45] Blatt, *The Plays of John Bale*, p. 222.
[46] John Guy, 'Thomas More and Christopher St German: The Battle of the Books', in Alistair Fox and John Guy, *Reassessing the Henrician Age: Humanism, Politics and Reform, 1500–1550* (Oxford: Basil Blackwell, 1986), p. 105.

Bibliography

Primary sources

Ackrill, J. L., ed., *A New Aristotle Reader* (Oxford: Clarendon Press, 1987).
Aquinas, St Thomas, *Summa Theologiae*, trans. Marcus Lefébure, 60 vols, vol. 38, 2a2æ (London: Eyre and Spottiswoode, 1975).
Axton, Richard, and Peter Happé, eds, *The Plays of John Heywood* (Cambridge: D.S. Brewer, 1991).
Beadle, Richard, ed., *The York Plays* (London: Edward Arnold, 1982).
Beadle, Richard, and Pamela King, eds, *The York Mystery Plays: A Selection in Modern Spelling* (Oxford: Clarendon Press, 1984).
Benson, Larry D., ed., *The Riverside Chaucer*, 3rd edn (Oxford: Oxford University Press, 1987).
Blake, N.F., ed., *Quattuor Sermones*, Middle English Texts 2 (Heidelberg: Carl Winter Universitätsverlag, 1975).
Brandeis, Arthur, ed., *Jacob's Well*, part 1, EETS OS 115 (London: Kegan Paul, Trench, Trübner, 1900).
Cawley, A.C., ed., *The Wakefield Pageants in the Towneley Cycle* (Manchester: Manchester University Press, 1958).
Christmas, Henry, ed., *Selected Works of John Bale*, Parker Society (Cambridge: Cambridge University Press, 1849).
Cigman, Gloria, ed., *Lollard Sermons*, EETS 294 (Oxford: Oxford University Press, 1989).
Craig, Hardin, ed., *Two Coventry Corpus Christi Plays*, EETS ES 87 (London: Oxford University Press, 1957).
Davidson, Clifford, ed., *A Tretise of Myraclis Pleyinge*, Early Drama, Art and Music Monograph Series 19, Medieval Institute Publications (Kalamazoo: Western Michigan University, 1993).
Davis, Nicholas, 'Allusions to Medieval Drama in Britain: A Findings List (3)', *Medieval English Theatre*, 5:2 (1983), pp. 83–6.
Davis, Norman, ed., *Paston Letters and Papers of the Fifteenth Century*, 2 parts (Oxford: Clarendon Press, 1971).
Eccles, Mark, ed., *The Macro Plays*, EETS 262 (London: Oxford University Press, 1969).
Embree, Dan, and Elizabeth Urquhart, eds, *The Simonie: A Parallel-Text Edition*, Middle English Texts 24 (Heidelberg: Carl Winter Universitätsverlag, 1991).
Erbe, Theodore, ed., *Mirk's Festial: A Collection of Homilies by Johannes Mirkus*, EETS ES 97 (London: Kegan Paul, Trench, Trübner, 1905).
Farmer, John S., ed., *The Spider and the Fly, by John Heywood*, Early English Dramatists (Guildford: Charles W. Traylen, 1966).
Foster, Frances A., ed., *The Northern Passion*, 2 vols, EETS OS 145, 147 (London: Kegan Paul, Trench, Trübner, 1913, 1916).
Furnivall, Frederick J., ed., *Robert of Brunne's 'Handlyng Synne'*, parts 1 and 2, EETS OS 119, 123 (London: Kegan Paul, Trench, Trübner, 1901, 1903).

Grattan, J.H.G., and G.F.H. Sykes, eds, *The Owl and the Nightingale*, EETS ES 119 (London: Oxford University Press, 1935).
Happé, Peter, ed., *English Mystery Plays* (London: Penguin, 1975).
Happé, Peter, ed., *The Complete Plays of John Bale 1*, Tudor Interludes IV (Cambridge: D.S. Brewer, 1985).
Hudson, Anne, ed., *Two Wycliffite Texts*, EETS OS 301 (Oxford: Oxford University Press, 1993).
Hulme, William Henry, ed., *The English Harrowing of Hell and Gospel of Nicodemus*, EETS ES 100 (London: Kegan Paul, Trench, Trübner, 1907).
Lucian, *Icaromenippus, or the Sky-Man*, trans. A.M. Harmon, 7 vols, vol. 2, Loeb Classical Library (London: William Heinemann, 1915).
Lumiansky, R.M., and David Mills, eds, *The Chester Mystery Cycle*, 2 vols, EETS SS 3 (London: Oxford University Press, 1974), EETS SS 9 (Oxford: Oxford University Press, 1986).
Lyall, Roderick, ed., *Ane Satyre of The Thrie Estaitis*, Canongate Classic 18 (Edinburgh: Canongate Publishing, 1989).
Manzaloui, M.A., ed., *Secretum Secretorum*, vol. 1, EETS 276 (Oxford: Oxford University Press, 1977).
Matthew, F.D., ed., *The English Works of Wyclif Hitherto Unprinted*, EETS OS 74 (London: Trübner, 1880).
Meech, Sandford Brown, ed., *The Book of Margery Kempe*, vol. 1, EETS OS 212 (London: Oxford: University Press, 1940).
Mills, David, ed., *The Chester Mystery Cycle*, Medieval Texts and Studies 9 (East Lansing, Mich.: Michigan State University, 1992).
More, St Thomas, *Responsio ad Lutherum*, ed., John M. Headley, *The Complete Works of St. Thomas More*, vol. 5 (New Haven: Yale University Press, 1969).
More, St Thomas, *A Dialogue Concerning Heresies*, ed. Thomas M.C. Lawler, Germain Marc'hadour, and Richard C. Marius, *The Complete Works of St. Thomas More*, vol. 6, part II (New Haven: Yale University Press, 1980).
More, St Thomas, *The Confutation of Tyndale's Answer*, ed. Louis A. Schuster, Richard C. Marius, James P. Lusardi, and Richard J. Schoeck, *The Complete Works of St. Thomas More*, vol. 8 (New Haven: Yale University Press, 1973).
Morris, Richard, ed., *Dan Michel's Ayenbite of Inwit*, EETS OS 23 (London: Trübner, 1866).
Nelson, Venetia, ed., *A Myrour to Lewde Men and Wymmen*, Middle English Texts 14 (Heidelberg: Carl Winter Universitätsverlag, 1981).
Neuss, Paula, ed., *Magnificence* (Manchester: Manchester University Press, 1980).
Nolcken, Christina von, ed., *The Middle English Translation of the Rosarium Theologiae*, Middle English Texts 10 (Heidelberg: Carl Winter Universitätsverlag, 1979).
Ogilvie-Thomson, S.J., ed., *Richard Rolle: Prose and Verse*, EETS 293 (Oxford: Oxford University Press, 1988).
Pearsall, Derek, ed., *Piers Plowman: Tthe C-text*, Exeter Medieval English Texts and Studies (Exeter: University of Exeter Press, 1994).
Powell, Susan, ed., *The Advent and Nativity Sermons from a Fifteenth-Century Revision of John Mirk's Festial* (Heidelberg: Carl Winter Universitätsverlag, 1981).
Ramsay, Robert Lee, ed., *Magnyfycence: A Moral Play by John Skelton*, EETS ES 98 (London: Kegan Paul, Trench, Trübner, 1908).
Ross, Woodburn O., ed., *Middle English Sermons*, EETS OS 209 (London: Oxford University Press, 1940).
Salter, F.M., 'Skelton's *Speculum Principis*', *Speculum*, 9 (1934).
Scattergood, John, ed., *John Skelton: The Complete English Poems* (London: Penguin, 1983).

Spector, Stephen, ed., *The N-Town Play*, 2 vols, EETS SS 11, 12 (Oxford: Oxford University Press, 1991).
Steele, Robert, ed., *Secreta Secretorum*, vol. 1, EETS ES 74 (London: Kegan Paul, Trench, Trübner, 1898).
Swinburn, Lilian M., ed., *The Lantern of Li3t*, EETS OS 151 (London: Kegan Paul, Trench, Trübner, 1917).
Thomas, A.H., and I.D. Thornley, eds, *The Great Chronicle of London* (London: George W. Jones, 1938).
Tyndale, William, *The Practice of Prelates*, ed. Henry Walter, Parker Society (Cambridge: Cambridge University Press, 1849).
Tyndale, William, *The Obedience of a Christian Man*, Christian Classics Series V (London: Religious Tract Society, n. d.).
Tyndale, William, *The New Testament*, ed. David Daniell, (New Haven: Yale University Press, 1995).
Weber, Robert, ed., *Biblia Sacra: iuxta vulgatam versionem* (Stuttgart: Deutsche Bibelgesellschaft, 1969).
Windeatt, B.A., trans., *The Book of Margery Kempe* (Harmondsworth: Penguin, 1985).
Wright, Thomas, *Letters Relating to the Suppression of the Monasteries*, Camden Society, series 1, 26 (1843).

Criticism

Aers, David, *Culture and History 1350–1600* (Hemel Hempstead: Harvester Wheatsheaf, 1992).
Aers, David, ed., *Medieval Literature: Criticism, Ideology and History* (Brighton: Harvester, 1986).
Altman, Joel B., *The Tudor Play of Mind* (Berkeley: University of California Press, 1978).
Ariès, Philippe, and Georges Duby, eds, *A History of Private Life* (Cambridge, Mass.: Belknap, 1989).
Ashley, Kathleen M., 'Titivillus and the Battle of Words in *Mankind*', *Annuale Medievale*, 16 (1975), pp. 128–50.
Aston, Margaret, 'Corpus Christi and Corpus Regni: Heresy and the Peasants' Revolt', *Past and Present*, 143 (May 1994), pp. 3–47.
Aston, M.E., 'Lollardy and Sedition, 1381–1431', *Past and Present*, 17 (1960), pp. 1–44.
Baird, Lorrayne Y., ' "Cocke's face" and the problem of *poydrace* in the Chester Passion', *Comparative Drama*, 16:3 (Fall 1982), pp. 227–37.
Bakhtin, Mikhail, *Rabelais and His World*, trans. Hélène Iswolsky (Cambridge, Mass.: MIT Press, 1968).
Bakhtin, Mikhail, *The Dialogic Imagination*, ed. Michael Holquist, trans. Caryl Emerson and Michael Holquist (Austin: University of Texas Press, 1981).
Bartlett, Robert, *Trial by Fire and Water: The Medieval Judicial Ordeal* (Oxford: Clarendon Press, 1986).
Bawcutt, Priscilla, 'The Art of Flyting', *Scottish Literary Journal*, 10 (1983), pp. 5–24.
Bawcutt, Priscilla, *Dunbar the Makar* (Oxford: Clarendon Press, 1992).
Beadle, Richard, ed., *The Cambridge Companion to Medieval English Theatre* (Cambridge: Cambridge University Press, 1994).
Beadle, Richard, and Peter Meredith, 'Further External Evidence for Dating the York Register (BL Additional MS 35290)', *Leeds Studies in English*, n. s. 11 (1980), pp. 51–8.

Beckwith, Sarah, 'Ritual, Church and Theatre: Medieval Dramas of the Sacramental Body', in Aers, ed., *Culture and History*, cited above.
Bennett, Michael J., 'Education and Advancement', in Rosemary Horrox, ed., *Fifteenth-Century Attitudes: Perceptions of Society in Late Medieval England* (Cambridge: Cambridge University Press, 1994).
Bevington, David M., *From Mankind to Marlowe* (Cambridge: Harvard University Press, 1962).
Bevington, David M., 'Is John Heywood's *Play of the Weather* Really about the Weather?' *Renaissance Drama*, 7 (1964), pp. 11–19.
Bevington, David M., '"Blake and Wyght, fowll and fayer": Stage Pictures in *Wisdom*', in Milla Cozart Riggio, ed., *The Wisdom Symposium* (New York: AMS, 1986).
Billington, Sandra, *A Social History of the Fool* (Brighton: Harvester, 1984).
Billington, Sandra, *Mock Kings in Medieval Society and Renaissance Drama* (Oxford: Clarendon Press, 1991).
Billington, Sandra, 'Social Disorder, Festive Celebration, and Jean Michel's *Le Mistere de la Passion JesusCrist*', *Comparative Drama*, 29:2 (Summer 1995), pp. 216–47.
Blamires, Alcuin, *Woman Defamed and Woman Defended* (Oxford: Clarendon Press, 1992).
Blatt, Thora Balslev, *The Plays of John Bale: A Study of Ideas, Technique and Style* (Copenhagen: G.E.C. Gad, 1968).
Bowen, Barbara C., 'Metaphorical Obscenity in French Farce, 1460–1560', in Clifford Davidson, C.J. Gianakaris, and John H. Stroupe, eds, *The Drama of the Middle Ages: Comparative and Critical Essays* (New York: AMS, 1982).
Bowker, Margaret, 'The Henrician Reformation and the Parish Clergy', in Christopher Haigh, ed., *The English Reformation Revised* (Cambridge: Cambridge University Press, 1987).
Brawer, Robert A., 'The Characterization of Pilate in the York Cycle Plays', *Studies in Philology*, 69 (July 1972), pp. 289–303.
Brigden, Susan, *London and the Reformation* (Oxford: Clarendon Press, 1989).
Burnley, David, 'Courtly Speech in Chaucer', *Poetica International Journal of Linguistic Studies Tokyo*, 24 (1985), pp. 16–38.
Butterworth, Philip, 'The York *Crucifixion*: Actor Audience Relationship', *Medieval English Theatre*, 14 (1992), pp. 67–76.
Camille, Michael, *Images on the Edge: The Margins of Medieval Art* (London: Reaktion, 1992).
Cameron, Kenneth Walker, *John Heywood's 'Play of the Wether'* (Raleigh, N. C.: Thistle Press, 1941).
Cattley, Stephen Reed, *The Acts and Monuments of John Foxe*, vol. III (London: Seeley and Burnside, 1837).
Cawley, A.C., 'The "Grotesque" Feast in the *Prima Pastorum*', *Speculum*, 30 (1955), pp. 213–17.
Cawley, A.C., et al., *The Revels History of Drama in English*, vol. 1 (London: Methuen, 1983).
Chambers, E.K., *The Medieval Stage*, vol. 1 (Oxford: Clarendon Press, 1903).
Clopper, Lawrence M., 'Tyrants and Villains: Characterization in the Passion Sequences of the English Cycle Plays', *Modern Language Quarterly*, 41 (1980), pp. 3–20.
Clopper, Lawrence M., 'Lay and Clerical Impact on Civic and Religious Drama and Ceremony', in Marianne Briscoe, ed., *Contexts of Early English Drama* (Bloomington: Indiana University Press, 1989), pp. 102–36.
Cochran, Carol M., 'Flyting in the Mystery Plays', *Theatre Journal*, 31:2 (1979), pp. 186–97.
Cohn, Norman, *Europe's Inner Demons: An Enquiry Inspired by the Great Witch-Hunt* (London: Heinemann, 1975).

Coldeway, John C., 'The Non-cycle Plays and the East-Anglian Tradition', in Beadle, ed., *The Cambridge Companion to Medieval English Theatre*, cited above.
Colish, Marcia L., *A Mirror of Language* (Lincoln: University of Nebraska Press, 1983).
Cox, John D., 'The Devil and Society in the English Mystery Plays', *Comparative Drama*, 28 (Winter 1994–5), pp. 407–38.
Cox, John D., and David Scott Kastan, eds, *A New History of Early English Drama* (New York: Columbia University Press, 1997).
Craik, T.W., 'Violence in the English Miracle Play' in Neville Denny ed., *Medieval Drama*, Stratford-upon-Avon Studies 16 (London: Edward Arnold, 1973).
Craun, Edwin, *Lies, Slander, and Obscenity in Medieval English Literature* (Cambridge: Cambridge University Press, 1998).
Daniell, David, *William Tyndale: A Biography* (New Haven: Yale University Press, 1994).
Davidson, Clifford, 'Iconography and the York-Towneley *Harrowing of Hell*', *American Benedictine Review*, 28 (1977), pp. 260–75.
Davidson, Clifford, *Visualizing the Moral Life* (New York: AMS, 1989).
Davidson, Clifford, 'Positional Symbolism and English Medieval Drama', *Comparative Drama*, 25 (1991), pp. 66–76.
Davidson, Clifford, C.J. Gianakaris, and John H. Stroupe, eds, *The Drama of the Middle Ages: Comparative and Critical Essays* (New York: AMS, 1982).
Davis, Natalie Zemon, *Society and Culture in Early Modern France* (London: Duckworth, 1975).
Davis, Nicholas, 'The *Tretise of Myraclis Pleyinge*: On Milieu and Authorship', *Medieval English Theatre*, 12:2 (1990), pp. 124–51.
Denny, Neville, ed., *Medieval Drama*, Stratford-upon-Avon Studies 16 (London: Edward Arnold, 1973).
Dickens, A.G., *Lollards and Protestants in the Diocese of York 1509–1558* (London: Oxford University Press, 1959).
Dickens, A.G., *The English Reformation*, 2nd edn (London: Batsford, 1989).
Dickens, A.G., and John Tonkin, *The Reformation in Historical Thought* (Oxford: Basil Blackwell, 1985).
Diller, Hans-Jürgen, 'The Composition of the Chester *Adoration of the Shepherds*', *Anglia*, 89 (1971), pp. 178–98.
Diller, Hans-Jürgen, 'The Torturers in the English Mystery Plays', *Medieval English Theatre*, 11 (1989), pp. 57–65.
Dillon, Janette, *Language and Stage in Medieval and Renaissance England* (Cambridge: Cambridge University Press, 1998).
Dobson, E.J., 'The Etymology and Meaning of *Boy*', *Medium Aevum*, 9 (1940), pp. 121–54.
Duffy, Eamon, *The Stripping of the Altars: Traditional Religion in England 1400–1580* (New Haven: Yale University Press, 1992).
Duncan, Douglas, *Ben Jonson and the Lucianic Tradition* (Cambridge: Cambridge University Press, 1979).
Duncan, Robert, 'The Play as Tudor Propaganda: Bale's *King Johan* and the Authority of Kings', *University of Dayton Review*, 16 (1983–4), pp. 67–74.
Ebin, Lois A., *Illuminator, Makar, Vates: Visions of Poetry in the Fifteenth Century* (Lincoln: University of Nebraska Press, 1988).
Edwards, Anthony S.G., *Skelton: The Critical Heritage* (London: Routledge & Kegan Paul, 1981).
Elam, Keir, *Shakespeare's Universe of Discourse: Language Games in the Comedies* (Cambridge: Cambridge University Press, 1984).
Ferguson, Arthur B., *The Articulate Citizen and the English Renaissance* (Durham, N. C.: Duke University Press, 1965).

Ferster, Judith, 'Writing on the Ground: Interpretation in Chester Play XII', in Julian N. Wasserman and Lois Roney, eds, *Sign, Sentence, Discourse: Language in Medieval Thought and Literature* (Syracuse, N.Y.: Syracuse University Press, 1989).
Fichte, Joerg O., 'The Presentation of Sin as Verbal Action in the Moral Interludes', *Anglia*, 103 (1985), pp. 26–47.
Fichte, Joerg O., 'New Wine in Old Bottles: The Protestant Adaptation of the Morality Play', *Anglia*, 110 (1992), pp. 65–84.
Fish, Stanley, *John Skelton's Poetry* (New Haven: Yale University Press, 1965).
Fish, Stanley, *Is There a Text in This Class?* (Cambridge, Mass.: Harvard University Press, 1980).
Fletcher, Alan J., *Preaching, Politics and Poetry in Late Medieval England* (Dublin: Four Courts Press, 1998).
Fletcher, Alan J., 'The N-Town Plays', in Beadle, ed., *The Cambridge Companion to Medieval English Theatre*, cited above.
Foucault, Michel, *Discipline and Punish: The Birth of the Prison*, trans. Alan Sheridan (London: Penguin, 1977).
Fox, Adam, 'Ballads, Libels and Popular Ridicule in Jacobean England', *Past and Present*, 145 (November 1994), pp. 47–83.
Fox, Alistair, and John Guy, eds, *Reassessing the Henrician Age: Humanism, Politics and Reform, 1500–1550* (Oxford: Basil Blackwell, 1986).
Gairdner, James, ed., *Letters and Papers, Foreign and Domestic, of the Reign of Henry VIII*, vol. VII (London: Longman, 1883).
Gardner, John, *The Construction of the Wakefield Cycle* (Carbondale and Edwardsville: Southern Illinois University Press, 1974).
Garrett Epp, P.J., 'Passion, Pomp, and Parody: Alliteration in the York Plays', *Medieval English Theatre*, 11 (1989), pp. 150–61.
Gash, Antony, 'Carnival Against Lent', in Aers, ed., *Medieval Literature: Criticism, Ideology and Literature*, cited above.
Gibson, Gail McMurray, *The Theatre of Devotion* (Chicago: University of Chicago Press, 1989).
Gibson, Gail McMurray, 'Writing before the Eye: The N-Town *Woman Taken in Adultery* and the Medieval Ministry Play', *Comparative Drama*, 27 (Winter 1993–4), pp. 399–407.
Goldberg, P.J.P., 'Women in Fifteenth-Century Town Life', in John A.F. Thomson, ed., *Towns and Townspeople in the Fifteenth Century* (Gloucester: Alan Sutton, 1988).
Gordon, Ian A., *John Skelton: Poet Laureate* (Melbourne: Melbourne University Press, 1943).
Gowing, Laura, 'Gender and the Language of Insult in Early Modern London', *History Workshop*, 35 (Spring 1993), pp. 1–21.
Gray, Douglas, 'Rough Music: Some Early Invectives and Flytings', in Claude Rawson, ed., *English Satire and the Satiric Tradition* (Oxford: Basil Blackwell, 1984).
Greenblatt, Stephen, *Learning to Curse* (New York: Routledge, 1990).
Guy, John, *Tudor England* (Oxford: Oxford University Press, 1988).
Guy, John, 'Thomas More and Christopher St German: The Battle of the Books', in Alistair Fox and John Guy, eds, *Reassessing the Henrician Age*, cited above.
Haigh, Christopher, *English Reformations: Religion, Politics, and Society under the Tudors* (Oxford: Clarendon Press, 1993).
Haigh, Christopher, ed., *The English Reformation Revised* (Cambridge: Cambridge University Press, 1987).
Hair, Paul, ed., *Before the Bawdy Court* (London: Elek, 1972).
Hanawalt, Barbara, *The Ties that Bound* (New York: Oxford University Press, 1986).
Hanawalt, Barbara, and David Wallace, eds, *Bodies and Disciplines: Intersections of Literature and History in Fifteenth-Century England*, Medieval Cultures vol. 9 (Minneapolis: University of Minnesota Press, 1996).
Hanning, R.W., ' "Your have begun a parlous pleye": The Nature and Limits of Dramatic Mimesis as a Theme in Four Middle English "Fall of Lucifer" Cycle Plays', in Davidson, Gianakaris, and Stroupe, eds, *The Drama of the Middle Ages*, cited above.

Happé, Peter, *Medieval English Drama*, Casebook Series (London: Macmillan, 1984).
Happé, Peter, 'Acting the York Mystery Plays: A Consideration of Modes', *Medieval English Theatre*, 10:2 (1988), pp. 112–16.
Happé, Peter, 'Fansy and Foly: The Drama of Fools in *Magnyfycence*', *Comparative Drama*, 27 (Winter 1993–4), pp. 426–52.
Happé, Peter, *John Bale* (New York: Twayne, 1996).
Happé, Peter, *English Drama before Shakespeare* (London: Longman, 1999).
Happé, Peter, 'Dramatic Images of Kingship in Heywood and Bale', *Studies in English Literature*, 39 (Spring 1999), pp. 239–53.
Happé, Peter, ed., *The Complete Plays of John Bale*, vol. 1 (Cambridge: D.S. Brewer, 1985).
Happé, Peter, and Wim Hüsken, ' "Sinnekins" and the Vice: Prolegomena', *Comparative Drama*, 29 (Summer 1995), pp. 248–69.
Harris, William O., *Skelton's* Magnyfycence *and the Cardinal Virtue Tradition* (Chapel Hill: University of North Carolina Press, 1965).
Heisermann, A.R., *Skelton and Satire* (Chicago: University of Chicago Press, 1961).
Helterman, Jeffrey, *Symbolic Action in the Plays of the Wakefield Master* (Athens, Ga: University of Georgia Press, 1981).
Hicks, Michael, *Bastard Feudalism* (London: Longman, 1995).
Hogrefe, Pearl, *The Sir Thomas More Circle* (Urbana: University of Illinois Press, 1959).
Holt, Richard, and Gervase Rosser, eds, *The Medieval Town: A Reader in Medieval Urban History 1200–1540* (London: Longman, 1990).
Horner, Olga, '"Us Must Make Lies": Witness, Evidence, and Proof in the York *Resurrection*', *Medieval English Theatre*, 20 (1998), pp. 24–76.
Horrox, Rosemary, ed., *Fifteenth-Century Attitudes: Perceptions of Society in Late Medieval England* (Cambridge: Cambridge University Press, 1994).
Hudson, Anne, *Lollards and their Books* (London: Hambledon Press, 1985).
Hughes, Geoffrey, *Swearing: A History of Foul Language and Profanity in English* (Oxford: Basil Blackwell, 1991).
Hunt, Alison M., 'Maculating Mary: The Detractors of the N-Town Cycle's "Trial of Joseph and Mary"', *Philological Quarterly*, 73:1 (Winter 1994), pp. 11–29.
Hunt, Ernest William, *Dean Colet and his Theology* (London: SPCK, 1956).
Hussey, S.S., 'How Many Herods in the Middle English Drama?' *Neophilologus*, 48 (1964), pp. 252–59.
Hutton, Ronald, *The Rise and Fall of Merry England: The Ritual Year 1400–1700* (Oxford: Oxford University Press, 1994).
Hutton, Ronald, *The Stations of the Sun* (Oxford: Oxford University Press, 1996).
Ingram, Martin, 'Ridings, Rough Music, and Mocking Rhymes in Early Modern England', in Barry Reay, ed., *Popular Culture in Seventeenth-Century England* (London: Croom Helm, 1985)
Ingram, Martin, *Church Courts, Sex, and Marriage in England 1570–1640* (Cambridge: Cambridge University Press, 1987).
Jack, R.D.S., *Patterns of Divine Comedy* (Cambridge: D.S. Brewer, 1989).
James, Mervyn, 'Ritual, Drama, and the Social Body in the Late Medieval Town', *Past and Present*, 98 (February 1983), pp. 3–29.
Johnson, Robert Carl, 'Audience Involvement in the Tudor Interludes', *Theatre Notebook*, 24:3 (Spring 1970), pp. 101–11.
Johnston, Alexandra F., 'The Procession and Play of Corpus Christi in York after 1426', *Leeds Studies in English*, n.s. 7 (1974), pp. 55–62.
Johnston, Alexandra F., 'The Plays of the Religious Guilds of York: The Creed Play and the Pater Noster Play', *Speculum*, 50 (1975), pp. 55–90.
Johnston, Alexandra F., 'Chaucer's Records of Early English Drama', *Records of Early English Drama Newsletter*, 13, (1988), pp. 13–20.
Johnston, Alexandra F., 'Evil in the Towneley Cycle', *Medieval English Theatre*, 11 (1989), pp. 94–103.

Kauper, Richard W., *War, Justice and Public Order: England and France in the Later Middle Ages* (Oxford: Clarendon Press, 1988).
Kendall, Ritchie D., *The Drama of Discontent: The Radical Poetics of Nonconformity, 1380–1590* (Chapel Hill: University of North Carolina Press, 1986).
Kermode, Jennifer I., 'Obvious Observations on the Formation of Oligarchies in later Medieval English Towns', in John A.F. Thomson, ed., *Towns and Townspeople in the Fifteenth Century* (Gloucester: Alan Sutton, 1988).
Kiechhefer, Richard, *Magic in the Middle Ages* (Cambridge: Cambridge University Press, 1989).
King, Pamela M., 'Morality Plays', in Beadle, ed., *The Cambridge Companion to Medieval English Theatre*, cited above.
Kinsman, Robert S., 'Skelton's *Magnyfycence*: The Strategy of the "Olde Sayde Sawe"', *Studies in Philology*, 63 (April 1966), pp. 99–125.
Knott, John R., *Discourses of Martyrdom in English Literature 1563–1694* (Cambridge: Cambridge University Press, 1993).
Kolve, V.A., 'The Drama as Play and Game', in Happé, ed., *Medieval English Drama*, cited above.
Lerud, Theodore K., *Social and Political Dimensions of the English Corpus Christi Drama* (New York: Garland, 1988).
Lester, Geoff, 'Idle Words: Stereotyping by Language in the English Mystery Plays', *Medieval English Theatre*, 11 (1989), pp. 129–33.
MacCulloch, Diarmaid, *Thomas Cranmer* (New Haven: Yale, 1996).
Mann, Jill, *Chaucer and the Medieval Estates Satire* (Cambridge: Cambridge University Press, 1973).
Marshall, John, ' "Fortune in the Worldys Worschyppe": The Satirising of the Suffolks in *Wisdom*', *Medieval English Theatre*, 14 (1992), pp. 37–66.
Marshall, John, 'O 3e Souerens þat Sytt and 3e Brothern þat stonde Ryght Wppe: Addressing the Audience of *Mankind*', *European Medieval Drama* 1 (Turnhout: Brepols, 1997), pp. 189–202.
Marshall, Mary H., 'Aesthetic Values in Liturgical Drama', in Jerome Taylor and Alan H. Nelson, eds, *Medieval English Drama* (Chicago: University of Chicago Press, 1972).
Martin, Leslie Howard, 'Comic Eschatology in the Chester *Coming of AntiChrist*', *Comparative Drama*, 5 (1972), pp. 163–76.
May, Stephen, 'Good Kings and Tyrants: A Reassessment of the Regal Figure on the Medieval Stage', *Medieval English Theatre*, 5:2 (1983), pp. 87–102.
McCain, John Walker, 'Heywood and Classical Mythology', *Notes and Queries*, 19 (1938), p. 368.
McCain, John Walker, 'Oratory, Rhetoric and Logic in the Writings of John Heywood', *Quarterly Journal of Speech*, 26 (1940), pp. 44–7.
McGavin, John J., 'Sign and Transition: The Purification Play in Chester', *Leeds Studies in English*, n. s. 11 (1980), pp. 90–104.
McGavin, John J., 'Chester's Linguistic Signs', *Leeds Studies in English*, 21 (1990), pp. 105–18.
McGavin, John J., 'The Dramatic Prosody of Sir David Lindsay', in R.D.S. Jack and Kevin McGinley, eds, *Of Lion and of Unicorn: Essays in Anglo-Scottish Literary Relations in Honour of Professor John McQueen* (Edinburgh: Quadriga, 1993).
McGavin, John J., 'Robert III's "Rough Music": Charivari and Diplomacy in a Medieval Scottish Court', *The Scottish Historical Review*, 74:2, 198 (October 1995), pp. 144–58.
McKane, W., 'Poison, Trial by Ordeal, and the Cup of Wrath', *Vetus Testamentum*, 30 (1980), pp. 474–92.

McNeir, Waldo F., 'The Corpus Christi Passion Plays as Dramatic Art', *Studies in Philology*, 48 (1951), pp. 601–28.
Meredith, Peter, 'The Towneley Cycle', in Beadle, ed., *The Cambridge Companion to Medieval English Theatre*, cited above.
Miller, Edwin Shephard, 'The Roman Rite in Bale's *King Johan*', *PMLA*, 64 (1949), pp. 804–22.
Mills, David, 'Characterisation in the English Mystery Cycles: A Critical Prologue', *Medieval English Theatre*, 5:1 (1983), pp. 5–17.
Mills, David, 'The Chester Cycle', in Beadle, ed., *The Cambridge Companion to Medieval English Theatre*, cited above.
Monter, William, *Ritual, Myth and Magic in Early Modern Europe* (Brighton: Harvester, 1983).
Morgan, Margery M., ' "High Fraud" in the Shepherds' Plays: Paradox and Double-Plot in the English Shepherds' Plays', *Speculum*, 39 (1944), pp. 676–689.
Munson, William F., 'Audience and Meaning in Two Medieval Dramatic Realisms', in Davidson, Gianakaris, and Stroupe, eds, *The Drama of the Middle Ages*, cited above.
Murphy, James J., *Medieval Eloquence* (Berkeley: University of California Press, 1978).
Nelson, William, *John Skelton Laureate* (New York: Russell and Russell, 1964).
Neuss, Paula, 'Active and Idle Language: Dramatic Images in "Mankind"', in Denny, ed., *Medieval Drama*, cited above.
Neuss, Paula, 'Proverbial Skelton', *Studia Neophilologus*, 54 (1982), pp. 237–46.
Nichols, Ann Eljenholm, 'Costume in the Moralities: The Evidence of East Anglian Art', in Clifford Davidson and John H. Stroupe, eds, *Drama in the Middle Ages*, 2nd series (New York: AMS, 1991).
Nichols, Ann Eljenholm, *Seeable Signs: The Iconography of the Seven Sacraments 1350–1544* (Woodbridge, Suffolk: Boydell Press, 1994).
Nicholson, R.H., 'The Trial of Christ the Sorcerer in the York Cycle', *Journal of Medieval and Renaissance Studies*, 16 (1986), pp. 125–69.
Owst, G.R., *Preaching in Medieval England* (Cambridge: Cambridge University Press, 1926).
Owst, G.R., *Literature and the Pulpit* (Cambridge: Cambridge University Press, 1933).
Palliser, D. M., *Tudor York* (Oxford: Oxford University Press, 1979).
Palmer, Barbara D., 'Corpus Christi "Cycles" in Yorkshire: The Surviving Records', *Comparative Drama*, 27 (Summer 1993), pp. 218–31.
Parker, Roscoe, 'The Reputation of Herod in Early English Literature', *Speculum*, 8 (1933), pp. 59–67.
Peristiany, J.G., ed., *Honour and Shame* (London: Weidenfeld and Nicholson, 1965).
Pettitt, Thomas, '"Here Comes I Jack Strawe": English Folk Drama and Social Revolt', *Folklore*, 95 (1984), pp. 3–20.
Phillips, Norma, 'Observations on the Derivative Method of Skelton's Realism', *Journal of English and Germanic Philology*, 65 (1966), pp. 19–35.
Phythian-Adams, Charles, *Desolation of a City: Coventry and the Urban Crisis of the Late Middle Ages* (Cambridge: Cambridge University Press, 1979).
Phythian-Adams, Charles, 'Ceremony and the Citizen: The Communal Year at Coventry 1450–1550', in Holt and Rosser, eds, *The Medieval Town*, cited above.
Pietropoli, Cecilia, 'The Characterisation of Evil in the Towneley Plays', *Medieval English Theatre*, 11 (1989), pp. 85–93.
Pineas, Rainer, 'William Tyndale's Influence on John Bale's Polemical Use of History', *Archiv fur Reformtiongeschichte*, 53 (1962), pp. 79–96.
Pineas, Rainer, 'The English Morality Play as a Weapon of Religious Controversy', *Studies in English Literature*, 2 (1962), pp. 157–80.

Pineas, Rainer, 'More versus Tyndale: A Study of Controversial Technique', *Modern Language Quarterly*, 24 (1963), pp. 144–50.
Pineas, Rainer, *Tudor and Early Stuart Anti-Catholic Drama* (Nieuwkoop: B. de Graaf, 1972).
Pineas, Rainer, 'The Polemical Drama of John Bale', in W.R. Elton and W. Long, eds, *Shakespeare and the Dramatic Tradition* (Newark: University of Delaware, 1989).
Pitt-Rivers, Julian, 'Honour and Social Status', in J.G. Peristiany, ed., *Honour and Shame*, cited above.
Platt, Colin, *King Death* (London: UCL, 1996).
Plummer, John F., 'The Logomacy of the N-Town Passion Play 1', *Journal of English and Germanic Philology*, 88 (1989), pp. 313–31.
Pollard, A.J., *North-Eastern England During the Wars of the Roses* (Oxford: Clarendon Press, 1990).
Potter, Robert, *The English Morality Play* (London: Routledge & Kegan Paul, 1975).
Rastell, Richard, *The Heaven Singing: Music in Early English Religious Drama*, vol. 1 (Cambridge: D.S. Brewer, 1996).
Reese, Jesse Byers, 'Alliterative Verse in the York Cycle', *Studies in Philology*, 48 (1951), pp. 639–68.
Rigby, S.H., *English Society in the Later Middle Ages* (Basingstoke: Macmillan, 1995).
Rigby, Stephen, 'Urban "Oligarchy" in Late Medieval England', in John A.F. Thomson, ed., *Towns and Townspeople in the Fifteenth Century* (Gloucester: Alan Sutton, 1988).
Riggio, Milla Cozart, ed., *The Wisdom Symposium* (New York: AMS, 1986).
Robinson, J.W., *Studies in Fifteenth-Century Stagecraft*, Early Art, Drama, and Music Monograph Series 14 (Kalamazoo: Medieval Institute Publications, 1991).
Rosen, Barbara, *Witchcraft in England 1558–1618* (Amherst: University of Massachussetts Press, 1991).
Roth, Cecil, *A History of the Jews in England* (Oxford: Clarendon, 1949).
Rubin, Miri, *Corpus Christi: The Eucharist in Late Medieval Culture* (Cambridge: Cambridge University Press, 1991).
Rubin, Miri, 'The Eucharist and the Construction of Medieval Identities', in Aers, ed., *Culture and History*, cited above.
Russell, Jeffrey Burton, *The Devil: Perceptions of Evil from Antiquity to Primitive Christianity* (Ithaca, N.Y.: Cornell University Press, 1977).
Schell, Edgar, 'The Limits of Typology in the Wakefield Master's *Processus Noe*', *Comparative Drama*, 25 (1991), pp. 168–87.
Schmitt, Natalie Crohn, 'The Idea of a Person in Medieval Morality Plays', in Davidson, Gianakaris, and Stroupe, eds, *The Drama of the Middle Ages*, cited above.
Scott, James C., *Domination and the Arts of Resistance* (New Haven: Yale University Press, 1990).
Sharratt, Bernard, 'John Skelton: Finding a Voice – Notes after Bakhtin', in Aers, ed., *Medieval Literature*, cited above.
Simeonova, Kristina, 'The Aesthetic Function of the Carnivalesque in Medieval Drama', in D. Shepherd, ed., *Bakhtin: Carnival and Other Subjects* (n. p., Rodopi, 1993).
Simon, Eckehard, ed., *The Theatre of Medieval Europe: New Research in Early Drama*, Cambridge Studies in Medieval Literature (Cambridge: Cambridge University Press, 1991).
Spector, Stephen, 'Anti-Semitism and the English Mystery Plays', in Davidson, Gianakaris, and Stroupe, eds, *The Drama of the Middle Ages*, cited above.
Spivak, Bernard, *Shakespeare and the Allegory of Evil* (New York: Columbia University Press, 1958).

Squires, Lynn, 'Law and Disorder in *Ludus Coventriae*', in Davidson, Gianakaris, and Stroupe, eds, *The Drama of the Middle Ages*, cited above.
Staines, David, 'To Out-Herod Herod: The Development of a Dramatic Character', in Davidson, Gianakaris, and Stroupe, eds, *The Drama of the Middle Ages*, cited above.
Stevens, Martin, 'Language as Theme in the Wakefield Plays' *Speculum*, 52 (1977), pp. 100–17.
Sugano, Douglas, ' "This game wel pleyd in good a-ray": The N-Town Playbooks and East Anglian Games', *Comparative Drama*, 28 (Summer 1994), pp. 221–34.
Swanson, R.N., *Church and Society in Late Medieval England* (Oxford: Basil Blackwell, 1989).
Taylor, Andrew, '"To Pley a Pagyn of the Devyl": *Turpiloquium* and the *Scurrae* in Early Drama', *Medieval English Theatre*, 11 (1989), pp. 162–74.
Taylor, Jerome, and Alan H. Nelson, eds., *Medieval English Drama* (Chicago: University of Chicago Press, 1972).
Thomas, Keith, *Religion and the Decline of Magic* (London: Penguin, 1971).
Thomas, Keith, 'The Place of Laughter in Tudor and Stuart England', *Times Literary Supplement*, 21.1.77, pp. 77–81.
Thompson, E.P., ' "Rough Music": Le Charivari Anglais', *Annales E.S.C.*, 27 (1972), pp. 285–312.
Thomson, John A.F., *The Later Lollards 1414–1520* (London: Oxford University Press, 1965).
Thomson, John A.F., *The Transformation of Medieval England 1370–1529* (London: Longman, 1983).
Thomson, John A.F., ed., *Towns and Townspeople in the Fifteenth Century* (Gloucester: Alan Sutton, 1988).
Turberville, A.S., *Mediæval Heresy and the Inquisition* (London: Crosby Lockwood, 1920).
Walker, Greg, *John Skelton and the Politics of the 1520s*, Cambridge Studies in Early Modern British History (Cambridge: Cambridge University Press, 1988).
Walker, Greg, *Plays of Persuasion: Drama and Politics at the Court of Henry VIII* (Cambridge: Cambridge University Press, 1991).
Walker, Greg, *The Politics of Performance in Early Renaissance Drama* (Cambridge: Cambridge University Press, 1998).
Wasserman, Julian N., and Lois Roney, eds, *Sign, Sentence, Discourse: Language in Medieval Thought and Literature* (Syracuse, N.Y.: Syracuse University Press, 1989).
Weirum, Ann, 'Actors and Playacting in the Morality Tradition', *Renaissance Drama*, 3 (1970), pp. 189–214.
Welsford, Enid, *The Fool, His Social and Literary History* (New York: Anchor Books, 1961).
West, Michael, 'Skelton and the Renaissance Theme of Folly', *Philological Quarterly*, 50, (January 1971), pp. 23–35.
White, Paul Whitfield, *Theatre and Reformation: Protestantism, Patronage, and Playing in the Tudor Age* (Cambridge: Cambridge University Press, 1993).
Whiting, Bartlett Jere, and Helen Westcott Whiting, *Proverbs, Sentences, and Proverbial Phrases* (Cambridge, Mass.: Belknap Press, 1968).
Williams, Arnold, *The Characterization of Pilate in the Towneley Plays* (East Lansing, Mich.: Michigan State College Press, 1950).
Wilson, F.P., and G.K. Hunter, *The English Drama 1485–1585* (Oxford: Clarendon Press, 1969).
Womack, Peter, 'Imagining Communities: Theatres and the English Nation in the Sixteenth Century', in Aers, ed., *Culture and History*, cited above.
Woolf, Rosemary, *The English Mystery Plays* (London: Routledge & Kegan Paul, 1972).

Wright, Robert, 'Community Theatre in Late Medieval East Anglia', *Theatre Notebook*, 27, (1974), pp. 24–38.
Wrightson, Keith, 'Aspects of Social Differentiation in Rural England, *c.* 1580–1660', *The Journal of Peasant Studies*, 5 (1977), pp. 33–47.

Law

Arnold, Morris A., et al., eds, *On The Laws and Customs of England: Essays in Honour of Samuel E. Thorne* (Chapel Hill: University of North Carolina Press, 1981).
Baker, J.H., *An Introduction to English Legal History*, 2nd edn (London: Butterworth, 1979).
Bateson, Mary, ed., *Borough Customs*, vol. 1, Selden Society (London: Bernard Quaritch, 1904).
Bayne, C.G., and William Huse Dunham, eds, *Select Cases in the Council of Henry VII*, Selden Society (London: Bernard Quaritch, 1985).
Beckerman, John S., 'Adding Insult to Iniuria: Affronts to Honour and the Origins of Trespass', in Morris A. Arnold et al., eds, *Laws and Customs*, cited above.
Bellamy, John G., *The Law of Treason in England in the Later Middle Ages*, Cambridge Studies in English Legal History (Cambridge: Cambridge University Press, 1970).
Bellamy, John G., *Crime and Public Order in England in the Later Middle Ages* (London: Routledge & Kegan Paul, 1973).
Bellamy, John G., *Bastard Feudalism and the Law* (London: Routledge, 1989).
Donahue, Charles, 'Proof by Witnesses in the Church Courts of Medieval England: An Imperfect Reception of the Learned Law', in Morris A. Arnold et al., eds, *Laws and Customs*, cited above.
Elton, G.R., *The Tudor Constitution* (Cambridge: Cambridge University Press, 1962).
Gross, Charles, ed., *Select Cases from the Coroner's Rolls, A. D. 1265–1413*, Selden Society (London: Bernard Quaritch, 1896).
Haigh, C.A., 'Slander and the Church Courts in the Sixteenth Century', *Transactions of the Lancashire and Cheshire Antiquarian Society*, 78 (1975), pp. 1–13.
Helmholz, R.H., ed., *Select Cases on Defamation to 1600*, Selden Society (London: Selden Society, 1986).
Helmholz, R.H., *Canon Law and the Law of England* (London: Hambledon Press, 1987).
Holdsworth, William, *A History of English Law*, 12 vols (London: Methuen, 1925).
Hunnisett, R.F., and J.B. Post, eds, *Medieval Legal Records* (London: HMSO, 1978).
Kramer, Heinrich, and James Sprenger, *The Malleus Maleficarum*, trans. Montague Summers (New York: Dover, 1971).
Leach, Arthur, ed., *Beverley Town Documents*, Selden Society (London: Bernard Quaritch, 1900).
Longley, Katharine M., ed., *Ecclesiastical Cause Papers at York: Dean and Chapter's Court 1350–1843*, Borthwick Texts and Calendars: Records of the Northern Province 6 (University of York: Borthwick Institute, 1980).
Milsom, S.F.C., *Historical Foundations of the Common Law* (London: Butterworth, 1969).
Morris, Colin, '*Judicium Dei*: The Social and Political Significance of the Ordeal in the Eleventh Century', *Studies in Church History*, 12 (1975), pp. 95–111.
Plucknett, Theodore F.T., *A Concise History of the Common Law*, 5th edn (London: Butterworth, 1956).
Putnam, Bertha Haven, ed., *Proceedings before the Justices of the Peace: Edward III to Richard III* (London: Spottiswoode, Ballantyne & Co., 1938).

Riley, Henry Thomas, ed., *Munimenta Gildhallae Londoniensis: Liber Albus, et Liber Horn*, vol. 3 (London: Longman, Green, Longman and Roberts, 1862).
Sayles, G.O., ed., *Select Cases in the Court of Kings Bench under Richard II, Henry IV, and Henry V*, vol. 7, Selden Society (London: Bernard Quaritch, 1971).
Sharpe, J.A., *Defamation and Sexual Slander in Early Modern England: The Church Courts at York*, Borthwick Papers 58 (University of York: Borthwick Institute, 1981).
Sheils, W.J., ed., *Ecclesiastical Cause Papers of York: Files Transmitted on Appeal 1500–1883*, Borthwick Texts and Calendars, Records of the Northern Province 9 (York: University of York, 1983).
Smith, D.M., ed., *Ecclesiastical Cause Papers at York: The Court of York 1301–1399*, Borthwick Texts and Calendars 14 (University of York: Borthwick Institute, 1988).
Statutes of the Realm vol. 1 (n. p., n. pub., 1810).
Statutes of the Realm vol. 2 (n. p., n. pub., 1816).
Statutes of the Realm vol. 3 (n. p., n. pub., 1817).
Sutherland, Donald W., 'Legal Reasoning in the Fourteenth Century: The Invention of "Color" in Pleading', in Morris A. Arnold et al., eds, *On The Laws and Customs of England*, cited above.
Tanner, Norman P., ed., *Heresy Trials in the Diocese of Norwich 1428–31*, Camden Society, 4th series, vol. 20 (London: Offices of the Royal Historical Society, 1977).
Thorne, Samuel E., trans., and George Woodbine, ed., *Bracton on the Laws and Customs of England*, 4 vols, (Cambridge, Mass.: Belknap Press, 1968).

Bibliographies

Berger, Sidney E., *Medieval English Drama: An Annotated Bibliography of Recent Criticism* (New York: Garland, 1990).
Kolin, Philip C., 'Recent Studies in John Heywood', *English Literary Renaissance*, 13 (1983), pp. 113–123.
Staub, Susan C., 'Recent Studies in Skelton' *English Literary Renaissance*, 20 (Autumn 1990), pp. 505–16.

Index

abuse, ch. 2 *passim*, 166, 168, 171, 176–8, 194
  anti-Catholic, 176
  as a weapon, 166, 171–2
  of language, 194
  quarrelsome, 35, 42
abusive:
  allusions, 172
  exchange, 30, 33–6
accusations of falseness, 14
Act of Six Articles, 165–6, 187
acts of virtue, 46
affective piety, 68, 77–8, 80
alienation, 66–8, 191
allegory, 86, 100–101, 106, 110–11, 131, 136–7, 141–2, 152, 154, 162, 168, 174
alliteration, 30–3, 34, 47, 131–2
Anima, 94
anticlerical satire, 146–8, 155, 163
  complaint, 152–5
Antichrist, 148, 171–2
Aquinas, St Thomas, 7–13, 83
audience, ch. 2 *passim*, 85–92, 97–106, ch. 5 *passim*, 136–40, 167, 169, 172, 175
  challenged, 68–71
  Elizabethan, 180
  judgement, 129
  Protestant, 165, 179, 184, 187–9, 194
  response, ch. 3 *passim*, 50–59, 62, 85, 145
  Tudor, 111, 118, 120–1, 183
Augustine, St, 80
aureate language, 37, 46, 48, 102, 104, 120
authority, temporal and divine, 63–6

backbiting, 7, 11–13, 72
Bakhtin, Mikhail, 79–80, 103, 179
Bale, John, 54, ch. 7 *passim*
  'bilious' Bale, 166, 171, 193, 196
bawdy, 137–45, 161, 178

  scatology and schism, 155–161
Beverley Town documents, 55
biblical plays, *see* individual plays
binary structure, 148, 155–6
boasting of sin, 92, 106
  speeches, 131
Boleyn, Anne, 143, 157–9, 163
bombastic style, 31–3, 100
boots and spurs, 80
Boy Bishops, 22

Caiaphas, 38–40, 52–54, 69–70, 79–81
Cain, 23, 30, 36, 42, 63–4, 66–7, 84, 88
Canterbury cathedral, 150
Canterbury Tales, 14, 23, 145, 147
capital offences, 17–19
Castle of Perseverance, 25, 28–9, 32, 39, ch. 4 *passim*, 131, 133
caution, 165
characterization, ch. 2 *passim*, 51, 54, 86, 89, 101, 107, 117, 125, 142, 175
  of evil, 167–9, 171, 174, 177–80
charitable correction of sin, 9, 16, 51, 58
charivaris, 22
Chester, ch. 3 *passim*
  Balaam, 28
  Harrowing of Hell, 30
  Innocents, 12, 29, 34, 59–60
  Magi, 38
  Noah, 45
  Resurrection, 41
  Shepherds, 33, 36, 42, 45–6, 64, 86, 104–6
  Trial, 41, 70, 82
Christmas song, 102–4
chronological development, 107
civic disorder, 56–7
Clergye, 171, 173–4, 176, 181–3, 187–90
Colet, John, 146
colloquial insult, 130, 174–5

Index

comedy, 60–2, 65, 78–9
  anachronistic, 59
comic:
  interlude, 111–17, 135
  inversion, 65–6
  language, 60–61, 66–7, 72, 145
compurgation, 16
confession, 166, 168, 184, 189–91
conflicting signs, 119, 125, 128, 134
Confutation of Tyndale's Answer, 19, 148
consistory court, ch. 1 *passim*
contexts, ch. 2 *passim*, 34, 37, 45–49, 196
  dramatic, 40–44
  non-dramatic, 7
  social, 25, 35, 37
conventions of speech, 117
corn as the word of God, 103, 149–150
Corpus Christi, 56–7
corruption, 90–105, 110, 163–5, 172–3, 181–3, 191, 195
costumes, 38, 40, 46, 93–7, 111, 125–6, 135
courteous speech, 121
Cranmer, Thomas, 136, 141–2, 154, 165, 187
Cromwell, Thomas, 136–7, 141–2, 152, 156–7, 165
Croxton *Play of the Sacrament*, 30
cuckold, 16, 72, 145–6
cultural change, 108, 111–12, 115–16, 134–5
curses, 26–9, 30–33, 34, 36, 39, 45
  common, 194
Cyvyle Order, 173, 176–7, 181–3, 190, 194

De Heretico Comburendo, 18
deception, 111–17, 123–4, 128–9, 132, 134, 187
defamation, ch. 1 *passim*, 26, 27, 71, 81, 83
  of Christ, 68–71
defamation, doubt and sin, 71–6
  and witnesses, 16
delight in sin, 92, 95
detraction, ch. 1 *passim*, 71–6
devil oaths, 28, 30, 45
didactic intention, 100–105
difference and variation, 89
differing interpretation, 142
Dives and Pauper, 18
double entendres, 156

Duke of Suffolk, 97

ecclesiastical courts, 13, 23
elections, 57
emotional change, 40
Englande, 169–170, 175, 177–8, 192, 194, 196
entertainment, 6
Erasmus, 108, 148, 151–2
evil, 25, 85–6, 100, 140
  characters, 28, 29, 31–5, 42, 44, 46, 168, 171, 175, 177
  fool, 128
  lords, 30–3, 38–44, 80, 100, 131–2
  and mocking audiences, 51–9
  style, 30–33
  unregenerate, 42, 48
exasperation, 161, 163, 175
excommunication, 22–6, 194
exhibitory punishment, 20

Fansy, 112–17, 125
Felycyte, 119, 122, 128, 130, 132
female characters, 138–9, 156–162
Fergus (York *Coronation of the Virgin*), 79
festive disorder, 57
festive inversions, 20, 64, 66
flyting, 35–7, 48–9, 60–62, 64–5, 162, 167
folk rhetoric, 27
foolish naming, 115
fools, 82–3, 110–12, 117, 125–8
  artificial, 83
  natural, 83
fragmented allegory, 136–7, 142, 162

gendered insults, 60, 74–6, 88–9
Gentleman, 140–46, 149–150, 157
Gentlewoman, 139, 156–62
Grammarians' War, 109
Great Curse, *see* excommunication
Greek, 109
guilt, 50, 58, 72–9

hawk and owl, 113–14
Henry VIII, 108–9, 129, 135–7, 141–5, 154, 157, 160, 163, 165–167, 172, 174, 180, 187, 195
heresy, 17–18, 58, 69–71, 146, 154

Index

Herod, 27, 29, 31–2, 34–5, 38–42, 50
Heywood, John, 110, ch. 6 *passim*
hierarchy, 51, 62–8, 84
high-status characters, 28, 37, 42
historical figures, 80, 168, 179
horror, 60–2, 78–9
humiliation, 47
humility, 43
husbands and wives, 50, 62, 65

identity, ch. 5 *passim*
  princely, 129
Imperyall Majestye, 169, 174
indulgences, 188
injustices, 51
innovations, 137, 174, 176, 180
instability of signs, 112–17, 124–9, 196
insults, ch.1 *passim*, ch. 2 *passim*, 118,
    121–5, 130–33, 170, 177–8, 181,
    184, 194
  King Johan's, 172–3
  gendered, 60, 74–6, 88
  naturalistic, 168, 174–6
  and religious tension, 136, 146, 152,
    155, 162
  scatological, 67
  to a god, 141
insulting exchange, 161
inversion of moral significance, 168
irrational language, 112, 115

Jacob's Well, 10–13, 23–6, 62, 93, 102
Judas, 47

Katherine of Aragon, 136, 142–3, 145
Kempe, Margery, 18, 83
King Johan, 7, 88, 110, 138, 159, ch. 7
  passim
knights, 34–5, 38, 50–52, 59–62

language:
  of Catholicism, 189
  elite, 86
  against language, 194
  and the laws, 13
  non-actionable, 25
  power of, 173–4, 195
  self-revelatory, 168, 184–9
  as site of cultural conflict, 196
  transgressive forms of, 26

  of treason, 168, 181, 183
  virtuous, 176
  as vomit, 132
Lanterne of Li3t, 10, 13, 171
Latin, 37, 43, 45, 68, 98–100, 102–5,
    108–9, 112–15, 121–2, 134, 162,
    185–6, 190–1
laughter, 51–2, 61–2, 66, 79, 80, 83
Launder, 138–9, 143, 157–62
laws, 2, ch. 1 *passim*
lawyers, 183
lechery, 92, 96–8
licence to transgress, 144
licensed abuse, 20
  mockery, 21
linguistic change, 87, 91–2,
  excess, 44, 52
  signs, 114
  style, 30, 48, 120, 148, 163
local lords, 57–8, 100, 148
Lollards, 10, 13, 58, 99, 105, 109, 151
Lords of Misrule, 22
low status, 15
low-status characters, 26, 28–9, 40, 44, 48,
    62, 66–8
Lucian's *Icaromenippus*, 137, 153
ludic context, 52, 56, 58–9, 61, 72, 81, 103,
    132, 139–40, 144, 152, 160
  references, 184–5
Luther, 166–7, 172, 196
Lyberte, 119–23, 132
lying, ch. 5 *passim*, 187

Macro plays, ch. 4 *passim*, 85, 112
magic, 67–8
Magnificence's flawed condition, 110, 119,
    129–34
  soliloquy, 129–131
Magnyfycence, 6, 28, 43, 46, 49, 91, ch. 5
    passim, 139–41, 154, 169, 174, 177–
    81, 184, 187
Mahound references, 29–30, 33, 42
maintenance, 96
Mak, 46, 67–8
malice, 14, 42, 69, 76
malicious deception, 111, 129, 135
Mankind, 28–9, 43, 46, ch. 4 *passim*, 98,
    110, 117–18, 138, 141, 173, 196
marginalization, 61, 66, 68
masters and men, 50, 62, 64

Index

Merchant, 149, 155, 157, 163
Mery Report the Vyce, ch. 6 *passim*,
    insults, 140, 147–149, 152–3, 155, 163
metadramatic judgement, 112, 123–4, 135
metalinguistic references, 196
metaphors, 171
Middle English Sermons, 10
Mights, 91, 96–8
Mill of the host, 150
Millers' debate, 153, 161
    episode, 148–9, 153–6, 161, 163
minced oaths, 27–8
Mirk, John, 12, 27, 99
misinterpretation, 113, 116–7
misjudgement, ch. 5 *passim*
mnemonic mockery and abuse, 80–83
mockery, 8–11, 21, 26–8, 31, 38, 52,
    56–8, 82, 79–83, 90, 100, 128,
    132, 133, 145, 188
modulation, 167, 176, 193–4
moral identity, 117, 124, 133, 168
    significance, 6, 7
    significance inverted, 168
morality plays, *see* individual plays
More, Sir Thomas, 19, 136, 141, 146,
    148, 151, 154, 160, 166–7, 196
mothers, 34–5, 59–62, 170, 192
mowes, making, 11, 29
Myrour to Lewde Men and Wymmen,
    10–13, 26, 91–2
Myscheff, 29, 98–104

names, 81, 114–15, 119, 125–30, 168, 171–80
Noah's wife, 34, 43–4, 60, 65–7, 139
Nobylyte, 171, 173, 176, 182, 187, 190–1
N-Town, 11, 18
    Betrayal, 18, 69
    Cain and Abel, 63
    Conspiracy, 18, 69
    Crucifixion, 29, 82
    Fall of Lucifer, 89
    Magi, 32, 39–40, 82, 131
    Moses, 13
    Satan's Prologue, 114
    Trial before Herod, 52, 81, 175
    Trial of Mary and Joseph, 12, 16,
        71–8, 87–88, 106–7
    Woman Taken in Adultery, 74–8,
        87–8, 102

oaths, 26–32, 176, 191–2
Oldcastle, Sir John, 171

parodic prayer, 68
parody, 31, 98–9, 140, 153, 157, 168
    of confession, 189–91
    of the Litany, 192
    of Vespers of the Dead, 193
Paston, John, 55
Paston, Margaret, 15, 65
patter speeches, 161–2
perjury, 96–8
personifications, 26, 44, ch. 4 *passim*,
    86, 89, 110, 121, 138, 156–7,
    168, 175, 179
perversion of the law, 3, 86, 97–8, 101
Pilate, 31, 38–41, 43, 47, 68, 79, 81
pimp, 156–7
Play of the Wether, 6–7, 88, 103, 110,
    ch. 6. *passim*
Pride of Life, 32
processions, 57
prosodic style, 30, 34–5
Protestant polemical style, 166
proverbs, 127, 162, 171, 174
punishing language, 46–47, 60, 133,
    167, 173–4
punishment, 17, 20–6, 110, 112, 118,
    130, 133

quatrain form, 154
Quattuor Sermones, 10–12, 26

radical:
    changes, 165
    sentiments, 162–4
Ranger, 147–8, 155, 163
ranting, 30, 131
relationship of audience to action, 61
religious anxiety, ch. 6 *passim*
    debate, 153–5, 163
    dissent, ch. 3 *passim*
    instruction, 6
reputation, 14, 17, 19
resistance to God's will, 44, 49, 61, 66
rhyme royale, 131
rhyming couplets, 154
ridicule, 7, 24, 50–6, 80–3
Rolle, Richard, 10–11, 26–7
satire of Catholic rituals, 169, 184

satirizing of upstarts, 113
Scandalum magnatum, 19–21
scatological language, 5, 88–90, 102–6, 113, 138, 144–6, 163, 166–7, 178–9
scatology and divorce, 144–6
scorn, 26–9, 176, 181
Secreta Secretorum, 37–8
Secretum Secretorum, 130
secular courts, 13, 19
secular and ecclesiastical lordship, 50, 54
Sedicyon, 173, 175, 177–80, 181, 190, 192
semiotic instability, 111–12, 135, 196
sermons, 6–13, 25–7, 39, 58–62, 72, 91–4, 104
sexual:
 abuse, 74–6
 defamation, 15–17
 innuendo, 72–3, 143
 insult, 33, 75, 178
 slander, 16
shamelessness, 92, 96, 106
similarities and variations, 86–8
Simonie, 78
sinful language, ch. 1 *passim*, 102
sins of the mouth, 10, 13, 92, 95, 97
Skelton, John, ch. 5 *passim*
slander, 10–12
social:
 comment, 96
 functions, 35
 mockery, 56
 rank, 39
 subversion, 3, 62–8, 84
social and spiritual equality, 43
socio-political comment, 6, ch. 3 *passim*, 86, 93, 96–100, 182
soldiers, 59, 77–9
spiritual:
 change, 44–6, 91–5
 hesitant change, 46
 corruption and social evils, 97, 100
 degradation, 117–8, 133–5
 nourishment, 150
 reversed, 176–7
status:
 of language, 116
 social and spiritual, ch. 2 *passim*, 25, 50, 110, 168
stable signs, 112, 115, 117–18
stern virtue, 118
stichomythia, 33, 34
style, 30, 48
subversion, 50, 62–5, 68, 110, 152
Sumptuary laws, 21, 109

taxation, 186–7
tempters, 89, 102–6, 110, 113, 117–19, 125, 129–30, 138, 142, 177
tension resolved, 78
thematic change, 108
theological debate, 154–6, 161, 163
tithing, 63, 150
Titivillus, 43, 90, 102–4
torturers, 69, 78, 82
Towneley:
 Buffetting, 18, 39–40, 69–71, 80
 Caesar Augustus, 29
 Conspiracy and Capture, 53
 First Shepherds' Play, 42, 45, 46
 Herod, 15, 27, 34, 38, 60
 Murder of Abel, 23, 36, 42, 64, 88
 Noah, 34, 44, 65
 Scourging, 31, 82
 Second Shepherds' Play, 27–8, 46, 67, 86, 96, 99–100, 105
transgressive language:
 defined, 6–13, 26, 165–6, 168
 and evil lords, 19–20
 new forms, 180
 and virtuous characters, 169
transubstantiation, 136, 161, 165, 179, 187
treason, 17–19, 70, 168–70, 180–83
Tretise of Miraclis Pleyinge, 77, 78, 102
trial by ordeal, 72
truth-speaking, 171
Turk, as insult, 173
Tyndale, William, 142, 167

upstarts, 113
unstable signs and princely identity, 119, 124, 129, 134
urban communities, 51

vassals, 50, 59, 62, 68, 80, 101
verbal filth, 103
Veritas, 169, 173, 176

violence, 12, 50, 58–62, 65, 68, 74, 78, 83, 177
violent polemical style, 166
virtuous characters, 168–74, 177, 184, 195
Vyce and entertainment, 140
Water Miller, 142–3, 149–54, 159
whore, 17, 75, 160, 196
Whore of Babylon, 172
whoremaster, 16
Wife of Bath, 14–15
willingness to accept sin, 93, 106
wind and doctrine, 155
Wisdom, 25, ch. 4 *passim*, 110, 114, 133, 138, 173
witchcraft, 17–18, 69–71
witnesses, 6, 8, 14, 16–20, 53, 68–83, 125
word games, 117, 140
Worldlings, 27, 90–104
worth of language, 110, 115, 135
Wynd Myller, 151–5, 163

Wyclif, John, 54, 58
York, 55
   Cain and Abel, 23, 63–4
   Christ before Annas and Caiaphas, 52–3, 70
   Christ before Herod, 29, 31, 82
   Christ before Pilate (1), 18, 43, 69, 81, 131, 139
   Christ before Pilate (2), 18
   Conspiracy, 47
   Crucifixion, 77, 78, 80–82, 102
   Death of Christ, 29, 78
   Fergus, 79
   Flood, 34, 66
   Herod and the Magi, 35, 52
   Moses and Pharaoh, 27
   Remorse of Judas, 18
   Resurrection, 15
   Slaughter, 34, 59
York Proclamation, 56